The Post-War British Literature Handbook

**Literature and Culture Handbooks**

General Editors: Philip Tew and Steven Barfield

Literature and Culture Handbooks are an innovative series of guides to major periods, topics and authors in British and American literature and culture. Designed to provide a comprehensive, one-stop resource for literature students, each handbook provides the essential information and guidance needed from the beginning of a course through to developing more advanced knowledge and skills.

*The Eighteenth-Century Literature Handbook*
Edited by Gary Day and Bridge Keegan

*The Medieval British Literature Handbook*
Edited by Daniel T. Kline

*The Modernism Handbook*
Edited by Philip Tew and Alex Murray

*The Renaissance Literature Handbook*
Edited by Susan Bruce and Rebecca Steinberger

*The Seventeenth-Century Literature Handbook*
Edited by Robert C. Evans and Eric J. Sterling

*The Shakespeare Handbook*
Edited by Andrew Hiscock and Stephen Longstaffe

*The Victorian Literature Handbook*
Edited by Alexandra Warwick and Martin Willis

# The Post-War British Literature Handbook

Edited by

Katharine Cockin

and

Jago Morrison

continuum

Continuum

The Tower Building          80 Maiden Lane, Suite 704
11 York Road               New York
London SE1 7NX             NY 10038

www.continuumbooks.com

British Library Cataloguing-in-Publication Data
A catalogue record for this book is available from the British Library.

ISBN:    978-0-8264-9501-3 (hardback)
         978-0-8264-9502-0 (paperback)

Library of Congress Cataloging-in-Publication Data
A catalog record for this book is available from the Library of Congress.

Typeset by RefineCatch Limited, Bungay, Suffolk
Printed and bound in Great Britain by the MPG Books Group

# Contents

Contents

# Detailed Table of Contents

# General Editors' Introduction

The Continuum *Literature and Culture Handbooks* series aims to support both students new to an area of study and those at a more advanced stage, offering guidance with regard to the major periods, topics and authors relevant to the study of various aspects of British and American literature and culture. The series is designed with an international audience in mind, based on research into today's students in a global educational setting. Each volume is concerned with either a particular historical phase or an even more specific context, such as a major author study. All of the chosen areas represent established subject matter for literary study in schools, colleges and universities, all are both widely taught and the subject of ongoing research and scholarship. Each handbook provides a comprehensive, one-stop resource for literature students, offering essential information and guidance needed at the beginning of a course through to more advanced knowledge and skills for the student more familiar with the particular topic. These volumes reflect current academic research and scholarship, teaching methods and strategies, and also provide an outline of essential historical contexts. Written in clear language by leading internationally acknowledged academics, each book provides the following:

- Introduction to authors, texts, historical and cultural contexts
- Guides to key critics, concepts and topics
- Introduction to critical approaches, changes in the canon and new conceptual and theoretical issues, such as gender and ethnicity
- Case studies in reading literary and theoretical and critical texts
- Annotated bibliography (including websites), timeline, glossary of critical terms.

This student-friendly series as a whole has drawn its inspiration and structure largely from the latest principles of text book design employed in other disciplines and subjects, creating an unusual and distinctive approach for the undergraduate arts and humanities field. This structure is designed to be user-friendly and it is intended that the layout can be easily navigated, with various points of cross-reference. Such clarity and straightforward approach should help students understand the material and in so doing guide them through the increasing academic difficulty of complex critical and theoretical approaches to Literary Studies. These handbooks serve as gateways to the particular field that is explored.

All volumes make use of a 'progressive learning strategy', rather than the traditional chronological approach to the subject under discussion so that they might relate more closely to the learning process of the student. This means that the particular volume offers material that will aid the student to approach the period or topic confidently in the classroom for the very first time (for example, glossaries, historical context, key topics and critics), as well as material that helps the student develop more advanced skills (learning how to respond actively to selected primary texts and analyse and engage with modern critical arguments in relation to such texts). Each volume includes a specially commissioned new critical essay by a leading authority in the field discussing current debates and contexts. The progression in the contents mirrors the progress of the undergraduate student from beginner to a more advanced level. Each volume is aimed primarily at undergraduate students, intending to offer itself as both a guide and a reference text that will reflect the advances in academic studies in its subject matter, useful to both students and staff (the latter may find the appendix on pedagogy particularly helpful).

We realize that students in the twenty first-century are faced with numerous challenges and demands; it is our intention that the Handbook series should empower its readers to become effective and efficient in their studies.

*Philip Tew and Steven Barfield*

# 1 Introduction

## Katharine Cockin and Jago Morrison

## Surveying the Field: A Forest of Posts?

The aim of this book is to set out a range of frameworks for understanding British fiction and poetry in the post-war period. Since World War Two, an incredible range and variety of writing has emerged from these islands, and the forms of critical analysis that have been brought to bear on it have also varied enormously. From a mood of hesitancy and conservatism in the immediate post-war decades, contemporary literary studies developed from the 1970s and 1980s onwards into a thriving field of debate, with rival schools of criticism vying for status and popularity. In the twenty-first century, this spirit of debate and innovation continues, with no single critical perspective on the literatures of our times enjoying a position of dominance.

In this book we have tried to reflect this by offering a sense of the different ways in which the landscape of post-war and contemporary writing can be mapped, without trying to impose one particular approach as orthodoxy. In this introduction, however, we do focus on one extraordinarily resilient, recurring motif in the criticism of the last half century. That is, the idea of being 'post' or after something. To the un-initiated, the landscape of post-war criticism can seem like a forest of 'post-s', impenetrable to the casual explorer. We have been 'post-war', 'post-colonial', 'post-modern', 'post-feminist', 'post-human'. According to many critics working on the twenty-first century writing, it is important now to think of ourselves as 'post-9/11'.

These 'posts' reveal something interesting about the mood of post-war criticism, which transcends the arguments and differences between all the different schools and 'isms'. That is, a common perception of historical transition, the suggestion that we are living through the last gasps of something that is in the process of giving way to something else. Much more than the criticism of earlier literatures, post-war and contemporary criticism often involves the sensation of working in the shadow of open questions. New evidence and critical insights assert themselves, as they do for scholars in other periods, forcing a rethink of previous assumptions. For us, though, this process of intellectual renewal is complicated by the fact that we are often working with living writers and dynamically evolving cultural contexts. In such circumstances it feels much more difficult, for example, to begin assessing an oeuvre with the kind of confidence that Victorianists might take for granted, with all the texts before them.

In this introduction, then, we have used this recurrent motif of 'post-ness', to explore some of the different ways in which scholars of our period have attempted to position it in historical terms, and especially to understand it in terms of transition. Appreciating how each of these periodizing frames – these 'post-s' – have constructed the field as an object of study is essential to gaining a sophisticated understanding of many of its ongoing concerns and debates. We have tried to give a sense of the ways in which working in the absence of critical orthodoxy often involves experimenting with different historical shapes, playing with different sets of theoretical coordinates, to see which ones fit most convincingly or shed most light on the questions in hand. As should be clear, then, our aim here is not to offer an exhaustive or encyclopaedic account of post-war British Literature from Amis to Zephaniah, in the closed and comfortable style of a literary 'companion'. Instead, we explore six different ways of navigating a field whose character and topography continue to shift and change even as we write.

## Post-War

In the immediate post-war period, the experience of war itself must be recognized as having had a devastating effect on the British population. For authors, a common first response to war is to put writing aside or to question its relevance. Perhaps unsurprisingly, then, criticism of the immediate post-war period often reflects a fear that British literature had in some sense gone into hibernation. Most critics of the 1950s looked back to the early twentieth century to find writers whose work they regarded as worthy of serious study. For Anthony Thwaite (1957), for example, the contemporary was seen as beginning in the late-Victorian period with Gerard Manley Hopkins and reaching its peak in the early twentieth century with T. S. Eliot. The poetry of the post-war years is seen as hardly worthy of consideration. Kingsley Amis took a similar view, seeing post-war writing as infected with a damaging 'meagreness and triviality' (Thwaite 1957: p. 154). In the 1960s, similarly, influential critics like Frederick Karl saw the diminished ambitions of post-war fiction as a poor rival to the excitement and innovation of early twentieth-century modernism. According to Karl, the weight of recent history had simply proved too much for such writers as Graham Greene, Elizabeth Bowen, Evelyn Waugh and George Orwell, restricting their stylistic and imaginative palette. As he argued, 'the tremendous pressure of outside events in the last thirty years has resulted in withdrawal' (Karl 1963: p. 5).

In the post-war decades themselves, then, the critical establishment showed, by and large, little enthusiasm for contemporary writing. For students, as Alan Sinfield recalls in his book *Literature, Politics and Culture Post-War Britain* (2004), current writing was something to be read and debated in one's spare time, not in the lecture room. Frequently the focus of student's own choice of reading was not home-grown talent but the more exciting and radical work of European writers such as Eugène Ionesco and Jean-Paul Sartre, or Americans such as Allen Ginsburg and Jack Kerouac. Among British writers themselves, this mood of despondency can be detected as late as the early 1970s, when L. P. Hartley complained in interview with Peter Firchow that contemporary British culture seemed to exclude the spirit of individualism which he saw as underpinning great writing: 'you can't really write a novel about people who are all alike' (Thurley 1974: p. 167). In one of the defining critical works of that decade, *The Situation of the Novel*, Bernard Bergonzi repeated the familiar refrain, lamenting that the British novel had lost its defining characteristic of novelty. From its position as a purveyor of the new and surprising in the eighteenth and nineteenth centuries, fiction had become 'moderately con-servative', based on a technology (the printed book) which was now 'slightly old-fashioned' (Bergonzi 1970: p. 26).

From the mid-1970s, this pessimistic mood among critics underwent a sig-nificant shift, partly under the influence of the increasingly heated debates surrounding fashionable French theorists such as Louis Althusser, Roland Barthes and Jacques Derrida. From this time, contemporary writing began to enjoy a new renaissance in Universities and Colleges. One of the key features of the literary theories that began to gain popularity in that period was the way they encouraged readers to dispense with the idea that authors con-trolled the meaning of their works. Instead readers were invited to enjoy their encounter with the text and allow the play of possible meanings to engage them. The landscape of contemporary literary studies began to open up with increasing interest in the work of a new generation of writers, such as John Fowles and Angela Carter, as well as international literary figures such as Gabriel Garcia Marquez, Italo Calvino and Umberto Eco. In place of the somewhat negative orthodoxies espoused by earlier critics, new perspectives and methodologies began to proliferate. Certainly, the shift to 'theory' in literature departments was hotly contested, with Feminist, Marxist, Post-structuralist and Psychoanalytic critics (among others) waging long wars of attrition against the 'Liberal Humanist' establishment, as well as against each other. The re-emergence of contemporary literature into the curriculum took place against this background of debate, and an unexamined side-effect of this was that, while high modernists such as James Joyce and Virginia Woolf continued to be studied alongside current writers, fiction and poetry of the 1950s and 1960s was, for a significant period, relegated to the margins of the syllabus. In recent years, critical attention has shifted back to the writings of the post-war decades, with studies by such critics as Dominic Head (2002) on British fiction, Bruce King (2004) on the internationalization of English literature and Deborah Philips (2006) on post-war women's writing bringing a range of fresh perspectives to the field.

As all these commentators acknowledge, the Second World War was a defining moment in British culture, instigating a break which has had an enduring impact on British literature. It provided the principal focus for a reconstruction of the entire notion of 'Britishness' in the context of a radically changed international landscape. Anxieties about wartime endurance and the rebuilding of communities had affected the sensibilities of writers and readers alike. The devastating effects of war itself – the fear of invasion, the terrors of the holocaust and the use of the atomic bomb – forced intractable questions about the ethical implications of art to the fore. Was literature inadequate in the face of such terror, such dehumanizing experience? As Head and others show, Literature had a much more significant part to play in bearing witness to the traumatic experiences of war and to mediating survivor guilt, than earlier critics were able to recognize. As feminist critics have noted, dynamics of guilt and rivalry shaped the crisis in masculinity experienced by the post-war generation deprived of the proving ground of combat, a crisis played out in the writings of 'Angry Young Men' such as John Osborne and Alan Sillitoe. Themes of atonement, regeneration and redemption characterized many literary responses to combat and the restoration of peace, including in the work of later writers such as Ian McEwan. Relationships had to be redrawn at all levels from the international to the domestic. Some of these circumstances revisited the instabilities created during the First World War: the devastation of genocide; the contested territories of Eastern Europe. The terrifying power of the state and the anonymous forces at work in making such devastating decisions are highlighted in such works as Dylan Thomas' poem 'The Hand That Signed the Paper': 'The hand that signed the paper felled a city; / Five sovereign fingers taxed the breath, / Doubled the globe of dead and halved a country'. In the early 1960s, the shadow of genocide was still felt by many writers: in *The New Poetry* (1962), for example, the editor declares that the collection is explicitly devoted to a 'new seriousness' in the wake of the Holocaust.

In Virginia Woolf's posthumously published novel *Between the Acts* (1941), the image of a snake swallowing a toad figures the gendered conflict embodied by the impending war. Generation, inflected with gender, becomes a significant factor in defining post-war experience. Known as baby boomers, the generation born immediately after the war benefited from an optimistic drive to rebuild the nation, with the formation of the welfare state and the National Health Service, together with an extension of higher education. Those deprived of the opportunity to fight in the war, reaching young adulthood in the fifties as teenagers, formed a new, emergent and rebellious youth culture. Questions about the effectiveness of the post-war British government became a feature of public debate, especially in the wake of such crises as the Profumo affair. A sense of dispossession from the heroics of the Second World War was keenly felt by many, perhaps especially novelists and poets.

The fear of war, notably with nuclear weapons, and attempts to prevent another international conflict led to a new form of warfare in the Cold War, enacted through espionage, intimidation and posturing. In popular fiction, writers like Ian Fleming and John le Carré were among the most successful in harnessing the potential of these contexts for the novel. The war in Vietnam provoked challenges from a youth movement which collectively organized and demonstrated, relying on new cultural forms to mobilize support. A single year – 1968 – has come to signify the counter-culture of this period, which sought to expose the society of the spectacle and transform social relations entirely. Political theatre and performance poetry were forms which especially characterized this highly charged moment and have to some extent become restricted in literary history by their timeliness. While the location of these struggles appear to have been taking place principally elsewhere – Paris, California – the reverberations were felt in Britain, especially in cultural terms where a war of ideas was waged.

Warfare operates widely as metaphor in post-war British literature. The last two decades of the twentieth century have witnessed numerous conflicts: the improbable Falklands War; the civil unrest in Northern Ireland and during the miners' strike of 1984–85; the later revolutions in Europe in communist countries, the fall of the Berlin wall dividing East and West Germany, the wars in Yugoslavia; and those which have continued in Somalia, Burma, Tibet, Iran,

Iraq and Afghanistan. Since 11 September 2001, the continuing 'war on terror' challenges the principles of periodization once again. Since it is a war which appears to be virtual and open-ended, the impact it has on literature will be difficult to assess until we have gained the distance of time.

## Postcolonial

Since the eighteenth century, with the success of writers like Olaudah Equiano, Ignatius Sancho, Phyllis Wheatley, Mary Prince, Mrs Seacole and Dean Mahomet, works by Black and Asian authors have been a feature of the British literary scene. The notion of a distinctly 'Black British' sensibility in literature, however, is usually seen as a post-war phenomenon. In important ways, this has to do with the increasing confidence with which UK writers began to play with hybrid forms of English from the 1950s onwards. In fiction, Sam Selvon's *The Lonely Londoners* (1956) and in poetry, Linton Kwesi Johnson's *Dread, Beat, an' Blood* (1975) are two particularly celebrated examples. Selvon's text is, in one sense, clearly the product of European literary traditions, both realist and modernist. The influence of canonical figures like James Joyce is explicit in particular narrative passages. In the relatively conservative context of British writing in the 1950s, however, what is especially striking about Selvon's novel is the assurance with which it announces its hybrid sensibility. Written in a language that weaves between Trinidadian and 'Standard' Englishes, Selvon's novel depicts a different kind of London, a city seen through British Caribbean eyes.

Linton Kwesi Johnson's writing in the 1970s is presented in a very different idiom, but its debt to the innovations of *The Lonely Londoners*, as well as to the work of Caribbean writers such as Kamau Brathwaite, is clearly evident. Johnson's work is free in its use of Jamaican dialect, as well as improvisatory rhythmic and musical forms, especially drawn from reggae. In contrast to Selvon's writing, however, Johnson's writing is also explicitly political in tone. Collections such as *Inglan is a Bitch* (1980), published in conjunction with the album *Forces of Victory* (1979), take up a self-consciously oppositional, anti-Thatcherite position, drawing on the discourse of the Socialist Left but especially on that of the Black Arts Movement.

In screenwriting, British Asian writers like Hanif Kureishi were especially influential. As Writer in Residence at the Royal Court Theatre during the 1970s, Kureishi's early work is, like Johnson's, strongly and explicitly political, focusing on questions of class and race. With his 1985 screenplay *My Beautiful Laundrette* and later works such as *The Buddha of Suburbia* (1990), however, such concerns are mediated through other, perhaps more palatable elements, including humour and sometimes farcical explorations of sexuality. Kureishi's distinctive amalgamation of political themes with a light, quasi-comic sensibility in these works was a major influence on other British Asian writers. Works such as Ayub Khan-Din's *East is East* (1997) and *Rafta Rafta* (2007), and Gurinder Chadha's *Bend it Like Beckham* (2003) are three examples of box office successes which offer serious reflection on the changing experience of first and second-generation immigrants to the UK, but do so with an arch, provocative style that keeps its critical edge while avoiding a flavour of didacticism.

During this period, then, a diverse range of Black British and British Asian writing began to enter the literary mainstream, including school and college curricula. Wilson Harris' avant-garde representations of Guyana in *Palace of the Peacock* (1960) and subsequent novels, Buchi Emecheta's autobiographical *In the Ditch* (1972) and *Second Class Citizen* (1974), dealing with migrant experience in London and Salman Rushdie's provocative political fictions *Midnight's Children* (1981) and *Shame* (1983) were important examples of new writing which contributed to changing perceptions of what might constitute contemporary British Literature.

Within English departments the study of this new writing was frequently located under the umbrella of a new 'ism' – postcolonialism – which became associated with certain distinctive ways to approach writing and representation. To view British writing through postcolonial eyes typically means, first of all, to set it within wider historical and cultural frames. Working on writers such as Fred D'Aguiar or Jean Rhys, the history of slavery, especially in an American and Caribbean context, becomes an important area of concern. Reading the work of others, such as Buchi Emecheta, Ben Okri, Salman Rushdie or Ahdaf Soueif, the history of British colonialism in Africa, South Asia and the Middle East becomes an essential backdrop. In all these cases, a historical perspective encompassing the seventeenth century to the twenty-first centuries is likely to be called for, including some attention to the resistance towards the British mounted by colonized people, especially during the post-war period. As a critical methodology, then, postcolonialism places British Literature in relation to a complex of intercultural dynamics which mirror the historical relationships engendered by empire itself, from the beginning of the Modern period.

From a critical point of view, moreover, a particularly thought-provoking dimension of postcolonial theory is the way it calls into question long-standing assumptions about the function of literary studies in relation to the idea of nation and the concept of the English, or British, National Literary Tradition. Informed by such thinkers as Eric Hobsbaum and Benedict Anderson, a major theme of postcolonialism is to explore the ways in which nations – often established on unstable and discontinuous historical foundations – come to acquire an 'imagined' aura of timelessness and naturalness. With its hybrid, intercultural and international perspectives, postcolonial writing often finds itself in an uneasy or ambivalent relationship to ideological formations of nationhood and nationalism, including that of Britishness. For the postcolonial critic, this tension often affords the opportunity for some very interesting analysis.

Further, as Robert Young notes in his study *Postcolonialism: An Historical Introduction* (2001), postcolonialism is dialectical: the idea of opposing forces profoundly structures its approaches to texts and writers. Perhaps the most important of these is the opposition of colonialism *vs* resistance. At the same time, it is useful to recognize that postcolonial criticism and theory is almost always committed, ethically and politically. Critical readings of novels, poems and plays are usually situated, whether explicitly or implicitly, in the context of a critique of colonial ideology and practice, together with a desire to expose and/or undo some of their negative effects.

As this suggests, while postcolonial writing often conjures a medium-to-large scale historical perspective, this is not necessarily in the bland sense of historical 'context'. For example, one of the dominant tropes of postcolonialism is that of 'writing back'. Faced with textual representations of the past – both literary and non-literary – which are often saturated with colonial and euro-centric assumptions, postcolonial texts often take up a resistive stance. Salman Rushdie's *Midnight's Children* (1981), for example, offers itself not just as an alternative, but as an antidote to the 'Raj' view of India associated with writers like E. M. Forster and, in film, with the production company Merchant Ivory. Jean Rhys' *Wide Sargasso Sea* (1966) does not merely 'fill in the gaps' left by Charlotte Brontë's *Jane Eyre* (1847), but unsettles and reworks the story in crucial ways. Fred D'Aguiar's *The Longest Memory* (1994) casts a critical gaze on the language of Virginia slave-owners in the mid-nineteenth century, by juxtaposing them with the unrecorded testimony of slaves and slave sympathizers. While postcolonial writing often deals with historical representations, then, this is very often with a questioning rather than an accepting eye.

As a way into examining the antagonistic or revisionary relationships between post-war and older texts, 'writing back' may provide a useful starting point for thinking about texts as creative interventions that exist in dialogue with a complex economy of representation, both historical and current. In other ways, however, its dominance as a critical idiom can also become a problem. In the case of the Nigerian writer Chinua Achebe, for example, early criticism of *Things Fall Apart* (1958) and other fiction was so pre-occupied with tracing the writer's debt to the Western Canon (in the shape of Joseph Conrad, W. B. Yeats, T. S. Eliot, W. H. Auden and others) that a range of other concerns in the novels went largely unnoticed. With the development of an expanding canon of Black British and British Asian writing in the latter decades of the twentieth century, certainly, the default status of 'writing back' as the privileged mode for thinking about postcolonial texts has had to be reconsidered.

Indeed, it is important to recognize that the relationship between postcolonialism as a whole and Black British/British Asian writing is by no means one of happy equivalence. Indeed, in 1990s and twenty-first century writing, it is often possible to detect a significant strain of resistance among writers to the idea of 'writing back' or 'colonialism *vs* resistance' as the only – or at any rate the privileged – ways of writing or reading from a Black perspective. Although her first novel *White Teeth* (2000) has been celebrated by a number of postcolonial critics, Zadie Smith is one notable example among contemporary writers who regard the label 'postcolonial' as unhelpful and confining. Interviewed in the *New York Times* (Jordan 2005: p. 8), Smith was asked to name her key literary influences: her list of names explicitly avoided the 'postcolonial' canon, included no Black British writer at all and only one African American, Zora Neale Hurston, alongside a list of twenty three canonical white authors. Smith's response can probably be read as deliberately provocative, but it does offer a reminder that postcolonialism, as a framework for thinking about the forms and concerns of writing in our period, has sometimes proved to be more enabling for critics than it has for writers themselves.

In recent years, and especially in the wake of 9/11 (discussed below), postcolonialism's strong position within contemporary literary has been partially challenged by the emergence of a new, equally internationalist paradigm, that of 'globalization'. If postcolonial criticism tends to be organized around a dialectic of colonialism *vs* resistance, the oppositions set up by globalization are more likely to be region *vs* global, or tradition *vs* homogenization/hybridization. A potential advantage of 'globalization' as a critical idiom may be that it will encourage critics to extend their gaze beyond the limits of empire, as well as to think more broadly about empire itself as a manifestation of larger historical movements and transitions. A potential disadvantage is perhaps that, in its vastness and generality, a focus on 'globalization' might militate against the attention to cultural and historical specificity that underpins much of the best postcolonial criticism. Forging 'globalization' into a critical approach as productive as postcolonialism has proved to be will involve finding fresh ways to link global themes and processes with the *local* conditions that shape writers and their works.

## Postmodern

'Postmodern' is an umbrella term covering a range of different theoretical tendencies and aesthetic practices in the last half of the twentieth century. As a periodizing term it tends to frame post-war and contemporary writing in one of two ways, either in terms of post*modernism* or in terms of post*modernity*.

The first of these involves considering recent texts in terms of the ways in which they differ from the forms of writing associated with early-twentieth century modernism. In this account, postmodernist writing is seen as carrying forward modernism's commitment to formal experimentation, but with a move away from its dryly ascetic tendencies and with a big re-investment in pleasure. In place of the lean, pared-down style of some of the iconic modernists, postmodernists are said to experiment with more playful and flamboyant modes of expression, freely mixing past forms and influences along with a generous dose of self-parody. In British fiction, particularly celebrated 'postmodernists' include John Fowles and Martin Amis, both of whom play with their own status as authors and experiment provocatively with narrative form. During the 1980s and 1990s, the heyday of postmodernism, Angela Carter, Jeanette Winterson and Fay Weldon were among those seen as pioneering a new 'postmodernist feminist' aesthetic. In each of their work, what this tended to mean was that a feminist concern with interrogating gender representations was combined with radical modes of storytelling, often inspired by pioneers of Magic Realism such as Italo Calvino and Gabriel Garcia Marquez.

As can be seen from a range of critical studies of Fowles, Amis, Carter, Winterson and Weldon, reading contemporary fiction through 'postmodern' eyes can be a useful way of foregrounding the strategies of certain contemporary authors and texts. However, as a critical methodology postmodernism does tend to break down when the attempt is made to apply it more systematically. Inconveniently, it soon becomes apparent that iconic modernists such as T. S. Eliot, Virginia Woolf and James Joyce exemplify most of the celebrated postmodernist techniques, while acknowledged pioneers of the postmodern, such as Jorge Luis Borges, owe such a debt to modernism that it is difficult definitively to separate them from it.

The second generic way in which 'postmodern' can be used as a framing device for recent writing is by setting it up as some kind of break from the values and assumptions of a previous period, modernity. Modernity, characterized in terms of eighteenth- and nineteenth-century rationalism, individualism and colonialism, is contrasted to postmodernism's deconstructive play, its fascination with marginal, fractured and fluid identities and its commitment to anti-rational, self-defeating logics.

In poetry, as the critic Ian Gregson (1996) suggests, postmodernism can be useful in elucidating certain features of post-war and contemporary writing, which seem to echo these philosophical themes. However, as he argues, it is important to recognize that the formulations of postmodernism put forward by influential theorists tend to interlace much more convincingly with American verse, especially that of John Ashberry and his contemporaries, than they do with British poetry of the same period. Among such UK writers as John Ash, Peter Didsbury and Peter Ackroyd, classic postmodernist strategies such as the denial and deferral of meaning can certainly be detected by a critical eye attuned to the favoured strategies of postmodernism. However, viewing the work of these poets more broadly it is also apparent that their work is grounded strongly in a sense of time and place – Manchester, Hull and London respectively – which anchors their work to a rather un-postmodern sense of the 'real'.

When taken from the realms of pure theory to the process of application to works of fiction, poetry and drama, the attractiveness of the modernity/ postmodernity opposition seems, again, to lessen somewhat when deployed as a tool of critical analysis. The realist classics, against which postmodernist 'anti-realism' negatively defines itself, turn out to be more poly-vocal and self-divided than previously thought, when re-examined by contemporary critics. Early modern theatre, far from setting up a model of sovereign individualism for postmodernists to tear down, four centuries later, turns out to be at least as concerned with masquerade and self-fashioning as late twentieth- and twenty-first century literatures. In both aesthetic and philosophical terms, indeed, it is much easier to make out a case for modernist writing as a radical departure from eighteenth- and nineteenth-century work, than it is to make the same case for postmodernism.

In its attempts to frame the contemporary era in terms of discontinuity from the past, perhaps the most radical periodizing claim associated with postmodernism was that made by the American theorist Francis Fukuyama (1989) that we had reached the end of history itself. With the collapse of Soviet power and (he surmised) the unconditional victory of US-style consumer democracy, little more of sufficient interest to be deemed 'history' could now be expected to happen:

> What we may be witnessing, is not just the end of the Cold War, or the passing of a particular period of post-war history, but the end of history as such: that is, the end point of mankind's ideological evolution and the universalization of Western liberal democracy as the final form of human government. (Fukuyama 1989: p. 4)

In retrospect, Fukuyama's comments now seem decidedly premature, in such contexts as the Islamist challenge to US supremacy associated with the World Trade Centre attacks of September 2001 (see below). Another postmodernist favourite, French theorist Jean Baudrillard's (1981) characterization of contemporary society as an infinitely extended Disneyland, an endless circuit of self-referential representation, may seem similarly anachronistic amid the charged ethical and political sensibilities of the post-9/11 period: Baudrillard's own response to 9/11, *The Spirit of Terrorism* (2002) has received mixed critical reactions.

Undoubtedly, theorists such as Baudrillard have worked well for some critics, however, in drawing out the themes and concerns of certain texts. Julian Barnes' novel *England, England* (1998), in which an idealized simulacrum of England is re-created on the Isle of Wight, is one such example. Similarly, a text like George Orwell's *1984*, which concerns itself explicitly with the mediation and manufacture of social consciousness, can respond well to a postmodernist analysis. Set alongside the writing of authors such as Nadeem Aslam or Ahdaf Soueif, on the other hand, work which anticipates and explores the new challenges of East-West relations in the twenty-first century, postmodernism struggles to find the same purchase. In this sense, it is perhaps better to approach postmodernism as a distinctive set of reading practices, fruitful when used in conjunction with certain texts, rather than as a historicizing term that can separate late twentieth- and twenty-first century writing from everything that went before.

Viewed as a mode of critical reading, indeed, one of the most productive themes associated with postmodernism is its challenge to commonplace assumptions about the nature of historicizing itself. In the work of theorists such as Hayden White and Linda Hutcheon, the assumed distinctions between historical representation (as factual, objective) and literary representation (as fabricated, subjective) are explicitly called into question. The techniques of historical writing – the discovery, selection and arrangement of traces, the intellectual and imaginative leaps required to establish narrative coherence – are considered in explicitly literary terms. The insights of this work have interesting implications for the study of many contemporary writers, especially in their attempts to engage with questions of historicity. Linda Hutcheon's notion of 'historiographic metafiction' is one attempt to describe a particular mode of contemporary writing which deals with historical subject matter, while simultaneously questioning the nature of historical representation itself. In Salman Rushdie's *Midnight's Children* (1981), for example, the history of Indian Independence is laid out in gorgeous and colourful detail, but through the mouth of a narrator who admits his own unreliability, who suffers a bout of amnesia at a key historical moment and who revels in political point-scoring. Other novels, such as Ian McEwan's *Atonement* (2001), include sections of compelling historical narration which are then radically destabilized with questions about the tendentious and self-deluding nature of memory. Graham Swift's novel *Waterland* (1983), set in the Fens of East Anglia, plays with ideas of historical fluidity that intermix perfectly with the watery, metamorphosing landscape his novel describes. In this sense, postmodernism can be useful as an approach to important strands of contemporary writing, in describing a particular kind of *self-conscious* historical sensibility. It points to the distinctive ways in which such writers combine historical and imaginative elements in their work, in the knowledge that histories themselves are always partially speculative and present-minded.

As Katharine Cox suggests in her discussion of poststructuralism and postmodernism in Part III of this book, perhaps the most influential dictum to be dispensed by postmodernist theory was French Philosopher Jean-François Lyotard's (1979) designation of the postmodern as a condition of 'incredulity towards metanarratives'. The salient characteristic of our post-religious, techno-consumerist times, he suggested, was a prevailing attitude of scepticism towards grand systems of belief and periodizing schemes. Lyotard's formulation remains useful in suggesting how the notion of the 'postmodern' can best be deployed from a literary critical point of view. Its strengths are in its irreverent, sometimes sacrilegious approach to orthodoxies and its insightful questioning of the nature of representation. Applied to the literature of recent decades, postmodernism offers a vocabulary for analysing the self-conscious, deconstructive and playful strategies that have shaped and influenced the work of many writers. In postmodernism's more millennial manifestations as a historical thesis about the end of modernity itself, on the other hand, it is fair to say that its applications for criticism are rather more limited.

## Postfeminist

According to the 1985 anthology *Making for the Open: The Chatto Book of Post-Feminist Poetry*, edited by Carol Rumens, post-feminist writing can be traced at least as far back as 1964. If this is accepted, the question surely arises if, and when, feminism itself supposed to have ended. If it has ended, how we are to understand the difference between the two tendencies or positions? According to feminist critics such as Imelda Whelehan, the idea of postfeminism should always be approached with a sceptical eye, especially regarding the claims of some that 'the "post" signifies an engagement with feminism rather than a rejection of it' (Whelehan 2000: p. 91). If feminism is understood as firmly located in the past, what did it involve and where does that leave women today? Has feminism had its day because its ideals have become irrelevant, or have the goals of feminism been achieved and women have therefore moved on?

Among women writers of the last three or four decades, these questions have been addressed in a variety of interesting ways. Often, such influential figures as Angela Carter and Jeanette Winterson have enjoyed an uneasy relationship with their feminist readerships, including professional critics, partly because of their unorthodox and provocative approaches to the representation of gender and sexual identity. Such writers have therefore sometimes been labelled as 'post-feminist'. Others, such as Michèle Roberts and Jackie Kay have been clearer in their alignment to mainstream feminism. Among readers, such collections as *One Foot on the Mountain: An Anthology of*

*British Feminist Poetry, 1969–79* edited by Linda Mohin and *A Dangerous Knowing: Four Black Women Poets* edited by Barbara Burford, with their unambiguous commitment to a feminism uncompromised by 'post-ness', have continued to prove at least as popular and influential as Chatto's post-feminist anthology, often sitting side-by-side on the same bookshelf. As a critical category, 'post-feminist' is usually taken to refer to writing which engages with established feminist concerns, but which has at the same time, in some sense 'moved on' from feminist orthodoxies. The fact is, though, that women's writing and the women's movement have always had a complex relationship, as each has developed and evolved over the course of the post-war period. In one sense, then, 'what post-feminism' really points to is the continuation of debates that have always characterized feminism and its interest in the representation of women's experience.

Although the high point of feminism in post-war Britain is associated with the 1970s, this political movement which aims to transform society, to bring about equality, extends at least to the middle of the nineteenth century. The first wave of feminism concerning the agitation for legislative change to enfranchise women and to achieve equality as citizens under the law was accompanied by its own propagandist literature. The double standard, the constraints on women as wives and mothers, the demonization of the spinster and the limited education available to women were some of the issues which pre-war British literature considered. In Britain the enfranchisement of women occurred in two phases: the extension of the franchise to women of property and maturity following the First World War and finally its extension to all in 1928. Are women's rights, similarly, a feature of contemporary debates? The trend in political activism appears to have shifted in the later twentieth century from the mass movements of social class, gender and other identity-based groups to single-issue politics. Nevertheless, the feminist arguments on the right to abortion which led to the 1967 Abortion Act have become subject of scrutiny again forty years later, not as a result of explicitly anti-feminist or postfeminist campaigning but because of scientific developments in human reproductive technologies.

Feminists have argued for the need to change the role of the State in the relationships between women, work and childcare. The effect of material circumstances on the freedom of the imagination claimed by Virginia Woolf in *A Room of One's Own* (1929) to some extent continue long after the Second World War, not least with regard to the liberation of time and space for concentration. The demands on many women's time and energy from childcare and domestic work are increasingly supplemented by the demands of paid employment. At the end of the twentieth century multi-tasking women are admired (and feared) for achieving on all fronts while others experience the obstacle of a 'glass ceiling' preventing them from reaching the highest positions. Although many fields of work were opened up to women during the twentieth century, the potential women had to contribute to them was questioned, especially in times of peace. It was the necessary participation of women in support services and the workforce during the Second World War which proved to doubters the value of women in society. However, the late 1940s saw a revival of the ideology of domesticity which had been effective in the 1920s as a means of reinforcing the cultural and political power of the home and family in the rebuilding of the nation. After the end of the century the domestic interior has become more than ever a status symbol and, driven by the late twentieth-century boom in property development in Britain, the fascination with home improvement and interior design has crossed the gender barrier.

The separation of sex from reproduction and raising women's awareness of contraception was one significant element in the second wave of feminism. Its hopes for transforming society have been grounded in the education of women. The role of literature in consciousness-raising was crucial but feminists also needed to gather evidence of the prevailing conditions. Groundbreaking analyses were needed. Shere Hite's *The Hite Report: A Nationwide Survey of Sexuality* (1977) provided breadth while articles such as Anna Koedt's 'The Myth of the Vaginal Orgasm' (1968) exposed a single dominant idea, rejecting the necessary connection between penetrative sex and vaginal orgasm. The second wave of feminism coincided with a range of other challenges in the 1960s, extending the debate to female sexual desire. In *The Driver's Seat* (1970), Muriel Spark takes to an extreme the self-destructive effects of prevalent ideas about a subordinate femininity. The exposition of the deadly effects of patriarchy was found in the work of writers such as Margaret Atwood, Doris Lessing and Angela Carter. In 1963, the widespread dissatisfaction of women was identified by Betty Friedan in *The Feminine Mystique* which provided a comprehensive analysis of the state of the social condition as it affected women, followed by Germaine Greer's ground-breaking *The Female Eunuch* (1970) and Kate Millett's *Sexual Politics* (1970). Literary studies and psychoanalysis informed the work of Millett, in her scrutiny of the damaging images of women in the work of male literary authors and that of Juliet Mitchell in *Women: The Longest Revolution* (1984) which examined the novel in particular tracing its construction of woman from the eighteenth century onwards.

As Susan Watkins' essay in Part IV of this book explains, the relationship of sexuality to patriarchy has been of particular concern to feminism and was questioned by Adrienne Rich in her groundbreaking essay 'Compulsory Heterosexuality and Lesbian Existence' (1980). Rich's work sought to identify the institutional contexts to sexuality, to free it up from biological determinism and open it to choice. The broadcasting on television of various dramatizations featuring lesbian characters has contributed to a sense of visibility and acceptance. Notable moments included the first lesbian kiss on British Television in the soap opera *Brookside,* the serializations of Jeanette Winterson's *Oranges Are Not the Only Fruit* and Sarah Waters' novel *Tipping the Velvet.*

The influence of poststructuralist theories on feminist thinking inevitably raised questions about the claims of women's experience and perspectives attributed to women rather than men. A turning point in feminist theorizing came into view with Judith Butler's *Gender Trouble* (1990). Butler reassessed the sex-gender distinction, arguing that sex as well as gender is constructed rather than a given. The exclusivity of the universalizing category of woman was challenged together with an ethnocentric tendency in feminist thinking. When the constituents of women as a group went unexamined the risk was exclusion and the reproduction of the interests of a white, middle-class and heterosexual norm. Feminists such as bell hooks (1982) had already presented a challenge to this tendency. The development of queer theory has provided a position from which to challenge heteronormativity and drawn a coalition of people with a wide spectrum of desires.

The individualism and hedonism promoted in the 1980s at a time when more young women in Britain became economically independent provided a context for the backlash against feminism identified by Susan Faludi in 1991. The female body as object of scrutiny has long been a contentious issue in feminism and was reassessed by Naomi Wolf in *The Beauty Myth* (1990) where she controversially criticized feminists for imposing restrictions on other women no longer at ease in terms of their appearance. Postfeminism or the 'new feminism' seems to be characterized by individualism rather than collectivism and an approach to liberation which is presented as ideologically neutral.

The year 1996 saw the launch of the Spice Girls and their brand of 'girl power' as well as a publishing phenomenon which emphasized the commercial value of the predicament of young women. With the success of Helen Fielding's *Bridget Jones's Diary* (1996) and Candace Bushnell's *Sex and the City* (1996) came a reassessment of gender which prompted older feminists to challenge the effects of chick lit on the younger generation.

The contentious claim that the arguments of feminism are outdated has accompanied much discussion of postfeminism. According to Mary Joannou,

> The reader of women's fiction in the twenty-first century is likely to be faced with a disjunction between a sophisticated and potentially liberating understanding of the unstable nature of all gendered and sexual identities and of the institutions that sustain them, which is offered to her by a combination of poststructuralist ideas and feminist theory, and a desire for more permanent identities and representations to contest the demeaning

and restricted view of women which have historically prevailed. (Joannou 2000: p. 191)

Feminism has been accused of doing women a disservice yet the new ideas which have been proposed are rarely grounded in new evidence. To some extent the issues identified by second-wave feminism remain unresolved and continue to fascinate female authors.

## Posthuman

What is at stake when readers become so immersed in the world of a novel that they confuse characters with people? Is it tempting to assume we can envisage the thoughts and emotions of the writer on the basis of the skeletal words on the page? In close reading the literary text, the reader may be driven by a desire to fill in the gaps in her knowledge, to extend her experience and journey into another world view for the pleasurable hours spent reading. Driven in pursuit of an answer, the process may lead to the quest for a coherent self and the appreciation of a valuable truth. Contemporary culture frequently thwarts this pursuit by conceptualizing the human subject in a fundamentally different way. This can be a shock. Surely literature above all will provide insights into what it means to be human? The context for this question lies in a world where reproduction can be organized asexually, the body can be transformed and augmented and human consciousness can be altered by chemical or technological intervention.

Viewed as a frame for post-war and contemporary writing, an important effect of the idea of the post-human is to focus our attention on changing ideas of the self.

In the realist narrative, the coherence of the characters, the familiarity of the setting and the plausibility of the action all contribute to a picture of a world which seems to make sense; where people know themselves, learn to understand each other and overcome conflict to arrive at some other place. There is an implication of progress having been made, even while tragedies and misunderstandings have been part of the journey. The modernist project of the early twentieth century questioned this and arrived at an appreciation of the uncertainties of a split self. The rational, conscious, logical entity is at the same time driven by unpredictable impulses from the unconscious, emerging in dream, fantasy and linguistic expression. The relativity of time, the uncertainties of experience, the multiple perspectives at work in perception and the questioning of religion and science – those grand narratives which provide a solid framework to explain and guarantee a world view – were all new ideas which conspired to render the human subject vulnerable. The inner workings of the human consciousness became the object of scrutiny for writers.

In 1954 Aldous Huxley's *The Doors of Perception* provided an insight into the effects of consciousness-altering drugs. While the opportunities which this offered the individual for a personal journey of exploration was taken up by the counter-culture in the 1960s, Huxley had envisaged the use of drugs by the State to control its population in his novel *Brave New World* (1932). The recognizable behaviour of emotional responses and experience of family bonds are presented as abnormal curiosities exhibited by the savages:

> 'The Savage,' wrote Bernard, 'refuses to take soma, and seems much distressed because the woman Linda, his m-, remains permanently on holiday. It is worthy of note, that, in spite of his m-'s appearance, the Savage frequently goes to see her and appears to be much attached to her.' (Huxley 1932: p. 145)

Ideas about extending the experience and capabilities of the human by scientific developments – in prolonging life span, use of prosthetics, consciousness-altering drugs and interface with new technologies – were all common features of science fiction but are becoming more familiar as possible scientific developments of the very near future.

Where does the posthumanist perspective take us? It decentres the human and removes the privileged position automatically ascribed to it. The human-animal relationship is most obviously affected but the human-machine interface is becoming perhaps the more fascinating possibility for some authors. The hybrid figure of Fevvers in Angela Carter's *Nights at the Circus* (1984) takes the reader on a magic realist flight from the strictly human realm. Literary engagements with posthumanism are most apparent in post-war British literature in the field of science fiction, where the human is decentred in unfamiliar worlds inhabited by beings which cross the expected boundaries between human and machine or human and animal. In William Gibson's *Neuromancer* (1984) she has the retractable claws of a cat but this extension of her physical powers is brought about by technological means. The figure of the cyborg can take on animal as well as human properties.

Cyborgs or cybernetic organisms are commonplace in contemporary film and advertising. The point at which the cyborg is a strange figure has arguably passed. Donna Haraway's 'Manifesto for Cyborgs' (1985) claims for feminism the new subjectivity in the age of cyberspace which leaves behind the restrictions of the human. The cyborg is beyond gender, has no origins, traverses the boundaries of human-machine-animal; it rejects the assumptions of Western philosophy which opposes mind and body, culture and nature, wholeness and knowledge. Haraway cites science fiction as the form in which the cyborg has been tested out.

The powers of genetic engineering, and especially of cloning, have captured the imagination of writers such as Margaret Atwood, Kazuo Ishiguro, Zadie Smith and Caryl Churchill. In Ursula K. LeGuin's *The Left Hand of Darkness* (1969), the means of human reproduction and consequent social and emotional relationships are reimagined:

> They do not see one another as men or women. This is almost impossible for our imagination to accept. What is the first question we ask about a newborn baby?
>
> Yet you cannot think of a Gethenian as 'it'. They are not neuters. They are potentials or integrals. (LeGuin 1992: p. 85)

If human life can be created in the laboratory how does this affect the life created? How does it affect human development and social interaction? These questions were explored by Mary Shelley in *Frankenstein* (1831). To some extent, Frankenstein's 'creature' is the most human character in the novel. He puts forward the persuasive case for the right to a full life and makes a claim on his creator to fulfil his duty. He is driven to destructive acts because Victor Frankenstein refuses to accept his responsibility as parental figure and denies the creature the right to a companion. The creature evokes fear because he may reproduce a source of anxiety in numerous science fiction. Typically the robot or the human clone is feared because it is assumed that physiological similarity overrides the determining effects of nurture, and social circumstances. However this is rejected by scientists:

> [. . .] a clone would not and, indeed could not, be a mere copy of its progenitor. Unfortunately, however, the idea of clones as copies has found a prominent place in our cloning conversations [. . .] But people cannot be copied. Our mirror image will never come to life on our side of the looking glass. Reconstructing a new person using a single cell taken from a progenitor would duplicate only the genome. The clone would be a later-born identical twin. While the copying metaphor may lend itself more readily to clones than twins because, sequentially, the clone follows the progenitor, the term is as misleading applied to one as it is to the other. (Klotzko 2005: p. 148)

The worst scenario is explored in Ira Levin's *The Boys from Brazil* (1976) where the cloning of Hitler is accompanied by the engineering of the similar family circumstances with regard to parenting. Representations of human cloning in contemporary fiction may engage more with fears about the alienation of living in the modern world than with what is realizable scientifically.

N. Katherine Hayles (1999) defines the posthuman in terms of the separation of information from the body, the self as multiple and dispersed, the body as extendable and transformative and the human-machine interface as potentially seamless, quoting William Gibson's *Neuromancer* for a definition of the posthuman body as 'data made flesh' (Gibson 1984: p. 16).

Hayles argues that the posthuman is not anti-human:

> [. . .] the posthuman does not really mean the end of humanity. It signals instead the end of a certain conception of the human, a conception that may have applied, at best, to that fraction of humanity who had the wealth, power, and leisure to conceptualize themselves as autonomous beings exercising their will through individual agency and choice. What is lethal is not the posthuman as such but the grafting of the posthuman onto a liberal humanist view of the self. (Hayles 1999: pp. 2386–7)

If the cyborg has become a familiar figure in the science-fiction action film and while the use of computers in various forms has become a seamless part of daily experience, it seems feasible that the near future is posthuman. However, such rapid technological changes may simply be incorporated into the human condition. Although the extent to which new technology, the engagement with cyberspace and virtual reality, necessarily affects the perception of the self is not clear, some welcome this new world view. Given the cultural shifts associated with other technological revolutions of the past – the steam engine, the car, aviation, the telephone – it may be some time before the implications become clear but it is likely that artists and writers will be ready to explore them.

## Post-9/11

On 11 September 2001, a trio of passenger jets were flown into the two towers of the World Trade Centre in New York City, and into the west side of the Pentagon in Arlington Virginia. A fourth jet, possibly intended for an attack on Capitol Hill, Washington DC, crashed in a rural area of Pennsylvania. As the linguist Martin Montgomery (2005) shows in his work on responses to 9/11, the attacks triggered a major sea-change in political discourse within the United States, both in the media and in government. In the weeks, months and years that followed, a host of theorists and writers publicly grappled with the implications of the attacks, in a struggle to assign them coherent meaning.

Among the many and varied theoretical responses, one that is especially worthy of mention is the Slovenian theorist Slavoj Zizek's *Welcome to the Desert of the Real* (2002), in that it cuts across many of the rapidly solidifying reactions to 9/11. An important stress of Zizek's book is to counsel against unconsidered, reflex responses, whether in the form of an aggressive American nationalism or, on the Left, a certain kind of 'I told you so' satisfaction, 'with its *Schadenfreude*: the USA got what it deserved, what it had been doing to others for decades' (Zizek 2002: p. 51). Although written against the backdrop of America's rapid military mobilization and the commencement of its 'War on Terror', Zizek tries to resist such tendencies, capturing instead the strange sense of hiatus experienced by many writers and intellectuals at the time:

> Now, in the months following the attacks, it is as if we are living in the unique time between a traumatic event and its symbolic impact, as in those brief moments after we have been deeply cut, before the full extent of the pain strikes us. We do not yet know how the events will be symbolized, what their symbolic efficiency will be, what acts they will be evoked to justify. [. . .] So what about the phrase which reverberates everywhere: 'Nothing will ever be the same after September 11'? Significantly, this phrase is never further elaborated – it is just an empty gesture of saying something 'deep' without really knowing what we want to say. (Zizek 2002: pp. 44–6)

Fiction writers who have rushed to deploy the World Trade Centre attacks as an edgy backdrop to their fiction have certainly attracted wide readerships, but have also frequently attracted negative critical commentary. One such example is Jonathan Safran Foer's *Extremely Loud and Incredibly Close* (2005), which concludes with a sequence of pictures of a body falling from the North Tower. Foer's novel re-uses the work of Associated Press photographer Richard Drew, who captured scores of images of people falling to their deaths on the morning of September 11, and achieved major success with the most striking of these, a photograph he entitled 'The Falling Man'. If Drew's response to 9/11 illustrates a particularly chilling brand of professionalism, Foer's recycling of his work runs a different risk, perhaps inherent in all artistic negotiations of public trauma, that their handling may be found glib and unfitting.

Among British writers, Martin Amis has attracted exactly this kind of negative judgement from many critics, for his short story 'The Last Days of Muhammad Atta' (2006). Amis' work is well known for its fearlessness in handling controversial subject matter, as well as its experimental narrative strategies. In 'The Last Days of Muhammad Atta' he attempts to jar popular perceptions of September 11 by presenting its events through the eyes of one of the lead terrorists. In the actual text, though, his representation of Atta comes so close to caricature, complete with bad breath and a face 'growing more gangrenous by the hour', that there is little room for psychological or ideological insight.

In critical commentaries on '9/11' novels, films and poetry, it is interesting to note the ways in which a test or expectation comes over – that writers have to 'earn' the right to meddle with such public trauma. In Amis' case, the

21

overwhelming consensus seems to be that 'The Last Days of Muhammad Atta' fails that test of adequacy. Nevertheless, it is also interesting to see how heavily that collective judgement appears to rest on matters of taste, rather than on any more developed set of critical criteria. This, in itself, perhaps reveals something about the fledgling state of 'post-9/11' as a critical paradigm.

According to the critic Philip Tew (2007), one of the salient features of post-9/11 writing is that it captures and crystallizes a particular contemporary sensibility, that of trauma. One of the most thought-provoking early responses to the September 11 attacks, in this sense, was perhaps that offered by the Irish poet Seamus Heaney, in a 2003 graduation lecture at Emory University, Atlanta. Heaney reflected on the powerful public call for poets to respond to the trauma of the atrocity, on behalf of everyone; to create monuments of the imagination which might in some way replace the physical edifices that had been destroyed. For poets themselves, this call to build some kind of redemptive, collective vision out of the rubble of ground zero of course sets up extraordinary difficulties:

> These have been astounding events, yet our consciousness hasn't quite got
> the measure of them. Twin towers bursting into flame, human bodies
> falling like plummets, sorties of black-winged bombers taking off, as
> terrible and phantasmagorical as blackwinged devils of the medieval
> mind, explosions appearing in the coordinates of a reconnaissance camera,
> looking as harmlessly white and fluttery as snowflakes. (Caputi 2005: p. 1)

Within the post-war period in Britain, the negotiation of public trauma is certainly a challenge to which many writers have addressed themselves. According to Tew, what unites much of this writing pre-9/11, however, is the way such trauma is represented as a shattering force, both in terms of psychological representation and in terms of formal structure. This approach can undoubtedly be observed in the work of many leading writers. Peter Reading's *C* (1984) dealing with cancer and D. M. Thomas' *The White Hotel* (1981) dealing with the holocaust, though otherwise very different in tone and subject matter, both exemplify the use of fragmentation and self-conscious discontinuity as a way of negotiating traumatic subject matter. In post 9/11 writing, Tew argues however, there is a tendency to move away from this mode towards representations of trauma as public spectacle, not a shattering force but something which unifies and defines.

One example of this tendency is perhaps provided by Simon Armitage's elegy for the victims of the World Trade Centre attacks, 'Out of the Blue' (2006). In this poem's early sections, Armitage uses a single interior voice that of a British trader trapped in the North Tower at the moment of the attacks. As the terror and confusion of the event intensify, his stream-of-consciousness divides into many voices, with frequent formal and tonal shifts. As the poem draws towards its climax, however, the decisiveness with which Armitage moves to restore formal order is notable. In the final stanza of 'Out of the Blue' he shifts towards a disembodied, incantatory, public register, exhorting the reader to question what the collective, symbolic legacy of 9/11 should be.

Undoubtedly, the attacks of September 11, 2001, as well as America's response to them, brought with them a significant shift in the political discourse of the West. Within the field of contemporary criticism, this shift is reflected in the emergence of a new critical vogue, that of 'globalization', sometimes billed as the successor to postcolonialism (see above). Criticism keyed around the notion of globalization does not necessarily adopt 9/11 as a detailed focus, but it does usually retain it as a key cultural and political coordinate. More broadly, however, 'globalization' tends to frame critical discussions in relation to at least three recurring themes:

1 the worldwide expansion of consumer capitalism,
2 the homogenization of cultural difference in favour of ubiquitous corporate 'branding',
3 the hegemony of English as the global *lingua franca*.

As the critic James Annesley (2006) observes, these themes are vast in scope. One of the first challenges for critics wanting to work with the idea of globalization, then, is to focus their concerns tightly enough to enable productive analysis:

> Providing explanatory contexts for phenomena as diverse as global tourism, climate change, Jihadi terrorism, the power of transnational brands, mass migrations, the spread of the English language and the growth of global media, and understood as the product of complex, interrelated changes in the organisation of social, political and economic life that are in turn read in relation to technological developments, the danger is that globalization offers both a theory of everything and an explanation of nothing. (Annesley 2006: p. 4)

While postmodernism's view was often restricted to the analysis of 'late capitalist' or consumer society, and postcolonialism's view tended to focus on the dialectic of colonialism *vs* resistance, the potential of 'globalization' is to unite these concerns within one analytical framework. In order to be of genuine use to critics in their task of elucidating the imaginative and intellectual strategies of writers and texts, however, there is a need for its broad themes to be mediated through strategies for critical reading that, themselves, resist the urge to homogenize. As an emerging critical paradigm, like 'post-9/11', it should be recognized that 'globalization' remains a work-in-progress.

## Approaching Post-War British Literature

What is the relationship between post-war and contemporary writing and the historical period which produced it? This is a good question to start with in order to work through your approach to this field. Working with living writers, there may be little existing critical work to guide you. Some basic information might be useful such as biographical information about the author, the date when the text was written and published, who read it when it first appeared and how was it received. Studying reviews can help you establish how unusual your own response is and to what extent your evaluation of the text is confirmed by others. Newspapers, journals, television and radio programmes and book groups all regularly produce reviews of new writing and interview authors to ask them about their work. What kinds of questions would you put to the author of the book you are currently studying? Do you expect the author to have the definitive answer? These issues are all relevant to the task of situating your literary reading in a historical context.

Effective and persuasive criticism is always a marriage between fresh, personal insights on the one hand, and an understanding of existing debates on the other. This book aims to provide the tools to help readers manage both sides of this equation. Part I provides an historical overview of the period by one of the most influential and experienced critics in post-war literary studies, together with a series of short guides to key literary and cultural contexts. Part II offers a series of exemplary case studies in critical reading, encompassing literary, critical and theoretical texts. Part III includes a reference section covering the key critics, theorists and topics you are likely to encounter, together with five short essays outlining the most influential critical approaches. Finally, Part IV offers three 'position pieces' written by leading critics, giving a taste of contemporary scholarship as it is practised now. As we suggested at the beginning of this introduction, *The Post-War British Literature Handbook* is not intended as an exhaustive survey of all significant texts and writers to hit the UK literary scene since 1945, and does not attempt to lay down a monolithic interpretation of post-war writing. On the contrary, it is intended as an aid to readers in forming their own distinctive, individual engagements with the writing of our time.

# Timeline

|  | Literary | Cultural | Historical |
|---|---|---|---|
| **1945** | George Orwell, *Animal Farm* | *Brief Encounter* | |
| **1946** | | BBC Third Programme launched | |
| **1947** | | | Indian Independence |
| **1948** | | | Arrival of Empire Windrush Establishment of the National Health Service Republic of Ireland established |
| **1949** | George Orwell, *1984* | Simone de Beauvoir, *The Second Sex* *The Third Man* | |
| **1950** | C. S. Lewis, *The Lion, The Witch and the Wardrobe* | | |
| **1951** | John Wyndham, *The Day of the Triffids* | Festival of Britain | |
| **1952** | | | Coronation of Elizabeth II |
| **1953** | Ian Fleming, *Casino Royale* L. P. Hartley *The Go-Between* | | Death of Joseph Stalin |
| **1954** | William Golding, *The Lord of the Flies* Kingsley Amis, *Lucky Jim* Iris Murdoch, *Under the Net* | *The Belles of St Trinian's* | Beginning of the Vietnam War |
| **1955** | R. S. Thomas, *Song at the Year's Turning* | Launch of ITV Walter Benjamin, *Illuminations* *The Dam Busters* | |
| **1956** | John Osborne, *Look Back in Anger* Sam Selvon, *The Lonely Londoners* | | Suez Crisis |
| **1957** | Ted Hughes, *The Hawk in the Rain* John Braine, *Room At The Top* | Richard Hoggart, *The Uses of Literacy* Wolfenden Report | Ghanaian Independence Harold Macmillan becomes Prime Minister Britain tests H-bomb |

|  | Literary | Cultural | Historical |
|---|---|---|---|
| **1958** | Alan Sillitoe, *Saturday Night and Sunday Morning* Colin MacInnes, *Absolute Beginners* | Raymond Williams, *Culture and Society* | Race riots in Notting Hill and Nottingham |
| **1959** | Keith Waterhouse, Billy Liar Alan Sillitoe, *The Loneliness of the Long Distance Runner* Laurie Lee, *Cider with Rosie* | Obscene Publications Act | |
| **1960** | David Storey, *This Sporting Life* Stan Barstow, *A Kind of Loving* Raymond Williams, *Border Country* Lynne Reid Banks, *The L-Shaped Room* | *Lady Chatterley's Lover* trial | Nigerian Independence |
| **1961** | Iris Murdoch, *A Severed Head* Muriel Spark, *The Prime of Miss Jean Brodie* | | |
| **1962** | Anthony Burgess, *A Clockwork Orange* Doris Lessing, *The Golden Notebook* | | Cuban missile crisis Commonwealth Immigration Act |
| **1963** | Sylvia Plath, *The Bell Jar* Margaret Drabble, *A Summer Bird Cage* Nell Dunn, *Up The Junction* | Betty Friedan, *The Feminine Mystique* | Kenyan Independence Assassination of John F. Kennedy |
| **1964** | Philip Larkin, *The Whitsun Weddings* | Herbert Marcuse, *One-dimensional Man* | Harold Wilson becomes Prime Minister |
| **1965** | Sylvia Plath, *Ariel* Margaret Drabble, *The Millstone* | Death of T. S. Eliot | Death Penalty Abolished Beginning of Chinese Cultural Revolution |
| **1966** | Seamus Heaney, *Death of a Naturalist* | Bill Naughton, *Alfie* | |
| **1967** | Nell Dunn, *Poor Cow* Angela Carter, *The Magic Toyshop* | Jacques Derrida, *Writing and Difference* | Sexual Offences Act Abortion Act |

| | Literary | Cultural | Historical |
|---|---|---|---|
| **1968** | Barry Hines, *Kes* | Enoch Powell, 'Rivers of Blood' speech<br>E. P. Thompson, *The Making of the English Working Class*<br>Roland Barthes, *Writing Degree Zero* | Assassination of Martin Luther King<br>May 1968 Uprisings in France<br>Theatres Act |
| **1969** | John Fowles, *The French Lieutenant's Woman*<br>P. H. Newby, *Something to Answer For* | Kate Millet, *Sexual Politics*<br>*The Italian Job* | |
| **1970** | Muriel Spark, *The Driver's Seat*<br>Bernice Rubens, *The Elected Member* | | Equal Pay Act<br>Edward Heath becomes Prime Minister |
| **1971** | V. S. Naipaul, *In a Free State* | First Women's Liberation March, London | Beginning of the 'Troubles' in Northern Ireland<br>Bangladesh War<br>Immigration Act |
| **1972** | Stevie Smith, *Collected Poems*<br>Buchi Emecheta, *In the Ditch*<br>John Berger, *G.* | Wages for Work Campaign | Bloody Sunday |
| **1973** | J. G. Ballard, *Crash*<br>Ritae Brown, *Rubyfruit Jungle*<br>J. G. Farrell, *The Siege of Krishnapur* | Theodor Adorno, *Negative Dialectics*<br>*The Wicker Man* | |
| **1974** | Erica Jong, *Fear of Flying*<br>Nadine Gordimer, *The Conservationist*<br>Stanley Middleton, *Holiday* | Contraception available from NHS<br>Henri Lefebvre, *The Production of Space* | |
| **1975** | Linton Kwesi Jonson, *Dread Beat An' Blood*<br>Malcolm Bradbury, *The History Man*<br>Ruth Prawer Jhabvala, *Heat and Dust* | | Sex Discrimination Act |
| **1976** | John Fowles, *Daniel Martin*<br>Marge Piercy, *Woman on the Edge of Time*<br>David Storey, *Saville* | Shere Hite, *The Hite Report*<br>Richard Dawkins, *The Selfish Gene*<br>Michel Foucault, *The History of Sexuality, Vol. 1* | Death of Mao Zedong<br>Race Relations Act |

| | Literary | Cultural | Historical |
|---|---|---|---|
| **1977** | Lisa Alther, *Kinflicks*<br>Marilyn French, *The Women's Room*<br>Paul Scott, *Staying On* | | |
| **1978** | Iris Murdoch, *The Sea, The Sea* | Edward Said, *Orientalism* | Winter of Discontent |
| **1979** | Seamus Heaney, *Field Work*<br>Penelope Fitzgerald, *Offshore* | Feminist Review founded<br>Angela Carter, *The Sadeian Woman* | Margaret Thatcher becomes Prime Minister<br>Islamic Revolution in Iran<br>Soviet invasion of Afghanistan |
| **1980** | William Golding, *Rites of Passage* | The Long Good Friday | |
| **1981** | Salman Rushdie, *Midnight's Children*<br>D. M. Thomas, *The White Hotel*<br>Alasdair Gray, *Lanark*<br>Brian Patten, *Love Poems* | Gregory's Girl | Brixton riots<br>Beginning of the AIDS crisis<br>Death of hunger striker Bobby Sands<br>British Nationality Act |
| **1982** | Caryl Churchill, *Top Girls*<br>James Fenton, *The Memory of War*<br>Pat Barker, *Union Street*<br>Thomas Keneally, *Schindler's Ark* | Silver Jubilee of Elizabeth II<br>Establishment of Peace Camp at Greenham Common<br>*Boys From the Blackstuff*<br>*Gandhi* | Falklands War |
| **1983** | Fay Weldon, *The Life and Loves of a She-Devil*<br>Grace Nichols, *I is a Long-Memoried Woman*<br>Graham Swift, *Waterland*<br>Salman Rushdie, *Shame*<br>J. M. Coetzee, *Life and Times of Michael K* | Jean Beaudrillard, *Simulations* | |
| **1984** | Angela Carter *Nights at the Circus*<br>J. G. Ballard, *Empire of the Sun*<br>Martin Amis, *Money*<br>Seamus Heaney, *Station Island*<br>Anita Brookner, *Hotel du Lac* | Michel de Certeau, *The Practice of Everyday Life*<br>Jean Francois Lyotard, *The Postmodern Condition* | Miners' Strike<br>Assassination of Indira Gandhi<br>IRA bombing of Conservative Conference, Brighton |

|      | Literary | Cultural | Historical |
|------|----------|----------|------------|
| **1985** | Jeanette Winterson *Oranges are Not the Only Fruit*<br>Caryl Phillips, *The Final Passage*<br>Carol Ann Duffy, *Standing Female Nude*<br>Joan Riley, *The Unbelonging*<br>Tony Harrison, *V*<br>Keri Hulme, *The Bone People* | Hanif Kureishi *My Beautiful Laundrette*<br>*Edge of Darkness* | |
| **1986** | Kazuo Ishiguro, *The Artist of the Floating World*<br>Pat Barker, *The Century's Daughter*<br>Margaret Atwood, *The Handmaid's Tale*<br>Kingsley Amis, *The Old Devils* | Caravaggio | Chernobyl nuclear disaster |
| **1987** | Margaret Drabble, *The Radiant Way*<br>Ian McEwan, *The Child in Time*<br>V. S. Naipaul, *The Enigma of Arrival*<br>Ciarán Carson, *The Irish for No*<br>Penelope Lively, *Moon Tiger* | | |
| **1988** | Alan Hollinghurst, *The Swimming-pool Library*<br>David Lodge, *Nice Work*<br>Peter Carey, *Oscar and Lucinda* | | |
| **1989** | Kazuo Ishiguro, *The Remains of the Day*<br>Margaret Drabble, *A Natural Curiosity*<br>Jeanette Winterson, *Sexing the Cherry*<br>Janice Galloway, *The Trick is to Keep Breathing*<br>Martin Amis, *London's Fields* | Invention of the World Wide Web<br>The Rushdie Affair over *The Satanic Verses* | Fall of the Berlin Wall<br>Tiananmen Square massacre |
| **1990** | Hanif Kureishi, *The Buddha of Suburbia*<br>A. S. Byatt, *Possession*<br>Paul Muldoon, *Madoc: A Mystery*<br>Pat Barker, *Regeneration* | Judith Butler, *Gender Trouble*<br>Donna Haraway, 'A Manifesto for Cyborgs'<br>*Total Recall* | German reunification<br>Poll Tax protests<br>John Major becomes Prime Minister<br>Human Fertilisation and Embryology Act |

| | Literary | Cultural | Historical |
|---|---|---|---|
| **1991** | Ben Okri, *The Famished Road* Margaret Drabble, *The Gates of Ivory* | Fredric Jameson, *Postmodernism, or, the Cultural Logic of Late Capitalism* | First Gulf War Breakup of the Soviet Union |
| **1992** | Jeanette Winterson, *Written on the Body* Jim Crace, *Arcadia* Michael Ondaatje, *The English Patient* Barry Unsworth, *Sacred Hunger* | Francis Fukuyama, *The End of History and the Last Man* | Black Wednesday economic crisis |
| **1993** | Caryl Phillips *Crossing the River* Irvine Welsh, *Trainspotting* Adam Mars-Jones, *The Waters of Thirst* Roddy Doyle, *Paddy Clarke Ha Ha Ha* Jeff Noon, *Vurt* Vikram Seth, *A Suitable Boy* | Murder of Stephen Lawrence | |
| **1994** | James Kelman, *How Late It Was, How Late* | *Pulp Fiction* | Apartheid abolished in South Africa Rwandan genocide |
| **1995** | Irvine Welsh, *Marabou Stork Nightmares* Nick Hornby, *High Fidelity* Alan Warner, *Morven Callar* Pat Barker, *The Ghost Road* | | Disability Discrimination Act |
| **1996** | Meera Syal, *Anita and Me* Helen Fielding, *Bridget Jones's Diary* Graham Swift, *Last Orders* | | |
| **1997** | Arundhati Roy, *The God of Small Things* Sadie Plant, *Zeroes + Ones* | *The Full Monty* | Tony Blair becomes Prime Minister Death of Princess Diana |
| **1998** | Ian McEwan, *Amsterdam* Irvine Welsh, *Filth* Ted Hughes, *Birthday Letters* Sarah Waters, *Tipping the Velvet* | Natasha Walter, *The New Feminism* Stephen Hawking, *A Brief History of Time* *The Truman Show* | Good Friday Agreement European Human Rights Act |
| **1999** | J. M. Coetzee, *Disgrace* | N. Katherine Hayles, *How We Became Posthuman* *The Matrix* *Fight Club* | |

| | Literary | Cultural | Historical |
|---|---|---|---|
| **2000** | Zadie Smith, *White Teeth*<br>Jeanette Winterson,<br>*The.PowerBook*<br>Naomi Klein, *No Logo*<br>Margaret Atwood, *The Blind Assassin* | | |
| **2001** | Jonathan Coe, *The Rotters' Club*<br>Peter Carey, *True History of the Kelly Gang* | | World Trade Center attacks<br>US attacks on Afghanistan |
| **2002** | Slavoj Zizek, *Welcome to the Desert of the Real*<br>Yann Martel, *Life of Pi* | | |
| **2003** | Monica Ali, *Brick Lane*<br>D.B.C Pierre, *Vernon God Little* | | US Invasion of Iraq |
| **2004** | Andrea Levy, *Small Island*<br>Alan Hollinghurst, *The Line of Beauty* | | Madrid train bombings<br>Gender Recognition Act |
| **2005** | John Banville, *The Sea* | | Civil Partnerships Act<br>7/7 bombings on London Transport |
| **2006** | Simon Armitage, 'Out of the Blue'<br>Sarah Waters, *The Night Watch*<br>Kiran Desai, *The Inheritance of Loss* | | |
| **2007** | Sean O'Brien, *The Drowned Book*<br>Ian McEwan, *On Chesil Beach*<br>Anne Enright, *The Gathering* | | Gordon Brown becomes Prime Minister |
| **2008** | David Lodge, *Deaf Sentence*<br>Salman Rushdie, *The Enchantress of Florence*<br>Aravind Adiga, *The White Tiger* | | Election results withheld in Zimbabwe<br>Human Fertilization and Embryology Bill |

# Part I
# Contexts

# 2 The Historical Context of Post-War British Literature

## Patricia Waugh

## Post-War Britain: From Cautious Consensus to Cold War

Though 8 May 1945, VE Day, is the official beginning of the post-war period in Britain, radio broadcasts the day before had already spread the news of the end of the conflict. The very medium whose technical advancement had transformed modern warfare was to be the same vehicle which ushered in the start of a new globalized modern world. By lunch-time on 8 May, Trafalgar Square and Whitehall were thronged with crowds waving banners, packed against railings, and expressing the promise of a new start. At precisely 3 p.m., just as the 'leaden circles' of Big Ben's boom gradually died to an expectant hush, Winston Churchill announced the 'unconditional surrender' of the enemy, proclaiming that 'the evil-doers now lie prostrate before us' as the words 'Advance Britannia' resounded through strains of 'God Save the King' (Nicholson 1970: p. 461). The theme of evil would loom large in post-war intellectual life: though Orwell had suggested in his 1945 essay, 'Notes on Nationalism', that one of the assumptions of nationalism had always been that human beings, like insects, could be neatly classified and definitively labelled 'good' or bad', the question of value, of the conditions for a good society, are at the intellectual heart of the post-war period. As debates about the building of consensus gave way, some thirty years later, to obituaries on its demise, and to prognostications of the rise of postmodernism and the 'break-up' of Britain, so too, notions of good and evil and questions of value would become increasingly relativized by the late seventies. Indeed, this will form a central theme of the period and of this chapter.

How to define the 'post-war consensus'? In part, social and political consensus was the consequence of hard-fought and inspired social engineering and planning from the moment of the Beveridge Report in 1942, through the post-war Atlee government and on to the 'Butskellite' middle way, the compromise of Conservative and Labour, from 1951 onwards. However, it was built initially out of the sense of national unity fostered during the war. Although the First World War is the so-called 'People's War', in fact the Second World War penetrated far more deeply into the everyday lives of ordinary people: across the spectrum of class and social groups, there was a deeply shared sense of threat and emotional horror arising from experiences such as the Blitz. This sense of wartime unity lingered, often nostalgically, in much of the writing of the next twenty years. Even in literary works regarded as definitively 'fifties' in outlook, a curious adherence to a mildly sentimentalized vision of war solidarity lived on: Alan Sillitoe's defiant Arthur Seaton in *Saturday Night and Sunday Morning* (1958) harks back continuously to the working class solidarity of the war years, a time when everyone seemed to have been fighting for the same thing; even Kingsley Amis' Jim Dixon, of *Lucky Jim* (1954), keeps his precious notebooks in an RAF file and hankers for a life in a metropolis imagined through the sepia lens of war-time memories.

Virginia Woolf had expressed this collective mood of fear and longing in an essay, 'Thoughts on Peace in an Air Raid' (1942: p. 154):

> The Germans were over this house last night and the night before that.
> Here they are again. It is a queer experience, lying in the dark and listening
> to the zoom of a hornet which may at any moment sting you to death. It is
> a sound that interrupts cool and consecutive thinking about peace. Yet it is
> a sound – far more than prayers and anthems – that should compel one to
> think about peace. Unless we can think peace into existence we – not this
> one body in this one bed but millions of bodies yet to be born – will lie in
> the same darkness and hear the same death rattle overhead.

The essay goes on to suggest a gendered perspective on the war, but its opening lines confidently address a collective 'we' who share the threat to humanity that war represents – even to its unborn members. In the last years of the war, some two and a half thousand VI bombs ('buzz-bombs') were dropped on London and their familiar menacing roar, which cut suddenly to a suspenseful silence, was absorbed into the metropolitan psyche almost like the irrevocable chimes of Big Ben sounding away the hours. Fearful suspense, the moment of dread, is recorded in much literature of the time and draws on and evokes the experience of bombing even when ostensibly about other kinds of experience. One of the most memorable moments in the third section of 'East Coker', in T. S. Eliot's *Four Quartets* (2004), describes such an experience:

> Or as, when an underground train in the tube, stops too long
>   between stations
> And the conversation rises and slowly falls into silence
> And you see behind every face the mental emptiness deepen.

By 1944, the first ballistic missiles, the V2s, also the first cybernetic 'intelligent' weapons working on the principles of self-organization and feedback loops, had arrived silently, unannounced, sinister, dropping suddenly from clear skies, like the bomb that drops almost as the vehicle of a Fortunate Fall near the end of Graham Greene's *The End of the Affair* (1951). The dual experience of waiting for the predictable explosion and yet the unpredictability of its destruction of life and livelihood prompted George Orwell (in another uncanny anticipation of literary responses to the suicide bombings of 9/11) to pronounce that 'only the mentally dead are capable of sitting down and writing novels while this nightmare is going on' (1968: p. 72). But as war ended, Mass Observation reports noted heightened social expectations and hopes arising out of the war-time will to rise above narrow or sectarian interests in order to confront the threat of totalitarian occupation. After the war, such expectations fed into further hopes for a more consensual society which might benefit all of its members. In 1940, Ernest Bevin, the charismatic General Secretary of the Transport and General Workers' Union, entered the wartime coalition government as Minister for Labour and, in 1942, produced the report on social insurance which established the principles for a welfare consensus built on Keynesian mixed economic foundations that would last until the mid-seventies. By the end of the war, Beveridge's determination to flatten social hierarchies had expanded into a vision of a good society which would provide for and nurture the well-being and health of all its members, promising the eradication of what he saw as the five obstacles to social recovery: want, disease, ignorance, squalor and idleness. The vision included a free health service, expanded educational opportunities for all, child allowance, full employment and social housing. A series of subsequent Acts brought in the full panoply of the post-war settlement: the 1944 Butler Education Act; 1946 NHS Act; town and country planning acts with provision for Green spaces, social housing, traffic control and New Town planning; arts and media Acts covering broadcasting and sponsorship of culture.

There is no doubt that Butler was a visionary and indeed laid the foundations for radical social reform and a 'quiet' revolution in British culture and, although historians disagree on the extent to which a post-war consensus really was achieved, there is no doubt that the main political parties agreed on the broad principles of a good society underpinned by a welfare state and Keynesian economics. Under the temperamentally cautious Atlee's Labour government, however, and on into the period of 'Butskellism' which saw the Conservatives returned to office in 1951, the implementation of the process was necessarily gradual, conforming more to Karl Popper's recommendation of 'piecemeal' reform and to the anti-theoretical inclinations of the British, than to the apocalyptic picture of a New Jerusalem. This was especially the case given, too, a political atmosphere increasingly pervaded by Cold War fears of communist world revolution and invasion. Indeed, the years after the war were experienced for the most part as a continuation of suffering, deprivation and anxiety, and the landscape of Britain changed little. (The opening chapters of Doris Lessing's *The Four-Gated City* (1969) give one of the most forceful literary accounts of the grimy, down-trodden, suspicious and closed-minded atmosphere of Britain in 1949, seen through the eyes of a young and initially hopeful immigrant, Martha Quest). As the full economic consequences of the war gradually impinged, along with this came the recognition of Britain's economic dependence on America as well as her loss of world power as the (enormously costly) British Empire began to be dismantled in 1947. Domestic reform was, from the start, beset by economic obstacles and deep-seated if not always acknowledged ideological resistance to social planning and interference with the free market. The majority of literary intellectuals were gloomy, though for a variety of reasons, which therefore produced different orders of gloom: apocalyptic, melancholy, incensed, exasperated, nostalgic, envious, impatient and enervated varieties abounded and, indeed, even intensified at the beginning of the new decade, despite improved affluence, the end of rationing, and a general increase in popular optimism by this time.

In a short survey, one can only gesture at the complex mood evident in literary productions of the time, and a few examples will have to suffice. Best known, perhaps, is the editor of *Horizon*, Cyril Connolly's announcement in its last issue (1950), that 'it is closing time in the gardens of the West and from now on an artist will be judged only by the resonance of his solitude or the quality of his despair' (Hennessy 2006: p. 319). Significantly, gloom was neither a prerogative of the Right nor of the Left: in the late forties, and though their politics and personal predilections differed vastly, writings by Orwell, Eliot and Evelyn Waugh testify to a pervasive tendency to look backward with some nostalgia and to contemplate the future only through the lens of nightmare or the genre of dystopia. Orwell's *Nineteen Eighty-Four*

(1949) captured vividly the day-to-day experience of living in the immediate aftermath of war: the sense of bureaucratic regulation, managerial control and *lumpen* workers; the blackened and grimy public buildings (smog everywhere and no clean air act for another decade) and the narrow and tenebrous streets; the pallid faces emerging from shadows and drab utilitarian garments, chilblains and cheap alcohol that burned the digestive tract; the rubble and wasteland of 'decaying, dingy cities where underfed people shuffled to and fro in leaky shoes, in patched-up nineteenth-century houses that smelt always of cabbage and bad lavatories', a London 'vast and ruinous, city of a million dustbins' (1989: p. 77). Winston and Julia, of course, attempt to step into a pastoralized Golden Country which they (wrongly) imagine to be of their own making, and only the past, symbolized in the glass paperweight, seems to hold out any vision of the social good: 'such a depth of it, and yet it was almost as transparent as air ... enclosing a tiny world with its atmosphere complete. ... The paperweight was the room he was in, and the coral was Julia's life and his own, fixed in a sort of eternity at the heart of the crystal' (1949: p. 155): the paperweight stands too as an image of the novel, the book we are holding, and it also represents the importance of touch and of the tacit in a rationalized and bureaucratized world of newness, symbolizing the need to feel, to cradle something from the past, in one's hands.

Yet Orwell's insistence, like Eliot's too, on the responsibility of the writer to keep the language alive, 'purify the dialect of the tribe' in order to sustain a social vision, seemed curiously to falter in the writing of this immediate post-war generation. The writerly self-interrogation is there, but negatively, in the double association of the beauty of the paperweight with the aesthetic pleasures of the world of the ordinary, a better world, now irretrievably fled, but also with the pragmatism and intrusion of the police state which appropriates the aesthetic, building fictions and illusory belief systems, degenerate myths, for its own ideological and totalitarian purposes of social control. Under the brittle layer of social optimism lay a deeper and more resonant emotional stratum of fear, anxiety and trauma, not only lingering from the experience of the war, but also reflecting Cold War anxieties about totalitarian control and loss of national identity. Class and social group tensions were held only precariously in place by the 'the role of the state as the knitter of a safety net for society as a whole' (Hennessy 2007: p. 3). Muriel Spark's *The Girls of Slender Means* (1963), captured brilliantly the roots of this curiously mixed mood of 1945–50, the cloud of horror not quite dispersed, the sense of the human potential for evil lurking beneath the communitarian vision, the easy recourse to slogans and epithetical truisms as substitutes for hard moral thinking. With Austenesque irony, the novel begins: 'Long ago in 1945 all the nice people in England were poor, allowing for exceptions. The streets of the cities were lined with buildings in bad repair or no repair at all, bomb-sites piled with stony rubble, houses like giant teeth in which decay had been drilled out' (1966: p. 7). Phoenix-like, a vision of a Rousseauian republic of simple needs arises out of the rubble and waste of war, except that the class connotations of respectable English 'niceness' strike a discordant note amidst the raucous VE celebrations in Trafalgar Square. The 'girls of slender means', the impover-ished young ladies of the May of Teck Club, mingle with the demob happy, planning their economic futures and contemplating the 'new order', described as 'something between a wedding and a funeral on a world scale' (p. 17). But the novel closes with VJ day, a few months later, where, amidst the crowds of revellers and celebrants, random acts of rape, stabbing and intimate violence occur in pockets among the swaying carnival of the crowd. Poverty does not, it seems, guarantee 'niceness' or fellow feeling or communitarian solidarity, and as the slender hips of Selena squeeze through the narrow casement to rescue the Schiaparelli dress in preference to the trapped human being within, we recognize that 'slenderness' refers as much to the moral, as to the economic, circumstances and foundations of this brave new world.

One of Spark's patrons was T. S. Eliot, yet her novel has an ambivalent rela-tionship to his social and cultural vision, offering a more realistic (pessimistic?) antidote to his nostalgic vision of pre-Enlightenment feudal harmony in *Notes Towards the Definition of Culture* (1948), but in other ways sharing his concerns about the failures and blindnesses of liberalism as an adequate ethical value system with which to underpin the post-war 'good society'. Earlier, in *The Idea of a Christian Society* (1936), Eliot had disparaged the essentially negative ver-sion of liberty available in liberal societies and suggested that, in setting up freedom as its axiomatic value, liberalism had created an ethical vacuum into which the forces of Fascism, of blood and belief, had flown with alarming ease. But again there is no easy demarcation of Left and Right thinking on consensus and community at this moment: Orwell's essay, 'Hitler, Wells and the World State' (1941) had argued in essentially similar terms against the pre-war Wellsian vision of social planning and engineering and suggested, like Eliot, that the appeal of Fascism was to the human proclivity to abandon itself to irrational convictions, to what Isaiah Berlin would refer to in his *Two Concepts of Liberty* (1958) as a version of 'positive liberty', a substantive account of the good beyond and outside of justification in purely rational terms. Essentially, Eliot and Orwell, though at opposite ends of the political spec-trum, share anxieties about the extent to which humans can be herded into rationally planned orders and made to give enthusiastic assent to political and social systems which deliver only material comforts and rewards. New paganisms threatened to unite belief and behaviour through the technological and even aesthetic manipulation of the mob, and such Fascistic communities in turn threatened the sterilized orders of the planned societies of the post-war reconstruction. Interestingly, both Orwell and Eliot also regarded the family as under threat in this period. Orwell's novel begins with Winston Smith effectively, if inadvertently, betraying his mother and sister, while O'Brien functions as the charismatic figure substituting for the lost Victorian paterfamilias which Frankfurt school analysis would later regard as a potent source of Fascistic identification in the thirties. Meanwhile, Eliot was bewailing the transfer of the responsibility for the education of values from the rituals of church and family to those of the expert and the state educator, and viewing the growth of autonomous expert cultures, floating free of class or traditional attachment, as the source of inevitable cultural fragmentation, requiring a more radical cure than the palliative care of social planners. More profoundly than this, however, both see the new order as a thinning of the experiential, bringing a loss of sensory awareness and embodied consciousness, a disappearance of the dimension of the tacit as the locus of value which underpins all modes of human understanding and perception. For Eliot, culture cannot be planned by experts who have no feel for it, and for Orwell, cosmopolitan intellectuals have 'lost touch' with the working classes, whose emancipation they still claim as the goal of their new planned orders. Locked into abstract schemes far removed from any empirical or sensory grounding in the real, two and two might indeed come to equal five: but for Eliot and Orwell, true objectivity requires *moral* effort rather than mere ratiocination.

Wherever one looks in the literature of the time, one finds at best muted support for post-war planning and almost always a preference for retrospective idealization and anxiety about the loss of the tacit, the experiential, the roots that go back to the past. For unadulterated nostalgia arising out of outright condemnation of the present with its softening of the social hierarchy and its new economic planning, however, few pieces of writing proved as seductive as Evelyn Waugh's *Brideshead Revisited* (1945). The threat to the survival of the great aristocratic house is a symbol of the catastrophic threat to a naturalized hierarchical social order now under siege by the barbarous 'rational planning' of modernity. Ryder, an architectural writer, succumbs to the charms of the aristocratic Flyte family and attempts to reconcile commercial with sentimental promptings by taking up a new career, painting the great houses of Britain as a way of preserving for posterity their beauties (though in practice it would be the National Trust, set up under the new umbrella of town and country planning, that would largely guarantee the survival of this national architectural heritage). Waugh acknowledged as much in a preface written in 1959 for a new edition of the novel, reflecting with disdain that 'Brideshead today would be open to trippers, its treasures arranged by expert hands', but also, more cheerily, that the English aristocracy has managed to hold its identity and 'the advance of Hooper has been held up at several points' (Hooper in the novel designating the new reign of the sergeants): the work, he says, is a 'souvenir' of the second world war, 'a panegyric preached over an empty coffin' (1962: p. 10).

*(See Chapter 4: Nineteen Eighty-Four (1949); Chapter 3: Education Act)*

## A Literary Cold War: From the 'Less Deceived' to the 'Literature of Extremes'

Otherwise diverse in politics, what each of these writers fear is the loss of the organic and affective dimension of human experience in the new post-war mass society, a world of managerialism, planning, new technologies and social engineering. Such anxieties gradually merged with those arising out of Cold War concerns, the intellectual recognition of Britain's decline as a world power, fears of political and social surveillance, as well as threats to the perceived or imagined hegemony of particular social groups. The future looked less than certain. In 1948, the Joint International Committee drew up an assessment of the Soviet threat after the Communist coup in Czechoslovakia had fanned fears of a world-wide domination of Soviet-style Communism. Exacerbating such fears was the development of the atomic bomb, which Russia had begun to stockpile unbeknown to the West from the late forties, by 1953 developing the vastly more powerful hydrogen bomb. The literary movements of the fifties and early sixties are anchored in various ways in these pervasive anxieties: they include those novelists and intellectuals concerned with the need to defend, but also to acknowledge, the weaknesses and shortcomings of liberalism, or who introduce new moral perspectives on the problem of being human in the new world order (Murdoch, Angus Wilson, John Fowles, Spark, Golding); the ambivalent relation to social change and the complex class positioning and 'less deceived' mentality of the Movement with its anti-modernist and anti-mythical cool 'reason'; the somewhat politically ineffectual and often misogynistic railing of the 'Angry Young Men' and the often exaggerated but fragile machismo of the working class novel of the late fifties. An important place here, also, should be reserved for the immensely influential book by Richard Hoggart, *The Uses of Literacy* (1957), which set out both to attack the parochialism of British society and to expose as a myth the tendency of the Left-leaning middle classes to sentimentalize the working classes as a species of 'noble savage'. Like Orwell, Hoggart also strove towards an authentic portrayal of working class life by accentuating tactile and sensory experience: what it feels like to live in back-to-back housing alongside thundering railway lines, to walk everyday along littered streets spattered with dog dirt, drawing in smells of gasworks and bombarded by screams of street urchins with pasty faces. What it feels like to remain anchored all one's life to one small locality and never to experience a world outside.

Like those of the immediate post-war period, these very different writers can also be seen to be united in their suspicion of and resistance to mythical thought or misplaced metaphysical speculation. A concern with 'truth' emerges, a desire to see beneath the promises of politicians, but also to take seriously the writer's responsibility to resist the seductive and often dangerous fictions of mass society. One of the most interesting collections of essays to appear in 1963 because it pinpointed so astutely the concerns of the previous decade, was W. H. Auden's *The Dyer's Hand*, prefaced by a famous quotation from Nietzsche: 'We have Art in order that we may not perish from Truth'. The collection contained his essay, 'The Poet and the City', a penetrating and complex piece on the place of art and the responsibilities of the writer in contemporary mass society. The main focus of the essay though, a warning against the abuses of the magical in art, and of the potential ethical dangers of an unrestrained aestheticism, was close to the thought of Auden's friend, the philosopher Hannah Arendt, whose controversial *Eichmann in Jerusalem* also appeared that year. This was ostensibly a report on the Eichmann trial of 1961, but it was also a continuation of Arendt's preoccupation, since the publication of *The Origins of Totalitarianism* (1951), with the human craving for meaning. Arendt sees this expressed in the need to tell stories, but sees also its dangerous possibilities when mythopoeic craving finds release in the ominous construction of world-historical logics and utopian thinking as the projection of perfect aesthetic orders onto the contingency and muddle of history. Both Auden and Arendt are caught between, on the one hand, a recognition that the impulse might only be reined in by a vigilant separation of categories, to guard against tribal systems of belief and utopian myth-making and, on the other, the feeling that the positivist categorizations of the world into scientific facts separated from values, had placed the latter outside of the domain of thought and left the individual marooned, an isolate will in a world shorn of meaning and purpose.

Auden is partly responding to the revival of logical positivism in the fifties, which may now be read as propelled by a philosophical concern to protect against dangerous metaphysical thinking in its insistence on the grounding of philosophy in purely scientific 'facts'. From Orwell's ultimately Popperian orientation towards empiricism and falsification; to the Movement's insistence on commonsense and their anti-modernist resistance to myth-making and reference to the 'ordinary'; to the concerns of writers such as Auden, Spark, Golding, Eliot and Murdoch with the abuses of the aesthetic, of fiction-making, and the seeming inadequacy of liberalism to counter irrationalist belief systems or provide an adequate foundation for a moral society: each of these displays an ambivalence about the robustness of the new order in the light of the destructive, triumphalist and irrationalist aspects of human nature exposed in recent history. Throughout the fifties, Iris Murdoch's

philosophical essays concentrated their critique on the disastrous consequences of G. E. Moore's hugely influential 'naturalistic fallacy' as the
impetus for logical positivism which, in so axiomatically separating facts
from values, had left human beings stranded as isolate wills in a world bereft
of texture or embodiment. Murdoch, in effect, pinpointed the dilemma of the
fifties: the fear, on the one hand, of a loss of the 'experiential', the spiritual or
metaphysical dimensions of human experience, of tradition and rooted ness;
but set alongside this, the greater fear perhaps that, without the 'scientific'
patrolling of orders of knowledge and value, a variety of dangerous and
totalitarian pseudo-scientific metaphysical systems stood poised to destroy
altogether the liberal order of the West. For writers such as Murdoch, Hoggart
and F. R. Leavis, literature was perceived to be a vital source of cultural value
in a positivist-driven age precisely because literary experience revealed axiomatically how values are themselves an intrinsic aspect of knowledge. In this
view, human knowledge arises out of a fundamentally tacit and already
value-laden understanding of the world that precedes the explicit knowledge
of science, technology and the discourses of social planning. It was this
difference in view, rather than a simple clash of science versus literature,
which substantially informed the so-called 'two cultures' debate between
F. R. Leavis and C. P. Snow at the end of the decade.

For commentators such as Blake Morrison, however, the literary group
that set the tone for intellectual debate in the fifties (eventually sparking the
retaliatory aesthetics of Alvarez's 'literature of extremes') was the Movement.
Unsurprisingly, the Movement's common-sense avoidance of 'emotional
hoo-ha', its less-deceived mentality and its Orwellian insistence on the virtues
of ordinariness, decency and robust empiricism, provoked accusations of
parochialism and lowered sights, though it was probably its lower middle
class, suburban, grammar school scholarship boy composition that induced
writers such as Evelyn Waugh and Somerset Maugham to see its members as
the new boys of the welfare state and to provoke Maugham's entirely unwar-
ranted verdict in a *Sunday Times* review on Christmas day 1958, that 'they are
scum'. A more measured view, retrospectively, might be that they were in
part responding to the kinds of Cold War fears outlined above, but by making
a virtue out of necessity: Britain's diminishing world role perhaps required a
literature determined to be stoically 'less deceived' as well as a resolute commitment to looking at the new world free of aristocratic myth-making and
genuflection to moribund ritual. By way of example, Larkin's poem, 'Dockery
and Son' (1963) offers a characteristic tone, the voice of one who is initially an
onlooker, 'death-suited', as he stops off to attend a funeral before he meets
the son of an old university acquaintance, Dockery. The title is suggestive of
some honourable and established family trade, passed from father to son and
evocative of a world of commerce and reproduction from which the speaker

presents himself as excluded. By the end of the poem, however, a more inclusive 'we' reasserts itself, a reminder of our common humanity that reunites this speaker with the rest of his tribe and its condition, in the level recognition that, 'life is first boredom and then fear/Whether or not we use it, it goes'. And then, to death, is added sex: 'what something hidden from us chose' (1988: p. 153). But if Larkin's tone is characteristically controlled, urbane, expressing only faint bewilderment at the essential absurdity of the human lot, there were more strident edges to Movement writing. At the end of *Lucky Jim* (1954), the lower middle class, provincial Dixon, short and fair 'with an unusual breadth of shoulder' (1961: p. 8), looks on at the ensemble of Welch (snobbish and aristocracy-aping Professor of medieval literature), sporting a fishing hat, and his son, Bertrand (lanky and foppish), in his father's beret, and observes that 'in these guises and standing rigid with popping eyes, as both were, they had a look of being Gide and Lytton Strachey, represented in waxwork form by a prentice hand' (p. 251). In one sentence, Amis conjures up and ridicules: foreignness (the beret); middle class social pretension to upper class barbarianism (the fishing hat); Bloomsbury, Bohemianism and aristocracy (Strachey); homosexuality and effete leisure classness (Strachey and the popping eyes) and homosexuality, foreignness and class-slumming (Gide).

Whether one regards Larkin's lugubrious stoicism or the somewhat adolescent prankishness of Dixon's rebellion as characteristic of the 'gentility' of the Movement or as symptomatic of the kind of Little Englandism derided by writers such as Doris Lessing and Charles Tomlinson (who, from the midfifties, were urging a greater cosmopolitanism), a number of contemporaries felt that expressions of secularized reverence in bicycle clips, poetic invocations of the shires, and controlled reasonableness, might not be entirely adequate responses to the time. It was this sentiment that ushered in the characteristically more apocalyptic tone of the sixties. Robert Conquest, the Church Father of the Movement, in the preface to the second volume of the *New Lines* anthology (1963), insisted (in characteristically measured and even mildly prim and certainly overtly moral tones), that 'it seems both egotistical and insensitive to proclaim that the circumstances of modern life are so different from anything that has gone before that they open up hitherto unsuspected depths to be exploited' (1963: xxiv). Conquest was responding to Al Alvarez's attack on 'gentility' and his insistence that the only art which might truly resist the lure of populism and conformism was, 'an art which forces its audience to recognize and accept imaginatively, in their nerve-ends, not the facts of life but the facts of death and violence: absurd, random, gratuitous, unjustified and part of the society we have created' (1974: pp. 282–3). Equally insistent had been Doris Lessing's *The Golden Notebook* (1962), where her protagonist, Anna Wulf, expostulates: 'I don't want to be told when I wake up, terrified by a dream of total annihilation, because of the H-bomb exploding, that people felt that way about the cross-bow. It isn't true. There is something new in the world' (1962: p. 459). For if Conquest's voice is characteristic of the intellectual mood of the fifties in insisting that scientific modes of thinking and planning can furnish human means but not human ends, that of the sixties is more given to revolutionary and liberatory discourses. Apocalyptic and always about *deferral*, of living in the shadow of a promised or imagined end, this sixties' mode persisted through Cold War catastrophism, through fears of the Bomb, to postmodernism and even to contemporary anxieties about the 'clash of civilizations' between the West and Islam. For ironically, it is perhaps this shift in the sixties, towards the Dionysian, the acceleration of liberation, and the intensified insistence on freedom, rights and libertarianism, that helped both to realise most fully the vision of consensus but, as Britain began to 'break-up' in the mid-seventies (with devolution on the agenda, an economic crisis that heralded the end of Keynesianism, the emergence of new identity politics, the rise of postmodernism and the formation of the radical right and neo-liberalism), paradoxically also helped to bring about its demise.

*(See Chapter 3: The Movement, Angry Young Man)*

## From Sexual Liberation to Identity Politics: The Sixties and After

The period from the early sixties to the late seventies is one characterized by the impulse of liberation: from everything that had seemed to be screwed down, kept hidden and expertly harnessed under the state version of 'consensus' for the fifteen-year period after the war. During the next fifteen years, however, from 1960, the initial 'sexual' and emotional revolution associated with the Counterculture would gave way to a more genuine opening out of consensus to include issues of race, gender, nation and sexual orientation, a concern with rights and equality as well as with liberation, and with the diversification of citizenship and political identities. The trajectory, however, was by no means straightforward. The April 1966 headline of *Time* magazine announced the birth of 'Swinging London' just as Mary Whitehouse launched her 'clean-up TV' campaign. Britain was recovering from the Cuban Missile Crisis of 1962 which, after Suez, hammered in the final nail in the coffin of its former assumption of world Imperial power just as its relations with Europe were also taking a downward turn with refusal of entry into the Common Market. Perry Anderson's essay, 'Origins of the Present Crisis' (1963), published in *New Left Review*, attacked the literary and intellectual culture of the nation as parochial, sclerotic and devoid of theoretical vigour or original thinking, and writers sympathetic to the New left, such as Doris Lessing, bemoaned the retreat into the private sphere and the existence of a paralysing gulf between the public and the private. The July 1963 issue of *Encounter*, featuring the sexual shenanigans of the Profumo affair that had destroyed the Macmillan government, not surprisingly bore the sombre headline, 'Suicide of a Nation'.

Yet ironically it is Larkin, the most important writer associated with the Movement, who is most immediately associated with the sexual liberation of the sixties, for his poem 'Annus Mirabilis' famously announced that 'Sexual intercourse began/In nineteen sixty-three/(Which was rather late for me)'. As the poem indicates, the birth of sexual liberation was sandwiched between the end of the Chatterley ban (the beginning of the end of censorship) and the Beatles' first LP (the beginning of the new commercial culture of pop with its £6 million profits in one year). The heavily ironized reference to *'sexual intercourse'*, rather than plain *sex*, in the first line, captures wonderfully the prim legalese of the *Lady Chatterley* trial where defence and prosecution alike had blended vocabularies of Lawrentian physical passion with those of an often prim or medicalized moral hygiene (Larkin 1988: p. 167). But 'nineteen sixty-three' functions primarily as a vehicle for Larkin to address the issue of love in an age of consumer values – the new age of consumer affluence, of you've never had it so good – love freed up from the necessity of emotional, or a 'sort of', bargaining ('the wrangle for a ring') or indeed from any other kind of higher commitment or obligation. This is sex, welfare-capitalist style. And, even more so in what was poised to become the technological 'white heat' of the Wilson years, sex becomes a free for all, an activity that requires no bargaining at all. For everyone can share this 'brilliant breaking of the bank' (another line which mixes allusions to gambling, sexual defloration, and perhaps even to the Great Train Robbery in August of that year when the principal robbers escaped to be lionized by the popular press as romantic adventurers). In the new age of consumer liberation and the contraceptive pill, no one loses and 'everyone felt the same'. However, Larkin sees that without even a residually sacramental sense of marriage or a lively fear of unwanted pregnancy, the profanity of sexual transgression also dies. The Lawrentian myth of sex as the road to liberation, the profound source of selfhood, already finds its days numbered. The Romantic gleam, always ever in thrall to the exchange of the marriage economy, is now itself in danger of fading to a dying ember in the brave new commodified world of 'going, going, gone', of money, the cool store, and the new leisure and entertainment industries.

Although *sexual* liberation may have began in the early sixties, women's liberation would not get under way for a number of years. Betty Friedan's *The Feminine Mystique*, published the same year as Larkin's poem, offered the first analysis of 'the problem with no name' (that of affluent middle-class women's general unhappiness, despair and lack of fulfilment in the suburban home), though many women writers had already began to publish literary accounts of their sense of disaffection in the late fifties (Lessing, Drabble, Plath) and would later expose the shortcomings of the sexual revolution viewed from the perspective of women. Noting the increasing obsession with sex, its commodification, and its medicalization in the two Kinsey reports of 1948 and 1953, Friedan observed that although 'sex is the only frontier open to women who have always lived within the confines of the feminine mystique', it is also absolutely central to the construction of that mystique (1965: p. 228). The educated housewife, queen in her suburban palace, with its array of labour-saving devices, enters what Friedan contentiously referred to as 'the comfortable concentration camp' (p. 245) of middle-class home-making via myths of romantic love and domestic bliss. Her escape into extra-marital affairs and consumer fantasies is simply more of the same. The condition analysed by Friedan was already producing a proto-feminist exposé of the oppressions of the suburbs to match those of male writers such as Orwell, Amis and Wain. In Plath's novel, *The Bell Jar* (1963), for example, the 'motherly breath' of the suburbs closes in on Esther, 'the white, shining, identical clapboard houses with their interstices of well-groomed green proceeded past, one bar after another in a large but escape-proof cage' (1963: p. 120): suburban existence as a home-maker is a life imagined as an endless vista of identically spaced and perspectivally retreating telegraph poles.

The new loosening up of reticence about expressing feelings, the return of the confessional mode and the new explicitness about sex, as the sixties wore on and brought the liberatory slogans of the Counterculture, began to offer women writers the opportunity to raise awareness of the construction of femininity, and in particular, to deconstruct the exclusivity of the constrained choice between Bluestocking or Domestic Goddess. The countercultural emphasis on expressivity was required so that women might begin to recognize that, as Shulamith Firestone would observe, 'the tool for representing, for objectifying one's experience in order to deal with it, culture, is so saturated with male bias that women almost never have a chance to see themselves culturally through their own eyes' (1971: p. 157). Perhaps because the Women's Liberation Movement only lasted for a decade, from 1968 to 1978, after which it seemed to splinter into a bewildering diversity of identity politics and abstruse theoretical disputes, commentators often argue for sharp distinctions between a pre-1968 and a post-1978 generation of women writers, with the latter far more alert to the instabilities of the very category of woman. But there is an anxious dialogue on the nature of feminine identity and female authorship from the early sixties onwards.

The Movement for Women's Liberation emerged out of the upsurge of counter-cultural political activism of the sixties and alongside radical movements such as Gay Liberation, Black Power, and the Civil Rights Movement. In 1968, the grass roots women's movement set out to analyse the sources of oppression within patriarchal societies and began its task of liberating women by campaigning for equal pay and opportunities, equal human rights, the eradication of sexist assumptions, and the deconstruction of woman as 'the second sex'. Almost immediately, however, feminists recognized that issues about rights and freedoms are not easily dissociated from representations of human needs, and that the procedural discourses of the legal system are woefully inadequate tools for the articulation of such human requirements as respect, affection, dignity, and recognition. Consequently, the energies of the movement came to be absorbed more and more with questions concerning identity: 'who am I?', as much as 'what is to be done?' Such questions are traditionally the concern of literature and culture rather than activist or campaigning politics. Early on, therefore, feminists turned to art and literature as a means of working through contradictions that seemed intractable when addressed through traditional political and philosophical discourses. The power of symbolic representation and cultural embodiment in constructing and containing identities and subjectivities was recognised from the first as a definitive aspect of a new kind of political movement.

But without an organized women's movement, the strategy was risky and without the later recognition that 'the private is the public' – the most important slogan of the early women's movement – confession seemed already to be so much a part of the 'feminine mystique' and the perceived emotionality and submissiveness of women. For these reasons, many politically aware writers in the years before the liberation movement officially began, writers such as Doris Lessing for example, were extremely reluctant to be explicitly construed in this fashion.

In some ways, the culture of confession and the sexual libertarianism of the sixties, was even *dangerous* to women writers, and we need now to examine carefully the Dionysian impetus of the Counterculture, broadly seen as liberatory for all, but actually, in many ways, exposing the contradictions of post-war inclusivity as it impacted, specifically, on women and issues of gender. If there is one authorial construct that perhaps subsumes all others and proves most problematic for women writers in the sixties, it is what Alvarez later referred to as 'the myth of the artist'. Defined as a 'general belief – by the public as well as the artists – that the work and the life are not only inextricable but also virtually indistinguishable', he went on to argue that 'out of this something new and disturbing emerged during the '60s and the '70s, and it is still around in a debased form. I call it the myth of the artist' (2005: p. 196). The myth took sustenance from the enormous influence of psychoanalysis in the sixties. Friedan blames Freud as the single most important source of the feminine mystique, while contradictorily offering a Freudian analysis of its consequences in creating misogyny, infantilization and dependencies in both men and women. Edmund Wilson's influential essay,

'Philoctetes: The Wound and the Bow' (1941) had explicitly married the Greek tale of the wounded artist to the Freudian account of the grounding of art in neurosis, pain and suffering. Wilson's essay argued that though art is rooted in psychopathology, the artist is the sacred pariah we cannot do without; the idea was revived in the work of R. D. Laing at the beginning of the sixties where, along with the Marxist critique of consumer capitalism, it became the intellectual lynch-pin of the Counter-culture and attractive to many writers searching for a justification of art as an antidote to an instrumentally rationalist culture of mediocrity and conformism. In Laing's account, all madness, including the frenzy of the creative artist, is a refusal of the slave morality whose violence destroys those ascetic fictions which compel our conformity through internalized guilt and shame. His work is pervaded with the metaphor of the Dionysian as daybreak, of madness as breakthrough, liberation and renewal, as much as breakdown, enslavement and existential death, facilitating 'the emergence of the inner archetypal mediators of divine power, and through this death a rebirth, and the eventual re-establishment of a new kind of ego-functioning, the ego now being the servant of the divine, no longer its betrayer' (1971: pp. 144–5). As in Nietzsche's writings, Dionysus comes to stand as a symbol of psychic renewal through a self-dissolution involving an ecstatic release of the instincts in primordial ritual. The revival informed writing as diverse as Lessing's *The Golden Notebook* (1962) and Marowitz's RSC *Theatre of Cruelty* season in 1964. In theatricalized language, Alvarez himself described the discovery of the body of Sylvia Plath in the performative terms of the 'myth of the artist' and Plath, in particular, has ever since been read as a woman whose suicidal drive is motivated by a desire to hone her body into the cold perfection of words. Berryman, Sexton and Lowell all wrote obituaries of Plath in the form of poems which play out a complex identification with the lure of death and sacrifice, and also expressed a thanetic enviousness about what Sexton, for example, referred to as 'the death I wanted so badly and for so long' (1981: p. 126). Like Alvarez, she too seems to blame Plath *herself* for the myth. But the body as waste, as fodder for the god Dionysus, is part of the current myth of the artist – and it must have been especially alluring for a woman writer in the sixties also inevitably caught up with the contradictions of the feminine mystique. For the female body must have seemed to be source of that debarment from 'transcendence' which de Beauvoir had read as central to the myth (of immanence) of the Eternal Feminine. In turning herself into words, Plath escaped one myth, only to fall willing victim perhaps, to the other. For surely part of the dangerous lure of the myth of the artist for women writers is its promise of escape from the gender-specific myth of the 'Angel in the House'. For the myth of the Angel as pure altruism had placed the role of authorship almost entirely out of bounds for women by identifying writing with egotism and selfishness.

The Countercultural myth of the artist appears to offer escape out of instrumental reason and into and then beyond the body in a kind of ecstatic ritualization of writing as a version of *jouissance*.

(See Chapter 3: Censorship, Feminism; Chapter 6: Myth)

## The Break-Up of Britain and the Thatcher Effect

The last national conference of Women's Liberation was held in Birmingham in 1978 and, by the 1980s, although internal differences and the rise of a more fragmented identity politics across race, class, sexual orientation and ethnicity, would break up the original movement, that decade witnessed a boom in feminist publishing and a huge interest and growth in women's studies and gender courses in Higher Education. The year before, in 1977, Tom Nairn had suggested that national consensus too had disintegrated and that the 'break-up' of Britain was imminent, the post-war consensus at an end. The development of Welsh and Scottish nationalism, the immigration into the UK since the late forties of overseas people from its former dominions, and the rise of new cultures around ethnic identities and youth sub-cultures, the influence of American popular culture, the Troubles in Northern Ireland and the entry into the EEC in 1975, all contributed to this sense of a breakdown of national unity. But the centre was failing to hold in economic terms too as monetarist ideas crept increasingly into circulation after 1975, when Margaret Thatcher won the Conservative leadership and set about using the IMF crisis to move her party towards free-market economics. As the Left moved towards demands for genuine democratic representation of all social groups and identities, and the Right towards a declaration of war on corporatism and the desire for neo-liberalist economics, each registered a withdrawal from the post-war consensus. A new era of polarized conviction politics and confrontational identity issues ensued. With the Conservative victory of 1979 and the installation of Mrs Thatcher as Prime Minister, the swing to neo-liberalist economics would also institute a backlash against the libertarianism and social emancipation of the sixties, and the introduction of a fiercely ideological campaign for a return to a more authoritarian state, to the family and 'Victorian values', with Thatcher standing as a second Britannia attempting to revive the faded Churchillian nationalism of the war. Even before this political shift, however, cultural trends were producing tendencies towards a more fragmented or 'postmodern' society. Industry was shifting from Fordist mass production to consumer-oriented flexible specialization using a freer floating workforce; service and 'knowledge' industries expanded, and the economy seemed to become both more complex and less stable even before the incisive moment of deregulation of the stock markets in 1986. Globalization was already well under way with the expansion of multi-nationals, the space–time compression effect of new technologies, world media coverage, satellite links, digital circuits and world marketing of goods, and with it a concomitant search for the recovery of lost traditions, identities, local attachments and ethnic roots which often transcended national or state boundaries. Daniel Bell declared that the nation-state was 'too small for the big problems of life and too big for the small problems of life' (1987: p. 14). Whereas writers of the sixties and earlier seventies had looked to throw off state and ideological oppression to uncover and liberate a buried and authentic identity, those of the late seventies and eighties would increasingly come to see identity as fluid, constructed and always in process, as hybrid rather than pure, invented rather than discovered. Consensus seemed to be over: Keynesian economics replaced by monetarism; the search for authentic essence replaced by plasticity, artifice and self-fashioning. For as well as the acceleration of communications and the compression of space and time, the history of the period is one of break-up of Empires, migrations of peoples, civil wars, generational conflicts, the economic and political decline of Europe.

Fredric Jameson provided one of the most resonant images of the cultural postmodern in his description of the architect and developer John Portman's Westin Bonaventura Hotel in Las Vegas. For Jameson, the building is an icon of and testimony to the 'incapacity of our minds, at least at present, to map the great global multinational and decentred communicational network in which we find ourselves caught as individual subjects' (1991: p. 44). Throughout the eighties, as the stable maps of the world shifted, literature too became self-reflexively preoccupied with the problematic nature of representation. Numerous writers explored the connections between the temporally and spatially disorientating experience of the fabricated worlds of postmodernity, and the ontology of the literary text as a world axiomatically constructed out of other textual worlds. As the nation-state began to 'explode', a new generation began to write from the margins and the process began to accelerate after 1980 as writers began to unite in response to the 'Thatcher-effect'. For, whether regarded as a force for radical change, or a lamentable reinvigoration of Little Englandism, it was evident that the entry into office of Mrs Thatcher coincided with a burgeoning era of trans- and multi-nationalism, globalization, neo-liberalism, postcolonialism, the proclaimed End of History, and the move away from party and towards identity politics.

Martin Amis' *Money* (1984) is perhaps the best known and most ferocious fictional critique of eighties' greed and the new entrepreneurialism associated with the deregulation of world money markets. In this Pandemonium, late capitalism has emphatically invaded every corner of existence: 'You can't drop out any more. Money has seen to that. There's nowhere to go. You cannot hide from money'. John Self, its protagonist, inhabits a modern inferno produced by the unpredictable global flows of money – 'I am a thing made up of time lag, culture shock, zone stuff' – and, even before his final descent into destitution, he feels chillingly excluded from the sidewalking middle management of Manhattan with their 'faces as thin as credit cards' and their 'fascinating' world of thought and culture (1985: pp. 153, 32, 26). But the appearance of Salman Rushdie's *Midnight's Children*, in 1981, was probably the most significant literary moment of the decade, ironically coinciding with a symbolically resonant political act of closure: the British Nationality Act, which deprived Black and Asian British people of citizenship rights by power of birth. Like the novel, the Act also served to provoke questions about the problematic nature of belonging, and the emotional and existential meanings of homelands, real and imaginary.

Initially located in the fiercely disputed border territories of Kashmir, *Midnight's Children* is a marvellously decentered allegory of the history of India from the first moment of Independence which was also of course the first significant moment of the end of Britain as an Imperial world power. The new state is immediately torn apart by partition, political factions, and the incompatibility between Nehru's technologically driven programme of centralization, and Mahatma Gandhi's advocacy of local and decentred trad-itional village networks. The pivotal conceit of the novel is that the body of Saleem, its narrator, and one of the children born on the midnight hour of Independence, begins to somatize the splits and schisms of the new Independent State. Opening comically with Aziz, Saleem's father-to-be, medically inspecting his future bride's body successively through a hole in a sheet, the conceit of the hole and the partitioned body soon dissolves into the aching cavern that has opened up at the heart of India. As partition turns to violence, those now bereft of history and place are left with an emotional vacuum to be filled only with the promises of new nationalisms or theocratic fervour. The fragile and disintegrating body is conflated with the emerging 'unrepresentable totality' of the new postcolonial and globalized worlds of the late twentieth century. The integrity of Saleem's personal identity is fur-ther jeopardized by telepathic powers connecting him to the thoughts of the other children born on the stroke of midnight, 15 August 1947. Effectively a transistor radio, his head is also a fictional device that fantastically reconciles Nehru's globalism and Gandhi's localism. He gradually becomes aware that 'consumed multitudes are jostling and shoving inside' him. For his head is also Rushdie's vision of the new transnational literary text, with its melange of voices resisting the fanatical purisms that are the destroyer of worlds. Sitting 'like an empty pickle jar in a pool of Anglepoise light', Saleem is the postcolonial writer, situated in a new and globalized world and opening himself to the possibility of mixing and mingling and preserving different versions of history (1981: pp. 10, 18).

But the nation-state both expanded and imploded during the eighties and nineties. The impulse came not only from writers from outside the British Isles but from those who felt internally colonized within it. Writers such as James Kelman and Irving Welsh began to experiment with Scottish vernacular and, like Rushdie, to globalize the local. In the early eighties, Kelman began experimenting with free indirect discourse, mixing standard and vernacular languages, without implying the usual hierarchization. By the time of James Kelman's *How Late It Was, How Late*, which won the Booker Prize in 1994, he had developed a unique modernist vernacular that bestowed on the disinherited and the underclass an inner life as real as that of Joyce's Bloom or Beckett's tramps and loners. Rushdie's trope of migrancy soon became the most powerful metaphor to describe contemporary experience. Just as the migrant writer is not tied to any one national tradition or 'legend-haunted' civilization, and may live in several places, so the migrant can choose his or her literary parentage from any number of traditions and mix them at will, and so literature, like the nation (in Homi K. Bhabha's account), must also become *disseminated*, can no longer remain parochial or stranded in this or that ghetto of nation, race or single tradition (Bhabha 1993: p. 4). Literary texts will now mix realism and fantasy in an ever-open sea of stories where 'we are inescapably international writers at a time when the novel has never been a more international form' (Rushdie 1992: p. 20).

*(See Chapter 3: Regional Novel, Magic Realism; Chapter 6: Homi K. Bhabha)*

## From Globalization to Terror

Yet Rushdie's metaphor continues to cause controversy. Migrancy might be a provocative catch-all image for a generalized postmodern condition, but there is risk of merging and conflating very different kinds of experience. That of the new and second generation black and Asian British, of refugees from Eastern Europe and of those fleeing war-torn and oppressive regimes: their experiences are different and also different again from the global tourists, the jet-setting affluent, and the transnational communities of the media and managerial classes of the new global economies. Not all migrants become cosmopolitan citizens of nowhere. For to be migrant, whether across nations, regions, classes or systems of belief, might mean to feel, painfully, that one no longer has a home, and to yearn to return to something which no longer exists except in the sepia tints of memory (reflected in the etymology of the word nostalgia). Other writers such as Hanif Kureishi, Monica Ali, Zadie Smith and Andrea Levy, for example, have written eloquently about the way in which the most familiar experience of the migrant is not so much celebratory hybridity as the feeling of having become altogether invisible: déclassé or downtrodden in the new culture. Many novels of the nineties began to explore new techniques for representing the pain and trauma arising out of the transitions, transformations and historical disjunctions of the post-war period. Pathology, disordered affect, and disassociation were common themes, dealing with subjects as various as the Holocaust, sexual abuse, stalking and compulsive erotic behaviours, death, terrorism, and other kinds of disaster.

A less sanguine view of the internationalization of the British novel is that the new globalized fiction market and the celebration of the 'hybrid' are simply evidence of a continuing Orientalism: a capitalist exoticization and appropriation of postcolonial experience. The 'internationalization' of prizes such as the Booker might be seen as further evidence of the commodification of writers from former colonies and the commercial control still exerted through neo-Imperialism. Kazuo Ishiguro has brilliantly fictionalized this controversial debate from the perspective of the writer in *The Unconsoled* (1995), set almost entirely in a hotel in an unidentified middle-European town: a place of nowhere, in a continent whose borders keep changing, and whose place in the world has become uncertain. Ishiguro began the novel after an exhausting world-promotional tour, part of the process where the contemporary writer, like the book, has now become a packaged commodity, the possession of publisher, marketing agents, booksellers and international audiences, critics and reviewers. For the novel is a meditation on the tension between historical ideas about the creative arts and their place in a culture, and the varieties of new external pressures on the contemporary writer in an internationalized culture market: the conflicting demands of political representation, ethical obligation, and the commercial implications of producing creative work within a global economy. Ryder, the lauded and serious contemporary international artist (a pianist), is expected to be part of a cosmopolitan world of 'caring professionals' as he tours the world to perform for expectant audiences, an international ethicist as well as artist, who must exercise a kind of impossible telescopic philanthropy as he is compelled to respond to local demands without knowledge or time to acquire customs and histories. Commercial forces control his schedule and global demands confiscate rehearsal and performance time; he has become a stranger to his family and loved ones and barely knows who he is.

Since the publication of Ishiguro's meditation on the problems of the cosmopolitan novel, debates about globalization, multiculturalism and the postcolonial have been taken over by those deconstructing or reconfiguring the various 'clash of culture' theses which have sprung up since the suicide bombing of the World Trade Center in 2001. Surprisingly, a Marxist critic such as Eagleton seems to have returned to another revival of the Dionysian, analysing the phenomenon of the suicide bomber as a kind of internalized self-hatred projected out into the extravagant gesture of a thanetic drive intended to redeem a life otherwise swallowed up and negated by the inflicted abjection of Western capitalism (Eagleton 2005). For Martin Amis (2008), terrorism has functioned to expose both the misogyny of Islam, but also the pornographic violence of the West. Perhaps what Islamicist terrorism has most emphatically thrown up as a challenge to the literary imagination is a sense that, post-identity politics, the world seems fundamentally divided not so much between labour and capital or even between male and female or black and white or homosexual and heterosexual. In a strangely regressive loop, the world seems to be dividing again between those who believe in an afterlife, that human consciousness survives the death of the body (whether in religious or scientific terms) and those who do not. Curiously, things come round: ironically, the post-modern seems to have returned to enchantment, to aspects of the world-view of pre-modernity.

# 3 Literary and Cultural Contexts

*Katharine Cockin and Jago Morrison*

---

### Chapter Overview

## Angry Young Man

The fury and frustration expressed by Jimmy Porter in a play called *Look Back in Anger* by John Osborne produced at the Royal Court Theatre, London in 1956 came to be associated with a whole post-war generation. The anger concerned the expectations of masculinity in peace time when the actions of an older generation, whether heroic or compromised, were felt to dominate. The characteristics of the angry young man included a hedonistic virility, a rejection of social class and conventional morality and an interest in popular culture and jazz music. The angry young man signalled the beginnings of a revolution from the younger generation and a new category emerging in the teenager. His female counterpart has a different agenda and may be seen in such plays as Sheila Delaney's *A Taste of Honey* (1962).

## Auto/Biography

Autobiography is often assumed to be a self-evident category comprised of the author's reflective account of her or his own life. The non-fictional status of autobiography is another orthodoxy which requires some scrutiny. Modern life-stories tend to include the self-consciously crafted, the ghost-written and even the fictionalized. The relationship with the reader is then different from that defined by Phillipe Lejeune (1991) as an 'autobiographical pact' whereby the reader is led to believe that the narrative is true. The propriety of the exposure of the private self was a concern for female autobiographers in the nineteenth century. In the late twentieth century the most private aspects of the self, including the experience of terminal illness, have been publicized and avidly consumed by readers. The experiences of cancer patients, such as those of John Diamond, have been serialized in newspapers and subsequently published in book form. The public realm of autobiography, occupied by leaders and statesmen in the nineteenth century, has been made accessible through the internet in the late twentieth century exemplified by Salam Pax's account, *The Baghdad Blog* (2003). Witnesses and combatants in wartime have used the form of autobiography to manage their traumatic response. The concept of auto/biography is used by Liz Stanley (1992) to address the involvement of the biographer in the biographical narrative and to explore the conventions of this narrative form.

## BBC

The British Broadcasting Corporation was formed in 1922. It played a central part in communications in wartime Britain. The broadcasting of the coronation of Queen Elizabeth II in 1953 marked a significant moment in the creation of a mass audience. The BBC had an educative role and played an important role in the development and sponsorship of new writing in the regular drama and arts programmes it broadcast in the 1960s.

## Blasphemy

Although the world depicted in much post-war British literature may be designated as secular, fiction tends to address itself to the dimension of spiritual beliefs, the wonder at the inexplicable and the trauma of newly conceived horrors. The propriety of depicting the deity and sacred teachings in literature was the subject of debate in a period when other boundaries were being tested. While Mary Whitehouse instigated the prosecution for blasphemy in 1977 of the publication of a poem by James Kirkup entitled 'The Love That Dares to Speak Its Name', the offence was to some extent a particular depiction of homosexuality as much as it was the representation of Christ. In 1988 the publication of Salman Rushdie's novel *The Satanic Verses* (1988) led to the pronouncement of a fatwa or death sentence from Iran which lasted for ten years. International debates about censorship and freedom of expression as well as blasphemy ensued. Pressure from the local community in Birmingham in 2004 led to the closure of a play *Bezhti* by Gurpreet Kaur Bhatti which depicted rape and murder in a Sikh temple. In 2007 the blasphemy law in England was tested with the case brought by Christian Voice against the production of *Jerry Springer: The Opera* but was rejected. The common law of blasphemy was abolished in 2008.

## Book Clubs

The history of book clubs in Britain extends at least as far back as the early eighteenth century, pre-dating the large scale establishment of circulating libraries. In the post-war period they have enjoyed increasing popularity, with combined memberships running well into six figures. Book clubs take a number of forms, ranging from regular, informal discussion groups geared around a series of agreed texts, through radio and television shows arranged along similar lines, to direct marketing arrangements involving little or no interaction between readers. In the latter case, readers typically agree to buy a minimum number of titles per year, in exchange for a regular magazine and a discount on the recommended retail price of books.

## Booker Prize

The Booker Prize, founded in 1968, has done a great deal to promote the work of the winning author and guarantee sales. The awarding of literary prizes has become the occasion for the publicizing of literature and provides an opportunity for debate. In 1994 when *How Late It Was, How Late* won the Booker Prize, James Kelman defended his right to employ the language of working-class Glasgow in his novel.

## Censorship

The censorship of literature can take place in different ways. The control of publicly performed plays in England was exercised by the Lord Chamberlain's office from 1737 to 1968. Publications tried in court for obscenity include D. H. Lawrence's *Lady Chatterley's Lover* (1928) and Radclyffe Hall's *The Well of Loneliness* (1928). In wartime the Defence of the Realm Act (1914) allows for action to be taken to preserve national security which may include control of publications. A variety of laws can be invoked to prevent the publication and dissemination of unorthodox ideas. To some extent authors may be unconsciously engaged in withholding certain ideas, images or terminology in response to dominant ideological forces but it is the gaps and silences in the literary text which expose its most significant meanings.

## Chick Lit

Chick lit is associated with the romantic, comic fiction concerning the adventures of young, single women, heralded by the bestseller *Bridget Jones's Diary* (1996) by Helen Fielding. Chick lit has a close relationship with journalism and the world of commercial publishing. New variations have emerged such as working-mum lit, exemplified by Alison Pearson, *I Don't Know How She Does It* (2003), which deals with the issues relevant to the female character who has responsibilities of childcare and employment. Genre fiction is very popular and perhaps for this and other reasons it often proves to be the site of much anxiety. Panics about the dangerous effects of reading certain types of fiction have a long history but the mass production and marketing of the novel in recent times possibly increase the sense of alarm. While Mary Wollstonecraft was concerned about the effect on female readers of the sentimental novel in the eighteenth century, feminists in the second half of the twentieth century have raised similar questions about the romantic novel in its most formulaic mode such as those published by Mills and Boon. Chick lit differs from earlier forms of romantic fiction in that it has been particularly constructed and marketed by publishers to the extent that female authors have found their books packaged in chick lit clothing – the pastel colours and decorative typography – although they envisaged them in other terms.

## Class

The career of 'class' in post-war British culture is an especially interesting one. From a position of centrality in social and political discussion after World War Two, its status as an analytical category went into significant decline in the final years of the twentieth century. In politics, class analysis began to be relegated to the fringes of mainstream debate from the 1980s onwards. In the literature of this period, however, writers' interest in class divisions and class interactions hardly seems to have lessened, remaining a key concern in such diverse works as Raymond Williams' *Border Country* (1960), Kazuo Ishiguro's *The Remains of the Day* (1989) and Sarah Waters' *The Night Watch* (2006). In contemporary British literature, writers working across a range of idioms, such as Tony Harrison in poetry, Hanif Kureishi in screen writing and Mark Haddon in the comic novel, all accord the theme of class a prominent position in their work. In this sense, 'class' provides an interesting example of the ways in which literary writing is often capable of pursuing a variety of social concerns beyond the point at which they become taboo among spin doctors and political commentators.

## Comic Novel

The difficulties arising from social class and the need to adapt to a new community and its conventions, have provided successful material for many writers from Kingsley Amis, in his treatment of a lower middle class university lecturer in *Lucky Jim* (1954) to Meera Syal in her novel of *Life Isn't All Ha Ha Hee Hee* (1999) which follows three Asian women growing up in Britain. A satirical approach, exposing folly or vice, was particularly fertile in the culture of the early 1960s, influenced by *Beyond the Fringe* (1960). In the novel it is found in the sequence, *A Dance to the Music of Time* (1951–75) by Anthony Powell (1905) and in the witty exploration of the fake and grotesque in such novels as *Anglo-Saxon Attitudes* (1956) by Angus Wilson (1913–91). The bizarre practices and distorted values of the Americans are satirized in Evelyn Waugh's *The Loved One* (1948). Martin Amis (b. 1949) has applied an incisive wit to his investigations of sex, violence and the amoral in such novels as *Dead Babies* (1975), *Money: A Suicide Note* (1984) and *London's Fields* (1989). Muriel Spark's novels create their comic effects by means of a representation of the peculiar or strange, with a witty insight and satirical tendency, whether in the depiction of an obsessive school teacher in *The Prime of Miss Jean Brodie* (1961) or old age in *Memento Mori* (1959).

## Copyright

Although poststructuralist theories, especially those of Roland Barthes, have decentred the author and privileged the pleasure of the reader, the rights of the author over the work created are legally circumscribed. In the preliminary pages of published books may be found a statement in which the author asserts her or his moral rights over the work. The legal field of rights, copyright, intellectual property and others, is complex as set out in the Copyright, Designs and Patents Act (1988). The moment when it becomes most obvious is when a work is quoted from or reproduced by others. This may involve securing permissions and must make appropriate acknowledgement through referencing. The failure to follow this procedure can result in the serious charge of plagiarism. Some postmodernist novels, like Alasdair Gray's *Lanark* (1981), play with these ideas.

## Crime Fiction

Crime Fiction in the post-war period has been influenced by the hard-boiled detective fiction from the United States and has opened itself up to different perspectives on crime and characterization. This has moved some way from the constraints of the Golden Age of detective fiction in the 1920s and 1930s when crimes were always punished and the detective always triumphed. The realities of unsolved crimes and injustices, the extremes of violent and sadistic acts and the possibilities of corruption in the courts and police forces are all given attention in contemporary crime fiction. The popularity of 'police procedurals' has perhaps been enhanced by the scientific discoveries of genetic fingerprinting and the increasing possibility of tracking down the criminal in cold cases using a practically invisible trace of matter. The exploration of the ethical implications of crime or the psychological effects on the perpetrator and the victim are dealt with in novels which are otherwise not designated crime fiction. The work of Ian McEwan typically engages with a curious and morally perplexing situation which is carefully unfolded. The crime itself – murder, rape, stalking, possible child abduction – becomes a stage in the spectrum of human interactions investigated in a possibly unresolved plot. The reader may find in the reading process that condemnation and revulsion may be exchanged for contemplation and curiosity. Crime writers, such as Patricia Cornwell in her reassessment of the Jack the Ripper case, have extended their interest to true crime narratives. A survey of crime in fiction might encompass most contemporary fiction since law-breaking events seem to be difficult to avoid in the modern world.

## Cyberpunk

According to Bruce Sterling, 'Cyberpunk is a product of the Eighties milieu [. . .] but its roots are deeply sunk in the sixty-year tradition of modern popular SF' (Sterling 1994: viii). Cyberpunk typically has an urban setting and a dystopian atmosphere, to some extent borrowing from hardboiled detective fiction. The novels of William Gibson are especially associated with cyberpunk, notably *Neuromancer* (1984) in which the central character Case connects physically with the matrix of computer networks. This interface which transforms the physical body and breaks down the boundaries with a form of technology is characteristic of the cyborg. Indeed Bruce Sterling's more detailed definition of cyberpunk emphasizes the centrality of the transformed body: 'Certain central themes spring up repeatedly in cyberpunk. The theme of body invasion: prosthetic limbs, implanted circuitry, cosmetic surgery, genetic alteration. The even more powerful theme of mind invasion: brain-computer interfaces, artificial intelligence, neurochemistry – techniques radically redefining the nature of humanity, the nature of the self' (Sterling 1994: p. xi).

*(See Cyborg)*

## Cyborg

Although Donna Harraway has defined the cyborg as 'a cybernetic organism, a hybrid of machine and organism, a creature of social reality as well as a creature of fiction' (Haraway 1991: p. 149), the application of the term seems to have changed in recent years. The extent to which the human-technology boundaries have been broken down in the late twentieth century has enabled the cyborg to pass for human. In this regard the cyborg generates similar fears to that raised by the automaton, the robot or the android. This image of the cyborg has been reinforced by the Terminator films and Philip K. Dick's *Do Androids Dream of Electric Sheep?* (1968), filmed as *Bladerunner* (1982). Some science fiction, such as Marge Piercy, *He, She and It* (1991) explores the fantasy of human-cyborg sex. The 'cyborg' figure may be particularly disturbing because it challenges the boundaries commonly assumed to exist (and be clearly drawn) between the human and the machine. The outsider status of the cyborg provides the potential for an oppositional politics and it is this challenge which Harraway mounts in her 'manifesto' (1991).

*(See Cyberpunk)*

## Education Act

The Education Act (1945) introduced major changes in Britain, signifying the central importance placed on education. The reorganization of the infra-structure involved the creation of a Minister for Education and the inclusion of education provision in the government's budget. The school leaving age was raised, religious education became a compulsory part of the curriculum and daily collective worship was introduced. More schools were created and made it more possible for a wider group to pursue higher education.

## Environmentalism

Environmentalism has been as longstanding concern within British writing, especially in poetry. In the literatures of the post-war and contemporary period, concern with the environment manifests itself in many ways, ranging from an aesthetic interest in representing the natural world to more cam-paigning modes of writing, explicitly connected to green politics. In the mid-1990s, a new branch of literary studies began to establish itself around these themes, under the term ecocriticism. Within this field, many of the most influential critical studies have focused on the Romantic period, but twentieth and twenty-first century writers have also been treated to new forms of scrutiny.

Within ecocriticism, one particular focus of interest has been the ways in which contemporary ecological concerns are often mediated through the elegiac mode. In such writing, notions of nature's awesome power associated with Romanticism are typically displaced by representations of its fragility and loss. The work of influential post-war writers such as Ted Hughes and R. S. Thomas provide important examples of this tendency, but environmentalism and the new elegy have been also yoked in powerful and distinctive ways by contemporary figures such as the Sussex poet Hugh Dunkerley. With the increasing prevalence of ecological concerns within public discourse more generally, especially surrounding the question of global warming, it is likely that environmentalism will become an increasingly important strand within contemporary writing.

## Experimental Novel

The *nouveau roman* of Alain Robbe-Grillet and Nathalie Sarraute challenged expectations about plot, characterization and causality in the novel. Notable experiments with narrative form include the work of B. S. Johnson (1933–73), Rayner Heppenstall (1911–81) in *The Connecting Door* (1962), Ann Quin (d. 1973) in Berg (1964) and Christine Brooke-Rose (b. 1926) in *Such* (1966). The disruption of narrative sequence was exploited by B. S. Johnson's *The Unfortunates* (1969), a book consisting of fragments of text in a box. The interior world of the protagonist is explored by James Kelman in *A Disaffection* (1989) and *How Late It Was, How Late* (1994), extending the modernist experiment with stream of consciousness by mediating it through Scottish dialect. Some authors have engaged with new technologies, such as Jeanette Winterson's *The.PowerBook* (2000), Ali Smith's *The Accidental* (2005) and Christine Brooke-Rose's *Xorandor* (1986), *Verbivore* (1990) and *Textermination* (1991). Brooke-Rose exploits numerous narrators and repetition in her later novels which engaged with science, especially the human-computer interface. Experiments with characterization including transformations, shape-shifting, change of sex or some other aspect of their identity are tested out in Fay Weldon's *The Cloning of Joanna May* (1989), Angela Carter's, *Nights at the Circus* (1984) and Michael Moorcock's *Cornelius Quartet* (1969–77). The disruption of chronology or scrutiny of a short period of time features in Christopher Isherwood's *A Single Man* (1964), Martin Amis' *Time's Arrow* (1991) and Ian McEwan's *Saturday* (2005).

## Feminism

The connection between women's writing and the struggle for gender equality has always been a strong one. While it is true that many texts by women project quite conservative representations of femininity, many other women authors, including such iconic figures as Virginia Woolf and Angela Carter, place a more radical gender politics at the heart of their writing. Following Woolf's meditation of the 'women's sentence' in *A Room of One's Own* (1929), there has been a repeated interest among feminist thinkers in the formal and linguistic distinctiveness of women's writing, as compared to that of men. This concern with the recovery of women's voices, coupled with the feminist project of critiquing the social and cultural constraints imposed upon women by patriarchy, inflects the work of many post-war writers, both male and female.

In recent years, nevertheless, feminism has begun to encounter an interesting conundrum. While its essential premises – that women have a right to autonomy and gender inequality, and should be free from oppression at the hands of men – have achieved historically unparalleled levels of social acceptance, feminism itself often seems to be held at arms length, especially by younger women. An expectation of gender equality often seems to be combined with an attitude of scepticism towards feminism as a political discourse. In some contemporary women's writing, such as Helen Fielding's *Bridget Jones's Diary* (1996) this ambivalent, post-feminist sensibility may shade into quite patronizing representations of women. In the work of other writers, such as Jeanette Winterson and Sarah Waters, there is a provocative playfulness with gender stereotypes which carefully avoids this tendency. In the 1970s, women writers were exhorted by theorists such as Arlyn Diamond to yolk their creativity to the mainstream of the feminist project. The sexist stereotypes purveyed by men's literature were to be supplanted by representations of strong minded female role models, living authentic lives. In the twenty-first century, it would be difficult to find many critics who would expect such a programmatic approach from writers. Feminism has undoubtedly been one of the key formative influences of post-war culture in Britain, but there is recognition that its ideas manifest themselves in a variety of ways across the range of contemporary writing.

## Free Verse

Free verse or *vers libre* was a radical rejection of fixed meter, giving the impression of freedom of expression or liberation from the constraints of regular, predictable form. While in the period of modernism, poets became fascinated by the novelty of the language of ordinary speech, the interaction of word and image or word and music, it is difficult to identify any dominant poetic forms in the later twentieth century. Anthologists frequently categorize their selection as new in some way. A. Alvarez described the work in his collection in terms of its response to the devastating events of the Second World War and consequently characterized by a 'new seriousness'. To some extent the influence of drama and performance is discernible in the work of Tony Harrison, Jackie Kay and Simon Armitage. The sound of the spoken word, especially with the local flavour of accent and dialect, and a dialogic exploration of different, sometimes ventriloqual voices, is a tendency in contemporary poetry. To what extent have concerns about place and identity in contemporary poetry replaced the adoption by poets of a particular poetic form? The work of Tony Harrison, Sean O'Brien and Carol Ann Duffy could be used to address this question.

## Gothic

The gothic novel in the eighteenth century dealt with a plot driven by suspense and fear in a remote, enclosed setting, often a castle or large house. Some typical elements of the plot include kidnapping, rape and murder, the concealment of some secret and the appearance of ghosts or supernatural forces. The modern gothic novel has developed some of these conventions for different purposes. Angela Carter's novels often use a gothic form to explore (and challenge) the mechanisms whereby girls and women are trapped, controlled and destroyed by patriarchy and to identify the desires which drive such processes. Female authors such as Sarah Waters, Margaret Atwood and Angela Carter transform the genre by liberating the female character.

## Internet Publishing

The internet (or net) is an international computer network also known as the information super highway. The internet developed from a US military network (ARPAnet) in 1969 used for exchanging intelligence for nuclear defence. Computers connect to the internet through a server or internet service provider. The World Wide Web is a service which operates on the internet and was developed by Tim Berners-Lee at CERN laboratory in 1990. Cyberspace is a vaguer term for the spatial relationships in the world of electronic data in which text and images are created and exchanged and users may activate an avatar to relate to others in a virtual world. Hypertext is a term used by Ted Nelson in 1965 to describe the linking of fragments of text, providing layers of meaning which are activated by the user who chooses to click the hypertext link. Since the opening of the internet to public access in the 1990s, an enormous amount of literary writing has begun to be distributed in a range of online formats. By the twenty-first century, it was possible to buy both individual short fictions and whole novels to print-on-demand or read via a digital book display. Given the low cost of paperback fiction and the general consensus that paper remains the best display medium for extended prose texts, however, traditional print publishing has continued to dominate the fiction market.

In contemporary poetry, however, the situation is rather different. The high unit cost of short-run printed collections, coupled with the fact that few poets derive significant financial rewards from their work, has created an environment in which internet publication has started to become an important feature of contemporary literary culture. Online gateways such as Poetry Portal list dozens of e-zines and other fora, while the Poetry Library provides subscription free access to many established poetry journals. With the unprecedented opportunities that these kinds of publication offer for poets to find new audiences, as well as to enjoy dynamic, interactive relationships with their readers, the advent of internet publishing may prove to be a significant milestone in the history of British poetry.

## Kitchen Sink Drama

The kitchen sink became iconic in the drama of the mid fifties to early sixties signalling the lives of working-class people depicted in the naturalist play. The ground-breaking production of John Osborne's *Look Back in Anger* at the Royal Court Theatre in London in 1956 became associated with a gendered representation of the younger generation – the Angry Young Man – and explored the impact of the crises of the period on an alienated, resentful but rebellious youth, prepared to embrace the unconventional. Sheila Delaney's *A Taste of Honey* (1959) provides a relevant counterpoint to Osborne's play and foregrounds women as agents rather than objects of a masculine anger. A parallel narrative concerns the dangers faced by women in the risks of premarital sex and illegal abortions.

*(See Angry Young Man; Chapter 6: Social Realism)*

## Lad Lit

Like chick lit, lad lit finds its origins in the mid-1990s and portrays the vicissitudes and pleasures of the single young person. Nick Hornby's *Fever Pitch* (1992) holds a similarly canonical place in lad lit to that occupied in chick lit by *Bridget Jones's Diary* (1996). The uncertainties about identity are explored in imperfect romantic relationships and in the generational differences and conflicts between parent and child. To some extent lad lit and chick lit constitute the *Bildungsroman* of the late twentieth century and their didactic potential has caused much consternation among some readers. As this highly commercialized new popular form developed and lost its novelty, the characters grew up and found themselves in marriages, divorces and parenting relationships. Tony Parsons' *Man and Boy* (1999) exemplifies this wider exploration of the complex social fabric of the male protagonist's life, including an insight into his vulnerability and insecurity.

## Literary Canon

In the post-war period, the notion of a British Literary Canon, comprising a definitive list of elite, representative works, has continually been subject to contestation. Even arch-defender Harold Bloom, in his book *The Western Canon* (1994) says of his list of great twentieth-century books 'I am not as confident about this list'. An important reason for the breakdown of confidence in previously uncontroversial notions of canonicity is the unprecedented diversification of literary production in the post-war period. With new voices drawing on – and self-consciously hybridizing – a much wider complex of cultural traditions than in earlier eras, lists of canonical books rooted in trad-itional conceptions of cultural inheritance and value are easily subject to criti-cism. In Bloom's attempt, for example, it is easy to question on what basis the writers of India are seen as having produced only three really worthwhile books during the whole of the twentieth century, in comparison to one hundred and fifty two supposedly produced by the writers of the United Kingdom and Ireland.

One of the key, unintentional insights yielded by Bloom's book is that what canons express is as much a set of expectations and reading habits as any more objective criteria for comparing texts. Many literary works produced in recent years self-consciously trouble the boundaries between literary and (mere) genre writing. Others – notably by postcolonial authors – explicitly contest the canonical status of previous works, and thereby the institution of canonicity itself.

As ever, particular texts can be seen to have achieved consistent inclusion on the reading lists of schools and universities. Particular authors have cer-tainly been recognized with literary honours. Acknowledging this, however, in no way compels us to start drawing up a new list of privileged, compulsory reading for the post-war period, as if we were never going to evolve as readers, reconsidering our notions of cultural significance and value.

## Magic Realism

Magic Realism has been associated with visual art and the novels of Gabriel García Márquez and Jorge Luis Borges, but is also applicable to some post-war British fiction. In Angela Carter's *Nights at the Circus* (1984), a female character takes flight. In Salman Rushdie's *The Satanic Verses* (1988), two characters similarly transform themselves into other beings. Magic realist narratives explore a world in which the impossible becomes probable and the imagined is realized. As such they share some similarities with utopian and fantasy fiction.

## Mass Media

From the beginning of the 1960s to around the end of the 1980s, literary culture was widely predicted to be approaching extinction. Poetry and the novel, even the book itself, were seen by many popular commentators as poor competition for the immediacy of film, television and (in later years) computers. As expanding book sales and a thriving literary marketplace show, these predictions were clearly misplaced. In poetry, online technologies have not displaced, but complemented traditional print technology, with the emergence of a thriving contemporary scene in online publication and discussion. At both the 'popular' and 'literary' ends of the fiction market, many novelists have established a collaborative rather than antagonistic relationship with the film and TV industries, as screen adaptations help to build readerships for future works. The Harry Potter phenomenon, credited with sparking a major revival of reading among children, is a notable example from genre fiction, but there is also a burgeoning trade in adaptations of more 'literary' works by writers such as Ian McEwan and Sarah Waters.

In one sense, as this implies, the development of mass media can be seen as having rather different effects in the poetry and fiction worlds. The British poetry scene has enjoyed a diversification of voices and readerships with the aid of new communications technologies, whereas in fiction, media take-up of a few titles, with enormous accompanying marketing, has helped to contribute to a culture in which readerships are funnelled towards the consumption of a narrower and narrower selection of texts. Notwithstanding these pressures, nevertheless, it is clear that literary readership in Britain remains both buoyant and varied. Such recent developments as the alliance of independent publishers (*see Small Press Publishing*) can only help to bolster that strength and diversity.

## Metafiction

Metafiction is self-conscious; it displays its mechanisms and devices rather than concealing them. The act of story-telling is foregrounded and the narrative may even address the reader directly, introduce an author-figure or provide alternative endings. Many postmodernist novels by writers such as Wilson Harris, Will Self, John Fowles and Jeanette Winterson employ metafictional devices but some of these features have a longer history, demonstrated by the playfulness of Laurence Sterne's *The Life and Opinions of Tristram Shandy*.

## The Movement

A distinctive reaction to the emotional intensity and anxiety of the 1940s was claimed as a characteristic of a group of writers identified in an article by J. D. Scott, published in the *Spectator* on 1 October 1954. A more controlled, detached position was apparent in an aesthetic which used irony and detachment to survey the modern world. Novels associated with The Movement include John Wain's *Hurry on Down* (1953) and Kingsley Amis' *Lucky Jim* (1954) while in the field of poetry principal figures were Philip Larkin, Thom Gunn, Elizabeth Jennings and John Holloway as well as those included in *Poets of 1950s* (1955) edited by D. J. Enright and *New Lines* (1956) edited by Robert Conquest. Later George Macbeth, Anthony Thwaite and Alan Brownjohn were all linked to this grouping.

*(See Chapter 6: Irony)*

## Obscenity (and Pornography)

In 1971 the 'schoolkids' edition of the magazine *Oz* was tried under the Obscene Publications Act (1959) which had been tested on D. H. Lawrence's novel *Lady Chatterley's Lover* (1928) in 1960. The publicity attached to the *Oz* trial provided a moment for public criticism of hippy culture and freedom of expression. Pornography had become a contentious issue in the 1960s. Experimentation with different forms of sexual expression was politicized. The power of desire was also recognized and exploited commercially in the pornography industry. Feminist critics such as Catherine McKinnon and Andrea Dworkin have argued about the damaging effects of pornography and the objectification of women. The writings of the Marquis de Sade were rediscovered and such writers as Angela Carter reassessed them, as demonstrated in *The Sadeian Woman* (1979). In the late twentieth-century pornography and sex-industry products have become more generally visible and familiar, if not accepted. One consequence is that the shock factor which was powerful in early twentieth-century literature is now, in the twenty-first century, hard to achieve.

## Open University

The Open University developed from ideas which had begun in 1926 but were realized by the Labour government under Prime Minister Harold Wilson and education minister Jennie Lee. The 'university of the air' was intended to take advantage of the mass communication of broadcasting. The mission of the Open University is to be 'open to people, places, methods and ideas'. It had its first intake of students in 1971 and has led the way in best practice of distance learning and teaching methods which take advantage of the latest technology. The principle of extending the opportunity of education at a higher level to the widest possible constituency using new media has become the mission of many British universities in the twenty-first century (see www.open.ac.uk/about).

## Orange Prize

The Orange Prize for fiction, founded in 1996, is awarded to the best novel in English by a female author. It prompted debates which arose with post-feminism about the relevance or advisability of evaluating women's writing as a separate category based on the assumption that female authors who entered other literary prizes were treated equally. In 2005 Orange launched an award for new writers and is active in the support of reading groups (see www.orangeprize.co.uk).

## Nationalism

Nationalism is a political philosophy which has inflected post-war and con-temporary British literature in a variety of ways. In England, especially in the early part of the period, a form of soft nationalism, often with imperialist inflections, colours a great deal of literary writing. As late as the 1970s, colo-nial adventures of the kind written by Joyce Cary and works in the thriller genre associated with such figures as Ian Fleming continued to enjoy enor-mous popularity. During the same period, however, a group of newly emer-gent writers such as Sam Selvon and Linton Kwesi Johnson began to contest the view of England purveyed by such writing, with new, hybrid forms of expression which drew philosophical and political inspiration from anti-colonial movements in South Asia and Africa, and from Black Nationalism in the United States.

   In poetry, questions of national identity pervade the writings of many influential figures. For example, Seamus Heaney, although born north of Belfast, positions himself explicitly in terms of affiliation to the Irish Republic: 'Be advised, my passport's green'. In Wales, the theme of resistance towards English hegemony similarly colours the work of many poets, often combined with a distinctively working-class sensibility. Post-war Welsh literature is often considered exclusively in terms of the anglophone writing of figures such as Dylan Thomas and R. S. Thomas, while comparatively little critical attention is accorded to literature in Welsh itself, by writers such as Harri Webb and Gerallt Lloyd Owen. The appreciation of such work, often lin-guistically experimental and fiercely nationalistic in tone, is limited by the modest (although expanding) levels of fluency in the Welsh language, even within Wales itself. In Scotland, a long-standing tradition of anglophobia and nationalism asserts itself across a very wide range of writing, notably in the new wave of fiction associated with male writers such as Alasdair Gray and Irvine Welsh, which began to attract international acclaim from 1980s onwards. 'The United Kingdom of Great Britain, Northern Ireland and the Channel Islands' is in many ways a strange and ramshackle construct, framed over several centuries via a long series of coercions, negotiations and compromises. Lacking a single coherent cultural identity, its literatures necessarily reflect a range of political persuasions and affiliations.

## Net Book Agreement

The Net Book Agreement was a commercial arrangement between UK publishers which partly structured the book market from 1900 to 1995. The agreement prevented retailers from selling popular titles below the price fixed by the publisher. Booksellers who broke the agreement risked being refused further supply from the publishers at the discounted rates which enabled them to make a profit. Defenders of the Net Book Agreement argued that, while this system kept the price of some books artificially high, it also sustained the viability of a broad catalogue of titles, including many books of importance and value that would not otherwise stand on their own in terms of pure profitability.

In the mid-1990s, the Net Book Agreement was effectively terminated when several major booksellers, including W. H. Smith and Dillons, began to offer popular titles at reduced prices, in defiance of its terms. This was followed by the exponential growth of a new supermarket trade in books, in which a very limited range of titles began to be offered to shoppers at a very low price point. According to most analysts, the demise of the Net Book Agreement has led to an overall increase in book buying by the general public, notably on the back of publishing sensations such as J. K. Rowling's *Harry Potter* series. However, it has also led to a sharp narrowing in the range of books that are now considered viable by major publishers. Inclusion in promotions such as the 3-for-2 table at Waterstones and attention from popular media outlets such as *The Richard and Judy* show are now considered essential components of literary marketing, without which a writer will struggle to obtain publishing contracts for future books.

Exactly how far these developments in the book trade have changed the character of writers' work itself is difficult to quantify. In the poetry world, their effect may be very limited. In the world of fiction, however, anecdotal evidence suggests that the commercial imperative now impressed on writers to achieve 'market share' among a mass readership is now a major shaping force on contemporary literary production.

## Race and Racism

'Race' is essentially a nineteenth century concept, coined during debates about slavery and colonialism. In British culture, racism is powerfully linked to xenophobia (fear of the foreign) and nationalism (perhaps best glossed as commitment to an ideal notion of national identity). What is distinctive about racism as a political doctrine is its proposition that the human species can be broken down into a number of radically different and essentially incompatible sub-groups or 'races'. Under the system of Apartheid in post-war South Africa, there were four designated 'races': Black, White, Coloured and Asian. However, other versions of racism have claimed the existence of anything from three to several hundred racial groups. The lack of agreement among nineteenth and twentieth century racial theorists on the number of human races and how they should be categorized is, arguably, the inevitable result of the fact that racism's central premise – that humans are divisible into a set of biologically distinct sub-species – is impossible to sustain scientifically. Where it is encountered in post-war British culture, racism tends to mingle with nationalism and xenophobia in the form of a general antipathy towards successive immigrant groups, especially where these are seen as threatening livelihoods or creating competition for services.

In fiction, especially in the post-war decades, such racism often takes the form of a generalized, patronizing disdain for the other, mixed with a helping of imperial sentiment and/or 'little Englandism'. In children's fiction the work of Enid Blyton, in which unexamined classism and racism abounded, is one notable example. Reflecting many of the concerns of global anti-colonial writing from the 1950s onwards, Black and Asian writers working in the United Kingdom have often sought to contest this underlying strand of racism/imperialism/xenophobia in post-war British culture. On the more explicitly political end, Linton Kwesi Johnson's poetry of the 1970s focuses sharply on such themes as racist violence in the British police, while Buchi Emecheta's early novels expose the soft racism experienced by applicants for state benefits. In more contemporary Black British and British Asian writing, however, the theme of racism typically occupies a much less central position, perhaps reflecting the changing experiences of the second- and third-generation migrants who have emerged as dominant voices. Like the legacies of colonialism, racism takes its place as only one of a range of concerns to which contemporary writers are likely to address themselves.

## Reader Response

From the point of view of most writers, especially in the context of today's competitive literary marketplace, engaging a readership is of the utmost importance. The question of how readers actually interact with texts, however, often slips through the net of critical enquiry. In literary studies, reader response or reception theory was at its most popular in the 1970s and 1980s, revolving around the work of thinkers such as Wolfgang Iser, Norman Holland and Stanley Fish, all of whom attempted to theorize the relationship between texts and their readerships in different ways.

Along with Roland Barthes' proclamation of the 'Death of the Author' (1967), reader response theory did a lot to persuade critics to think more carefully about the relationship between literary production and consumption. Rather than being considered as a function of static words on a page, textual meaning began to be considered as the product of an interaction between literary works and readers, individually and collectively.

In the developing fields of Film and Media Studies, a significant new body of research on audiences and their behaviour emerged, using fieldwork techniques drawn from sociology. Among literary critics (with the exception of some work on children's literature), however, reception studies failed to sustain a similar momentum in the 1990s and beyond. As a result, it is fair to say that our understanding of the dynamic role of readers in producing and shaping British literary culture remains largely theoretical.

## Regional Novel

Although the regional novel may be located in a specific location it has tended to be a place distinct and separate from the metropolis or the perceived centre of life. Authors include Winston Graham (1909–2003), whose Poldark novels depicted the Cornish region, while Catherine Cookson (1906–98) and Leo Walmsley (1892–1966) represented Yorkshire life. The north is depicted in various novels in the 1950s by such authors as Alan Sillitoe and John Braine, which have led to stereotypes of the North as a site of deprivation and strife. A developing national consciousness in Wales and Scotland has had a positive influence on the novel, bringing James Kelman, *How Late It Was, How Late* (1994), Irvine Welsh, *Trainspotting* (1993) and Niall Griffiths, *Grits* (2000) to the fore. In *Anita and Me* (1996), Meera Syal's *Bildungsroman* provided an insight into the conflicts and confusions at work in the Black British adolescent experience, of second generation migrants to Birmingham. The experience of living in, and moving to, Manchester has been inspiring to many writers and has been the subject of much recent research (Moving Manchester: Mediating Marginalities Project see http://www.lancs.ac.uk/fass/projects/movingmanchester/about.htm).

## Science Fiction

Science fiction has affiliations with utopian fiction which has an ancient tradition. In Britain it is often assumed to be a twentieth-century phenomenon. H. G. Wells' *The War of the Worlds* (1898) typifies some of the central characteristics of science fiction. Its narrative mode is realist, concentrating on the depiction of a world which is both recognizable and in some significant ways made strange by some technological or scientific aspects. The strangeness of the world of the science fiction novel is sometimes attributable to time travel, the inclusion of alien beings and the interaction with new objects or processes, such as robots, computers, cyborgs, telepathy, telekinesis, travel in time and space. Science fiction (or SF) explores possibilities, whether utopian or dystopian. It is difficult to avoid science, technology and the possibilities that they offer in contemporary fiction as exemplified by the recent work of Margaret Atwood, Jeanette Winterson and Kazuo Ishiguro.

## Small Press Publishing

Small press publishing has always been a phenomenon within the British literary scene. It refers to the group of independent publishers who operate partially or wholly outside the commercial agency system. Although certain celebrated small presses, such as the Hogarth Press founded by Leonard and Virginia Woolf in 1917, have published some of the most iconic works of the last hundred years, independent publishers are more usually seen as providing a platform for less established writers and for work which falls outside the marketable mainstream.

Although financial returns to authors from small press publishing can be small, this should not be confused with 'vanity publishing', in which the writer pays the full production costs of a print run, in order to distribute copies privately to friends. Independent publishers have traditionally had strong relationships with small independent booksellers who aim to offer their readers a more thoughtful and targeted selection of reading than the major retail chains.

Since the demise of the Net Book Agreement and the opening up of the book trade to full commercial competition in the mid-1990s, many presses and bookshops have struggled to stay afloat. In 2006, the chief executive of Faber established an alliance of independent publishers and booksellers, with the aim of wresting influence over the future of the book trade away from the buying departments of Waterstones and Tesco's. The success or otherwise of this alliance may prove to have a significant influence on literary publishing over the next decade.

## Travel Writing

Travel writing has a long history, deriving from the autobiographical tradition in the spiritual or psychological journey of the author. In the 1950s,
notable travel writers include Norman Lewis (1908–2003) who published on
his trips to Indo-China and Burma in *A Dragon Apparent* (1951) and Eric
Newby (1919–2006), known especially for *A Short Walk in the Hindu Kush*
(1958). During the period of the Beat generation the idea of travelling, especially by car, was popularized by Jack Kerouac, *On the Road* (1957). The mode
of travel is highlighted in some travel writing, as in Dervla Murphy, *Full-Tilt:
Ireland to India with a Bicycle* (1965). Jan Morris (b. 1926), like a significant
number of travel writers worked in journalism. Her writings attracted further
publicity when she became a transsexual in 1972. Her writings on the Middle
East, Hong Kong, Venice and Oxford are distinctive in the restrained reference
to herself and to gender. Bruce Chatwin (1940–89), author of *In Patagonia*
(1977), experimented with hybrid forms in travel writing, blending fact and
fiction, the novel and history. Jonathan Raban's *Arabia: Through the Looking
Glass* (1979) revises the conventions of narratives of travel to the Middle East
including that of Wilfrid Thesiger's *Arabian Sands* (1959). Travel writing with a
specific focus in recent years includes accounts of genocide (Philip Gourevitch's *We Wish to Inform You That Tomorrow We Will Be Killed With Our Families*
(1998)), of places or practices under threat of rapid transformation such
as Sara Wheeler's *Terra Incognita: Travels in Antarctica* (1996) or Edward
Marriott's *Wild Shore: Life and Death with Nicaragua's Last Shark Hunters* (2000).
Bill Bryson's *Notes from a Small Island* (1995) attracted a wide readership and
provides an outsider's account of Britain. Some recent travel writing has
especially taken a comic turn (Dave Gorman's *Dave Gorman's Googlewhack
Adventure* (2004).

# Part II

# Case Studies

# 4 Case Studies in Reading Literary Texts

## Michael Greaney

| Chapter Overview | |
|---|---|
| George Orwell, *Nineteen Eighty-Four* (1949) | 81 |
| Philip Larkin, *The Whitsun Weddings* (1964) | 83 |
| Tom Stoppard, *Rosencrantz and Guildenstern are Dead* (1967) | 85 |
| Angela Carter, *Nights at the Circus* (1984) | 87 |
| Martin Amis, *Money: A Suicide Note* (1984) | 90 |
| Andrea Levy, *Small Island* (2004) | 92 |

This section examines six key literary texts from post-war British literature: George Orwell's *1984* (1949), Philip Larkin's *The Whitsun Weddings* (1964), Angela Carter's *Nights at the Circus* (1984), Tom Stoppard's *Rosencrantz and Guildenstern are Dead* (1967), Andrea Levy's *Small Island* (2004) and Martin Amis's *Money: A Suicide Note* (1984). My purpose is to examine the questions of reading and interpretation raised by each text and to show how they exemplify some of the major literary trends and innovations of the last fifty years.

### George Orwell, *Nineteen Eighty-Four* (1949)

The heretic, the enemy of society, will always be there, so that he can be defeated and humiliated over again. Everything that you have undergone since you have been in our hands – all that will continue, and worse. The espionage, the betrayals, the arrests, the tortures, the executions, the disappearances will never cease. It will be a world of terror as much as a world of triumph. The more the Party is powerful, the less it will be

> tolerant: the weaker the opposition, the tighter the despotism. Goldstein and his heresies will live forever. Every day, at every moment, they will be defeated, discredited, ridiculed, spat upon – and yet they will always survive. This drama that I have played out with you during seven years will be played out over and over again, generation after generation, always in subtler forms. Always we shall have the heretic here at our mercy, screaming with pain, broken up, contemptible – and in the end utterly penitent, saved from himself, crawling to our feet of his own accord. (pp. 280–1)

George Orwell's *Nineteen Eighty-Four* (1949) is the most celebrated piece of dystopian fiction in modern British literature. His vision of the future, in which Britain has been absorbed into a totalitarian super-state known as Oceania, has exerted such a powerful hold on the modern imagination that many of its coinages – 'Big Brother', 'Room 101' – have slipped into everyday language, while the adjective Orwellian is now commonly applied to situations in which state censorship and surveillance are felt to impinge oppressively on individual liberty.

In some ways the grim alternative-future fantasy of *Nineteen Eighty-Four* seems out of step with the dominant traditions of post-war British fiction. This period witnessed the resurgence of a tradition of hard-nosed provincial realism, associated with writers like Kingsley Amis, Alan Sillitoe and Keith Waterhouse, in which all forms of outlandish experimentation were wilfully spurned. There is, however, a significant tradition of post-war dystopianism to which we might relate Orwell's novel: Anthony Burgess's *A Clockwork Orange* (1962), which also deals with the brainwashing and comprehensive mental subjugation of a rebellious hero in an alternative future, is one obvious companion text. Less obviously, the world of *Lord of the Flies* (1954), William Golding's fable about a nightmarishly under-regulated and unsupervised desert island idyll, seems antithetical to – but no less disturbing than – the nightmarishly over-regulated society of Orwell's novel.

Despite the novel's obvious credentials as a futuristic fantasy, however, it seems fair to assume that it would have provoked a certain sense of déjà vu in Orwell's readership of the 1940s and 1950s. Its evocation of everyday life in Airstrip One is redolent of a post-war Britain of scarcity, rationing and deprivation from which any trace of colour or glamour is dismally absent: dilapidated and grimily inhospitable, the landscapes of *Nineteen Eighty-Four* will be familiar to anyone who knows the poetry of Philip Larkin. In Orwell's novel it is as though human experience has been systematically rationed and reality drained of all colour and variety; and it might well be argued that there is a curious sense in which these were the terms in which post-war Britain was most happy to imagine itself. The monochrome aesthetic of The Movement seems to be almost secretly in league with the Big Brother's own policy of shrinking the English language in order to prevent the thinking and articulation of subversive thoughts. *Nineteen Eighty-Four* therefore seems paradoxically to serve as both a cautionary tale about a wholly unendurable possible future *and* a lightly disguised portrait of a more-or-less comfortably lacklustre present.

One of the tasks that *Nineteen Eighty-Four* sets itself is to think the unthinkable: to imagine a future in which state power not only saturates itself into every corner of human subjectivity and snuffs out every impulse towards freedom – but in which the very impulse to freedom has been incited by the state in order to supply a pretext for every new vicious purge and crackdown. All thoughts of freedom, in Orwell's Oceania, are thus ghostwritten by the very powers that will brutally censor them. Thought, in Orwell's dystopia, is replaced by 'doublethink': a kind of non-thought or anti-thought that enables the defeated Winston Smith, in the end, to 'know' that 'TWO AND TWO MAKE FIVE' (p. 290). *Nineteen Eighty-Four* is thus a compellingly pessimistic story of the defeat of rational thought by unthinking power; one of its curious limitations, however, lies in its failure to think, or imagine, that there might be alternatives to its own alternative world. At moments in the novel, Smith absent-mindedly muses that 'Hope lies with the proles', but the working class in this novel are complaisantly absorbed in shallowly hedonistic pursuits such as gambling and drinking; culturally amnesiac and politically silent, they display no trace of solidarity or class consciousness. It is worth asking whether the image of the working class as an unthinking mass in this novel should be chalked up to Big Brother or to Orwell himself.

*(See Chapter 3: Science Fiction, Regional Novel; Chapter 6: Unconscious)*

 ## Philip Larkin, *The Whitsun Weddings* (1964)

Philip Larkin (1922–85) is the most prominent and significant writer associated with a generation of Oxbridge-educated post-war British poets and novelists, including Kingley Amis, Thom Gunn and John Wain, who came to be known as 'The Movement'. 'The Movement' was an almost comically lacklustre nickname for a group whose literary output was marked by its emphatic rejection of the ostentatiously experimental literary tactics of the modernist writers of the early twentieth century, such as James Joyce and Virginia Woolf, and by its equally strong suspicion of the bardic, rhapsodizing style that won acclaim in some quarters for Amis's bête noire, Dylan Thomas.

Larkin published just four slim collections of poetry in his lifetime, and his pursuit of a career as a librarian at the University of Hull helped secure him a reputation as a provincial hermit eking out a monastic existence well beyond the orbit of London literary circles.

Larkin's third collection, *The Whitsun Weddings*, is one of the high water marks of The Movement, and of post-war British poetry. It is a collection in which Larkin rejects self-advertising literary pyrotechnics in favour of a poetic style that is ironic, commonsensical, superbly (but unshowily) crafted, self-deprecating and guardedly lyrical. These poems are haunted by the themes of death and love; specifically, they are haunted by the dismally non-negotiable inevitability of the former ('Life is slow dying' is the fatalistic refrain of 'Nothing To Be Said') and the painful absence of the latter. Love, that 'much-mentioned brilliance' ('Love Songs in Age'), figures in this collection as a rumour, or a missed opportunity, or as something that happens to other people. The collection's title-poem, in which a dozen confetti-strewn newlyweds excitedly board the same London-bound train on a gloriously sunny Saturday afternoon, quietly excludes the poet from the festive romantic scenes he so benignly observes.

Larkin's poetry flirts ruefully with various kinds of consolation for the demoralizingly sober revelations of death-haunted poems like 'Ambulance' and 'Ignorance'. The tawdry visual language of advertising provides a target for the mordant satire of 'Sunny Prestatyn' and 'Essential Beauty', but Larkin's revulsion from modern consumer culture does not drive him into the arms of nostalgia; in 'Faith Healing', for example, he deplores the corruption of religion into show-business, without expressing any allegiance to a faith that 'all time has disproved'. Looking to the past, in Larkin, is more likely to provoke a queasy shock of recognition than a glow of nostalgia. Nowhere is this more painfully true than in 'Mr Bleaney', in which the poet-narrator rents a room whose previous occupant led a life so desperately uneventful as to make that of Eliot's J. Alfred Prufrock seem impossibly varied and colourful by comparison. Composed in heroic quatrains, the stanzas of 'Mr Bleaney' commemorate a life that is singularly unheroic – but one that the poet-narrator seems curiously willing to accept. As he settles into his cramped, austere, underlit new quarters, he seems happy – or at least not unhappy – to identify with his predecessor, to accept the straitened horizons and monochrome anonymity that his room represents, to re-live Bleaney's (non-)life in his coffin-like 'hired box'. Subtly, the poem invites us to measure the degree of ironic distance between Larkin and his narrator, and between his narrator and Mr Bleaney. One key difference between the narrator and his alter ego is, of course, the poem itself: Mr Bleaney could never have written 'Mr Bleaney'. But for all the distance it places between narrator and hero, particularly in the eloquent reservations of its final stanzas, the poem never seems quite wholehearted in its rejection of Mr Bleaney's intuitive sense of life as a dress rehearsal for death.

No introductory discussion of Larkin would be complete without some consideration of the fact that his reputation took an extraordinary nosedive in the 1990s, when the publication of Andrew Motion's biography and Anthony Thwaite's selection of letters revealed him as capable of voicing obnoxious political opinions, particularly on the issue of race (Thwaite 1992; Motion 1993). The poet, who died as recently as 1985, now seems to belong to a curious transitional phase of British cultural history, post-imperial but pre-multicultural, whose values feel unimaginably remote from our own. Larkin is now categorized in many quarters as a literary 'small islander' (to adapt a phrase from Andrea Levy's novel about the roots of contemporary multicultural Britain), a lamentably untravelled, narrow-minded, unambitious Little Englander, the Mr Bleaney of post-war British poetry. Whether this verdict on his status and significance is a fair one ultimately depends on the extent to which readers are happy to separate aesthetic judgements about Larkin-the-poet from moral judgements about Larkin-the-man.

*(See Chapter 3: The Movement)*

### Tom Stoppard, *Rosencrantz and Guildenstern are Dead* (1967)

GUIL: Hm?

ROS:　Yes?

GUIL: What?

ROS:　I thought you . . .

GUIL: No.

ROS:　Ah.

*(Pause)*

GUIL: I think we can say we made some headway.

ROS:　You think so?

GUIL: I think we can say that.

ROS:　I think we can say he made us look ridiculous.

GUIL: We played it close to the chest of course.

ROS:　*(Derisively)* 'Question and answer. Old ways are the best ways'! He was scoring off us all down the line.

GUIL: He caught us on the wrong foot once or twice, perhaps, but I thought we gained some ground.

ROS:　*(Simply)* He murdered us.

GUIL: He might have had the edge.

ROS:　*(Roused)* Twenty-seven-three, and you think he might have had the edge?! He *murdered* us.

'Rosencrantz and Guildenstern are dead' (*Hamlet* V. ii) is one of the less memorable lines from the most famous play ever written. The line is comparatively unmemorable because the off-stage demise of these two minor courtiers, who were tasked by the King to spy on Prince Hamlet and then to deliver him to be executed in England, seems like a relatively inconsequential footnote to the play's tragic finale, during which all of the surviving major characters die on-stage. But in taking this line as the title of his play, and in making Rosencrantz and Guildenstern its central characters, Tom Stoppard provides an excellent antidote to the sense of cultural déjà vu that can seem to cloud our reaction to a play that is – as the old joke goes – 'full of quotes'. If *Hamlet* is, in T. S. Eliot's famous phrase, the ' "Mona Lisa" of literature' (Eliot 1997: p. 85), then Stoppard's tragic-comic two-hander is a brilliant exercise in literary defamiliarization, providing an ingenious new perspective on what is probably the most widely performed, studied and criticized text in any culture.

The central conceit of Stoppard's play derives much of its comic impact from the contrast between the tragic Prince and the hapless courtiers: 'How would *Hamlet* look from the point of view of two of its minor characters?' While Hamlet is fascinatingly enigmatic and multi-faceted, Rosencrantz and Guildenstern are sketchily characterized; they have no back-story, and, crucially, they are given no chance by Shakespeare to soliloquize themselves into full-bodied subjectivity. An obvious irony of the play is that while Rosencrantz and Guildenstern outnumber the Prince, they have between them barely a fraction of his personality. Nor does Stoppard's play aim to 'flesh out' its central characters: the heroes of *Rosencrantz and Guildenstern* are afflicted by the same sense of near-anonymity and near-interchangeability that attaches to them in *Hamlet*. Indeed, Stoppard's play seems to corroborate the theory, widely circulated and discussed by twentieth-century critics, that the modern world simply is not the place for the kind of larger-than-life heroes that dominated classical or early modern drama. A key intertext for Stoppard in this regard is Samuel Beckett's *En Attendant Godot* (1953), whose English-language version *Waiting for Godot* is widely regarded as the most influential play of the last hundred years. Beckett's play, in which a pair of down-and-outs engage in aimless repartee, play games, bicker and generally kill time while they wait for the never-to-arrive Godot, evokes a world in which the epic grandeur of classical tragedy has been stripped away to expose a world that seems absurdly meaningless and inconsequential. Rosencrantz and Guildenstern might therefore be seen as Elizabethan precursors of Beckett's Vladimir and Estragon whose hapless role in *Hamlet* seems to prefigure the existential absurdity that would come to occupy centre-stage in the mid-twentieth century. If Stoppard uses Beckett's sensibility to 'modernize' Shakespeare, however, it could also be argued that it invokes Shakespeare in order to critique Beckett. *Rosencrantz and Guildenstern* particularly invites us to think sceptically about the mood of rueful defeatism that grips its heroes from the outset. Throughout the play, Rosencrantz and Guildenstern seem to be sleepwalking obediently towards death. Even the revelation, in Act III, that they are en route to England carrying orders for their own execution does not spur them into decisive action. Stoppard's heroes seem capable of 'acting' in the sense of play-acting or game-playing but incapable of carrying out genuine actions. Indeed, their Vladimir and Estragon-like fondness for games is symptomatic of their child-like eagerness to take refuge in a world of make-believe where human behaviour is never more than innocuously playful. For example, Rosencrantz and Guildenstern construe their inept attempt to cross-examine Hamlet as a game of questions in which they are roundly trounced by the Prince, though when Rosencrantz protests that 'He *murdered* us' at the game, he does seem to be involuntarily groping towards an aware-ness of the violent tragic outcome that awaits them once their games are through.

*Rosencrantz and Guildenstern are Dead* is thus both post-Beckettian and anti-Beckettian, owing a conspicuous debt to the stagecraft and verbal style of *Waiting for Godot*, but distancing itself emphatically from the acquiescence in absurdity and meaninglessness that became fashionable in the 1950s and 1960s. What makes Stoppard's play particularly intriguing, however, is the question of whether he manages to succeed where his heroes fail: after all, it might be argued that, in re-telling the story of *Hamlet*, *Rosencrantz and Guildenstern are Dead* has effectively been ghostwritten by the dead hand of Shakespeare, which suggests that Stoppard is every bit as unfree as his heroes. When Rosencrantz complains in Act III that 'I can't think of anything ori-ginal', he might almost be voicing an ironic *cri de coeur* on behalf of Stoppard and on behalf of all those postmodern writers who feel that any bid for creative originality has been emphatically pre-empted by the work of gener-ations of earlier writers. Original creativity in *Rosencrantz and Guildenstern are Dead*, as in many postmodern works, can only be achieved via the recycling of what Roland Barthes calls the 'already-written' (Barthes 1974: p. 21) and for this reason the play can be read as a symbolic obituary for the creative author as well as for his luckless heroes.

### Angela Carter, *Nights at the Circus* (1984)

'Lor' love you, sir!' Fevvers sang out in a voice that clanged like dustbin lids. 'As to my place of birth, why, I first saw the light of day right here in smoky old London, didn't I! Not billed as the "Cockney Venus", for nothing, sir, though they could just have well have called me "Helen of the High Wire", due to the

> unusual circumstances in which I came ashore – for I never
> docked via what you might call the *normal channels*, sir, oh, dear
> me, no; but, just like Helen of Troy, was *hatched.*'
>
> 'Hatched out of a bloody great egg while Bow Bells rang, as
> ever is!'
>
> The blonde guffawed uproariously, slapped the marbly
> thigh on which her wrap fell open and flashed a pair of vast,
> blue, indecorous eyes at the young reporter with his open note-
> book and his poised pencil, as if to dare him: 'Believe it or not!'
> (Carter 1984: p. 4)

The opening page of Angela Carter's *Nights at the Circus* is dominated by the voice of an irrepressibly loquacious trapeze artist who is busy spinning an outrageously improbable version of her own life story for the benefit of an as-yet unidentified listener. Variously identified here as 'Fevvers', the 'Cockney Venus', the 'Helen of the High Wire' and '[t]he blonde', Carter's heroine is clearly as much of a performer in her dressing room as she is in the big top, and the sustained analogy between the spectacular gravity-defying feats of the circus performer and the reality-defying feats of the imaginative storyteller is a central conceit of the novel. The circus thus functions as the novel's image of itself: an engrossingly riotous, slightly disreputable extravaganza in which virtuoso performance consorts with dazzling illusion, trickery and artifice in the course of a chaotic, increasingly ramshackle circumnavigation of the globe.

The question of whether Fevvers genuinely can fly is, in a broad sense, a question about fiction itself: should novelists keep their feet firmly on the ground and restrict themselves to down-to-earth realism? Or does the genre provide the freedom to indulge in magical, gravity-defying aesthetic performances? It would be fair to say that *Nights at the Circus* is 'about' these questions rather than a dogmatic answer to them. Indeed, Carter's novel stands as a remarkable contribution to the modern tradition of 'magic realist' fiction that originates with South American writers like Jose Louis Borges and Gabriel García Márquez, and has flourished in the work of European writers like Italo Calvino and Milan Kundera. Magic realist fiction flamboyantly liberates itself from the commitment to sober documentary verisimilitude that characterizes (and arguably constrains) traditional realism. It is not unknown for characters in magic realist texts to walk on water, as in Jeanette Winterson's *The Passion* (1987), or to emerge unscathed from mid-air explosions, as in Salman Rushdie's *The Satanic Verses* (1988), or to metamorphose into wild beasts, as in Carter's own *The Bloody Chamber* (1984). Outrageous conjunctions between the mundane and the fantastical, the vigorously earthy and the mind-bogglingly supernatural or marvellous are at the heart of magic realism; if a realist text is one in which everything is probable, a magic realist text is one in which anything is possible. For this reason, magic realism ostentatiously departs from mainstream English realist fiction and from the social-problem novels of the 1940s and 1950s to the 'kitchen sink' realism of the 1950s and 1960s. For generations, serious-minded novelists have sought to portray themselves as responsible truth-tellers or would-be historians, whereas the purveyor of magic realism is a mischievously and garrulously unreliable storyteller, a spellbinding charlatan whose tall tales are designed to seize our attention even as they brazenly defy our credulity. In terms of literary history, magic realism thus seems to emerge as a triumphant 'return of the repressed', a wildly unapologetic comeback for all the pre-novelistic genres – myth, fable, legend, folklore and fairy story – that modern fiction had written off as the stuff of infantile daydreams or escapist fantasy.

Fevvers's biological hybridity (she is, or at least claims to be, half-woman, half-bird) seems to replicate her ontological unclassifiability: is she fact or is she fiction? Her very existence is a scandalous affront to 'either/or thinking': that is, to the kind of fastidious classifying mentality that can only be happy if all phenomena can be unambiguously sorted into human or nonhuman, fact or fiction, authenticity or performance, and so forth. Jack Walser, the American investigative journalist whom Fevvers regales with her life-story in such bawdily coquettish fashion, is a callow personification of precisely this kind of truth-centred or truth-obsessed thinking. The confrontation between Fevvers and Walser is one between imaginative performance and hard-nosed scepticism in which the sceptical male realist appears naïve, bashful, and conspicuously incapable of getting a word in edgeways. On the face of it Fevvers's voice is that of a working-class East End Londoner, but the gestures of servile respect that punctuate her narrative ('sir ... sir ... sir') seem anything but sincere, not least when they are accompanied by nonchalant displays of classical erudition. It is not difficult to see Carter's credentials as a feminist writer emblazoned across this scene in which a female speaker runs rings around a dumbfounded male writer. And her vivid emphasis on the flesh-and-blood physicality of Fevvers offers a model of female selfhood that is powerfully at odds with the ethereal idealizations of women as angels or goddesses in traditional male fantasy. Carter's brand of magic realism is thus sharply political rather than airily escapist, and it is no coincidence that the numerous magic realist writers have found this sub-genre to be an excellent ground on which to take up radical or subversive positions. Carter's feminist magic realism thus takes its place alongside the comparably subversive postcolonial magic realism of Salman Rushdie and queer magic realism of such writers as Jeanette Winterson and Paul Magrs.

*(See Chapter 3: Magic Realism, Feminism, Gothic)*

## Martin Amis, *Money: A Suicide Note* (1984)

I was just sitting there, not stirring, not even breathing, like the pub's pet reptile, when who should sit down opposite me but that guy Martin Amis, the writer. He had a glass of wine, and a cigarette – also – a book, a paperback. It looked quite serious. So did he, in a way. Small, compact, wears his rug fairly long . . . The pub's two doors were open to the hot night. That seems to be the deal in early summer, tepid days and hot nights. It's a riot. Anything goes.

I was feeling friendly, as I say, so I yawned, sipped my drink, and whispered, 'Sold a million yet?'

He looked up at me with a flash of paranoia, unusual in its candour, its bluntness. I don't blame him really, in this pub. It's full of turks, nutters, martians. The foreigners around here. I know they don't speak English – okay, but do they even speak Earthling? (Amis 1984: p. 80)

In a discussion of his literary hero Saul Bellow, Martin Amis observes that 'Books are partly about life, and partly about other books' (Amis 2002: p. 448). Amis's most celebrated novel, *Money: A Suicide Note* (1984), exemplifies this notion. *Money* is vibrantly alive to the social reality of contemporary London and New York, viscerally responsive to human experience (sex, violence, eating, drinking), and implicitly critical of the world of consumerism where those appetites and instincts are variously exploited, commodified and debased. But *Money* is also a book-obsessed book, a sophisticated piece of metafiction, full of echoes and re-workings of other writings, including Shakespeare, Fielding and Orwell. For all its busy, first-hand engagement with reality, then, the novel frequently undermines its own 'reality-effect' by drawing our attention to the fictive status of its narrative. The scene quoted above, where the obnoxious film producer John Self stumbles across one 'Martin Amis' in a downmarket London pub, even floats the teasingly paradoxical idea that the author himself might be nothing more than a figment of the novel's imagination. To compound this paradox, the author appears in this novel not simply as 'Martin Amis', but also in the guise of Self's American friend 'Martina Twain', whose name suggests that she may be the author's female counterpart. Even the novel's narrator might be seen as another *alter ego* for the novelist. 'I'm called John Self', he remarks. 'But who isn't?' (p. 100). So for all its searching journalistic or anthropological curiosity about the contemporary world, *Money*'s attention is captured by fiction itself: it is an introvertedly, even decadently self-obsessed text, a labyrinthine hall of mirrors as well as a transparently realistic window on the world outside of books. This doubleness is, of course, an unsurprising quality of a novel obsessed with split and doubled identities.

In the course of the novel's riches-to-rags story, John Self squanders huge sums of money he does not have on a film (variously entitled *Good Money, Bad Money* and *Money*) that will never be made in search of fortune that will never be his. It seems likely that Amis found inspiration for his deluded hero in the work of Vladimir Nabokov, in which we find some of the most extravagantly deluded and unreliable narrators in modern fiction, from Hermann Hermann in *Despair* (1932) to Charles Kinbote in *Pale Fire* (1962). One of the distinctively post-Nabokovian traits of *Money* is that the novel obliges its readers to give their undivided attention to a narrator whom they cannot trust and whom they may actively dislike. Self emerges in the novel as an ingratiatingly unpleasant narrator whose tone is a curious blend of the aggressively streetwise and the touchingly clueless. His sweeping reference to London pubs frequented by 'Turks, nutters, martians' speaks of a world in which no one, including Self himself, is comfortably at home. The 'Martian' qualities of Amis's writings, especially their affinities with the so-called 'Martian Poetry' associated with his Oxford tutor, Craig Raine, have frequently attracted critical comment. Blake Morrison even noticed, in his review of *Other People* (1981), that the author's name is an anagram of 'Martianism' (Tredell 2000: p. 45) and the 'Martianism' of *Money* is visible in the positioning of the narrator as an outsider struggling to make sense of a culture to which he officially belongs. With his brutal *savoir-faire* and entrepreneurial hustle, Self seems like an exemplary citizen of the late twentieth century; yet he also strikes the note of a quizzical alien, a bemused extraterrestrial sightseer blundering through a mystifying ordinary world.

Much of the novel's action takes place in temples of consumption: pubs, cafes, restaurants, cocktail bars, fast food outlets, brothels and strip-joints. The encounter between John Self and Martin Amis takes place in a pub called The Blind Pig, a name that tells us all we need to know about the novel's gluttonously myopic hero. With his superhuman appetites for food, alcohol, drugs and pornography, Self is a larger-than-life personification of a consumer culture that attaches precious little value to the tradition of highbrow literature in which Amis is obviously deeply invested. When 'Martin Amis' strikes up an unlikely friendship with Self, the novel raises intriguing questions about the relationship between the highbrow author and the mass culture that seems both to fascinate and repel him. It has been influentially suggested, by Fredric Jameson among others, that one of the hallmarks of postmodernism is a certain erosion of the old hierarchical divisions between high and popular culture, but the uneasy confrontation between the philistine narrator of *Money* and his bookish creator suggests that those old barriers are not quite so easily surmounted.

*(See Chapter 3: Experimental Novel)*

## Andrea Levy, *Small Island* (2004)

In the breath it took to exhale that one little word, England became my destiny. A dining-table in a dining room set with four chairs. A starched tablecloth embroidered with bows. Armchairs in the sitting room placed around a small wood fire. The house is modest – nothing fancy, no show – the kitchen small but with everything I need to prepare meals. We eat rice and peas on Sunday with chicken and corn, but in my English kitchen roast meat with two vegetables and even fish and chips bubble on the stove. My husband fixes the window that sticks and the creaky board on the veranda. I sip hot tea by an open window and look on my neighbours in the adjacent and opposite dwelling. I walk to the shop where I am greeted with manners. 'Good day', politeness, 'A fine day today', and refinement, 'I trust you are well?' A red bus, a cold morning and daffodils blooming with all the colours of the rainbow. (Levy 2004: pp. 99–100)

Andrea Levy's *Small Island* is a cross-cultural family saga that reconstructs the story of black Britain during World War II and its aftermath. It focuses on the role of West Indian servicemen in the British armed forces during the war, and on the reception offered by post-war Britain to the so-called '*Windrush* generation' of West Indian immigrants in the later 1940s. The novel brings these large-scale cultural, political and demographic shifts into focus by parcelling its narrative out between four central characters: the working-class Londoners Bernard and Queenie Bligh and the Jamaican immigrants Gilbert and Hortense Joseph. *Small Island* is thus a multi-perspectival and polyphonic novel that bounces between different points of view in order to re-create the complex dynamics of fear, desire, suspicion and mutual incomprehension that characterized cross-cultural relations at this watershed moment of British history. The novel is, in part, a study of the ways in which colonial powers and colonized nations imagine each other, and of the tragicomic misconceptions that can blur or skew a given culture's view of its 'other'.

The novel's title is taken from the expression 'small islander', which is used by Jamaicans as a humorously disdainful shorthand for inhabitants of less sizeable Caribbean islands. But as the novel develops, and the geographical horizons of its characters expand massively, Jamaica and Britain are themselves implicitly re-classified as 'small islands'. Britain, the imperial 'Mother Country', might enjoy a reputation as a vast and vastly important part of the world, but is experienced by West Indian immigrants as a grey, claustrophobic world of cramped lodgings, inhospitable weather and entrenched xenophobia. Hortense Joseph's dream of cosy English domesticity, which is excerpted above, typifies the kind of discrepancies the novel continually discovers between cultures as they are fantasized and cultures as they are lived. One of the key images in the novel is that of an 'upside-down' (pp. 55, 287) or 'topsy-turvey' (p. 337) world in which landscapes have been violently disrupted by war or natural disaster, and in which stable world-views are up-ended by new forms of cross-cultural encounter. Throughout *Small Island*, grandiose expectations are ironically cut down to size, perhaps most subtly in the case of Hortense Joseph's relationship with English and Englishness. A trainee school-teacher, Hortense is steeped in English literature, history and culture before she joins her husband for a new life in London. Education, for Hortense, is paradoxically a source of both cultural power and cultural displacement. Having imbibed the works of Shakespeare, Wordsworth, Keats and Tennyson at college in Kingston, Jamaica, Hortense prides herself on her command of formal and correct standard English: 'Excuse me, sir, I am need-ing to get to Nevern Street. Would you perchance know where it is?' (p. 16). Her exaggeratedly formal dialogue is an intriguing example of what theorists call 'postcolonial mimicry'. One way in which colonial powers exercise their authority is by requiring colonized people to behave, linguistically and culturally, in accordance with the norms of the ruling society: to speak its language and generally mimic its official models of selfhood. While this prac-tice might seem designed to reduced colonized people to the role of servile impersonators, it also opens up the possibility of subversive mockery of colo-nial authority. There is a sense in which Hortense is more 'English' than the Londoners who greet her with suspicion and incomprehension, and for this reason 'Englishness' is one of the many cultural norms that the novel turns 'upside-down'.

It is also important to recognize that while Levy's novel leaves us in no doubt about the racism and ignorant hostility that greeted West Indian immi-grants in many quarters of post-war Britain, *Small Island* also has a strain of positive and even utopian thinking about the possibility of a multicultural society that might rise from the rubble of a blitzed wartime nation. So Hortense's reverie about an idyllic English lifestyle might be riddled with 'inaccuracies': the creaking veranda, the fish and chips bubbling on the stove, the hosts of multi-coloured daffodils, and so forth. But at the same time, her reverie functions not simply as a false version of English culture that the novel will debunk, but as a genuine attempt to envisage what an as yet unformed Anglo-Carribean culture might look and feel like; as such, it can be read as an optimistic first draft of the story of post-war multiculturalism.

*(See Chapters 6 and 7: Postcolonial Theory)*

# 5 Case Studies in Reading Critical/Theoretical Texts

## *Michael Greaney*

---

### Chapter Overview

---

This chapter offers readings of five critical and theoretical texts that explore key themes in post-war British literary studies: the author; mimicry; 'resistant reading'; simulation; and realism. Each section uses a quotation from the chosen text as a springboard into a discussion of its keynote theme.

### Roland Barthes 'The Death of the Author' (1968)

The image of literature to be found in ordinary culture is tyrannically centred on the author, his person, his life, his tastes, his passions, while criticism still consists for the most part in saying that Baudelaire's work is the failure of Baudelaire the man, Van Gogh's his madness, Tchaikovsky's his vice. The *explanation* of a work is always sought in the man or woman who produced it, as if it were always in the end, through the more or less transparent allegory of the fiction, the voice of a single person, the *author* 'confiding' in us (Barthes 1977: p. 143).

Roland Barthes' seven-page essay 'The Death of the Author' is arguably the single most famous contribution to modern theoretical debate. The essay crystallized the work of a generation of poststructuralist thinkers who sought to clear away traditional notions of human psychology and agency from their position at the heart of literary creativity and critical enquiry; and it has been the subject of extensive critical debate and rebuttal, perhaps most comprehensively in Seán Burke's major study, *The Death and Return of the Author*. But the notion of the death of the author has been disseminated well beyond the narrow academic circles to which theoretical concepts are normally restricted. Barthes is famously name-checked in John Fowles' *The French Lieutenant's Woman* (1969), a pioneering work of English postmodernism. His essay has supplied the title for at least one work of fiction, Gilbert Adair's campus whodunit *The Death of the Author* (1993); and the death of the author is the subject of detailed discussion among characters in Malcolm Bradbury's last novel, *To the Hermitage* (2000). It is still possible to suspect, however, that those who are familiar with the 'Death of the Author' as an outrageously controversial critical slogan comfortably outnumber those who are conversant with the finer detail of Barthes' argument.

The first thing to recognize about Barthes' essay is that its title and central argument are a calculated affront to common sense. How can there be writing without a writer? To question the presence of a creative human individual behind the production of a given text seems as preposterous as to assume that paintings paint themselves or that sculptures somehow emerge spontaneously from shapeless lumps of rock. On the face of it, 'The Death of the Author' does seem to commit the *'folie circulaire* of *authoring* and *authorising* the disappearance of the subject, of *declaring* that no-one speaks' (Burke 1998: p. 99), and there is of course a certain irony in the fact that the essay has done so much to make Barthes a famous author. But a careful reading of the essay reveals that it is not vulnerable to such facile rebuttal. For one thing, it is important to note the number of earlier writers whose work Barthes mentions. The work of Balzac, Mallarmé, Valéry, Proust, Baudelaire, Brecht and de Quincey is cited as offering notable precedents for the impersonal model of writing that 'The Death of the Author' advances. When the essay cites Baudelaire citing de Quincey, for example, it is clear that we are no longer (if we ever were) peering directly into the mind of Barthes, but rather tracing a web of connections between texts. In this sense, 'The Death of the Author' provides confirmation of its own claim that 'The text is a tissue of quotations drawn from the innumerable centres of culture' (p. 146). For Barthes, it is naïve to assume that an author enjoys an unchallenged monopoly on his/her words and their meanings. Every act of writing, however 'original', involves some adaptation of existing words, styles of expression, generic conventions and so forth. Writing thus emerges not from the author, but from what Barthes calls the 'immense dictionary' (p. 147) of literature and culture that pre-exists the writer. For this reason, Barthes even argues that the author – though at this point he prefers to use the term 'scriptor' – does not produce the writing but is an *effect* of the writing. There is a paradoxical sense in which the person we refer to as 'Proust' is a product of *A la recherche du temps perdu* just as 'Shakespeare' is a product of his sonnets.

None of this is to deny the existence of what Barthes calls 'the very identity of the body writing' (p. 142), the flesh-and-blood Proust or Shakespeare. Rather, it is to propose a model of reading in which the author is no longer granted pride of place as the God-like origin and master of the text. This move, for Barthes, is designed to create a radically open-ended model of reading. 'To give a text an Author', he argues, 'is to impose a limit on that text, to furnish it with a final signified, to close the writing' (p. 147). Without the Author, the text becomes an entity that 'ceaselessly posits meaning cease-lessly to evaporate it' (p. 147). The critic is no longer a detective who pro-vides rigorous solutions and comprehensive answers to the text by pinning everything on its author's psychological quirks and secrets; rather the critic must accept, even enjoy, the tantalizing anonymity and open-endedness of the text.

Though 'The Death of the Author' resonates strongly with much playfully tantalizing postmodern fiction, it is worth noticing that in many ways Barthes is recommending a return to a pre-modern model of writing. 'The author', he contends, 'is a product of medieval English empiricism, French rationalism, Reformation personalism, and capitalist individualism. In pre-medieval cul-tures, according to Barthes, narrative was never the exclusive property of one privileged individual, but was performed and mediated by a storyteller or shaman – the ancient precursor of the modern scriptor – who would never be regarded as the 'origin' of his material. And if texts no longer belong to their authors it seems entirely appropriate that 'The Death of the Author' should have enjoyed a cultural afterlife in fictional contexts that are unlikely to have figured in its original conception.

*(See Chapter 6: Intertextuality)*

In many ways the decentring of the author proposed by Roland Barthes challenged the dominant mode of literary criticism in the immediate post-war period which emanated from the works of F. R. Leavis. Notable for founding the journal, *Scrutiny*, and publishing key works of criticism such as *The Great Tradition: George Eliot, James and Conrad* (1948) and *The Common Pursuit* (1952), Leavis centralized the author in the practice of criticism. In *Marxism and Literature* (1977), Raymond Williams identified the relationship of tradition with power: 'For tradition is in practice the most evident expression of the dominant and hegemonic pressures and limits. [. . . .] What we have to see is not just "a tradition" but a *selective tradition*' (Williams 1977: p. 115). In Marxist and sociological approaches to literature in the post-war period, including Richard Hoggart's *The Uses of Literacy* (1957), the author has a significant role to play as producer and agent, with a determining effect on the text in the reader's hand. The extent to which the meaning attributed to the author is allowed to control, dominate or influence the readings produced by the reader has been of concern to other critics.

## Homi K. Bhabha, 'Of Mimicry and Man: The Ambivalence of Colonial Discourse' (1987)

[C]olonial mimicry is the desire for a reformed, recognizable Other, as *a subject of a difference that is almost the same, but not quite*. Which is to say, that the discourse of mimicry is constructed round an *ambivalence*; in order to be effective, mimicry must continually produce its slippage, its excess, its difference. The authority of that mode of colonial discourse that I have called mimicry is therefore stricken by an indeterminacy: mimicry emerges as the representation of a difference that is itself a process of disavowal. Mimicry is, thus, the sign of a double articulation; a complex strategy of reform, regulation, and discipline, which 'appropriates' the Other as it visualizes power. Mimicry is also the sign of the inappropriate, however, a difference of recalcitrance which coheres the dominant strategic function of colonial power, intensifies surveillance, and poses an immanent threat to both 'normalized' knowledges and disciplinary powers. (Bhabha 1996: p. 361)

Homi K. Bhabha's paper on mimicry is a densely argued but highly suggestive contribution to debates about national identity in contemporary critical theory. Like many postcolonial theorists, Bhabha addresses himself to the notion of the 'Other', which may broadly be defined as the not-self, or as everything that lies beyond the limits of one's own subjectivity. Self–Other relations tend to be fraught with complexity because it seems that while the Self likes to think that it enjoys priority over the Other, the Self also *needs* an Other: there can be no secure sense of 'I' without a secure sense of 'not I'. For this reason the Self's relationship to the Other is a paradoxical mixture of superiority and dependence.

It is not difficult to see why the Self–Other model has proved an immensely useful one in postcolonial studies, since it is applicable at the level of cultural and national as well as personal identity. Cultures, as well as people, have their Others; and the relationship between colonizing and colonized nations often seems to play out in these terms. The colonizing nation assumes all the privileges of the Self, while the colonized nation is relegated to the status of Other: a secondary, foreign, peripheral not-Self. Racist and xenophobic views of certain cultures often take the form of a violently pejorative 'othering' of those cultures, an egregious example of which is offered by the eighteenth-century historian, cited by Bhabha, who claims that 'I do not think an orangutang husband would be any dishonour to a Hottentot female' (p. 366). This remark is clearly designed to place maximum distance between the supposedly 'civilized' historian, and the black women whom he classifies as borderline inhuman. Elsewhere in his essay, however, Bhabha is less interested in attempts to banish the colonial Other beyond the pale of 'civilized' humanity, and more concerned with the significance of attempts to make the colonial Other *emulate* the imperial Self. Through missionary work, education and governance, there are all sorts of ways in which colonialists have sought to induce colonized people to *mimic* the normative beliefs and behaviour of the dominant culture. And the fact that English is now the most widely spoken language in the world is testament to the apparent 'success' of this project. But Bhabha's point is that colonial subjectivity cannot propagate replicas of itself without opening up the possibility for subversion, parody and mockery. For this reason, he concludes, 'mimicry is at once resemblance and menace' (p. 362).

In many ways, the history of postcolonial writing in English can be seen as a history of mimicry. Anglophone writers from former colonies frequently delight in adapting and subversively reinventing the 'Queen's English'. To take just one example, relatively close to home, the Northern Irish poet Seamus Heaney is extremely well-versed in the English literary tradition, but his political and cultural sympathies obviously lie with the Republic of Ireland. His 1975 poem 'Act of Union' represents the 1801 Act of Union, which brought Ireland under the direct control of the British Crown, as an act of sexual violation that produced Northern Ireland as its bastard offspring. On the face of it, the poem is an emphatically unambiguous critique of the British imperial presence in Ireland. What makes it problematic, however, is that 'Act of Union' takes the form of a pair of Shakespearean sonnets, which is to say that Heaney's pungent critique of British imperialism is spoken in the voice of England's national poet. Heaney's 'impersonation' of Shakespeare seems in part to represent a kind of cultural guerrilla warfare against British imperialism, in which he engages the enemy using its own tools on its own territory. A British reader of 'Act of Union' is thus likely to be confronted with an unsettling sense of 'resemblance and menace' from a writer whose impersonations of English lyric poetry continually sensitize us to what Bhabha calls 'the difference between being English and being Anglicized' (p. 364).

*(See Chapter 6: Ambivalence, Postcolonial Theory, Mimicry, Power)*

### Laura Doan, '"Sexy Greedy is the Late Eighties": Power Systems in Amis' *Money* and Churchill's *Serious Money*' (1990)

The invention of an outrageous anti-hero cannot mask a failure to fulfil the grander aim of unmasking the ideological under-pinnings of Thatcherism. Amis gestures towards the daring and radical in order to disguise his conservative appropriation of the classist stereotype of a protagonist who meets his expected demise. The character of John Self simply cannot work as a metonym for Thatcherism. The discourse of Amis's novel ostensibly exposes the false tenets of the new Toryism and impugns the greed of Thatcherite England in order to call for the transformation of the existing capitalist system. However, by casting his protagonist as a member of the working class, Amis endangers this purpose and instead devises a telos that valorizes the class and gender systems. (Doan 2000: p. 79)

Laura Doan's critique of Amis' *Money* exemplifies many of the political and ideological issues that have come to the fore in recent critical debate. She begins by raising sharp questions about the relationship between the novelist and his hero, John Self. When Self refers in quick succession to 'blacks', 'women', 'faggots' and 'diesels' (p. 324), for example, he seems to slide between neutral, inoffensive terms for race and gender, but casually homophobic ones for sexuality. Doan rightly raises the question of whether this inconsistency is Self's or Amis'. Doan also detects in the novel a curious blind-spot in relation to the issue of social class. Though Self is an arch-stereotyper, and therefore the butt of Amis' satire, he is himself a stereotype: a working-class *parvenu* whose attempts to make a fortune and climb the social ladder are farcically unsuccessful and self-defeating. As Doan argues, Self is 'nothing more than an upstart who tries to stick his nose where it doesn't belong and who is "rightfully" excluded by the upper middle-class types whose sensibility he offends and whose security, comfort and finan-cial resources he threatens' (p. 77). For Doan, the credibility of the novel's satirical attack on the unbridled acquisitiveness associated with Thatcherite capitalism is seriously compromised by Amis' allegiance to a deeply old-fashioned model of the class system. The fact that Self is reduced to pen-ury at the end of the novel as symbolic punishment for attempting to escape his working-class roots suggests, for Doan, that *Money* is not so much an attack on conservatism as a debate between different kinds of conservatism.

Doan is operating here as what Judith Fetterley calls a 'resisting reader'

(Fetterley 1978), that is, a reader who consciously declines a text's invitation to accept its unspoken ethical or political assumptions. This style of interpretation begins with the perception, obvious but always worth stating, that literature is resistible. Readers are not obliged to acquiesce in a given text's world-view or to take for granted its taken-for-granteds. *Against the Grain*, the title of a 1986 essay collection by the leading British Marxist Terry Eagleton, provides a neat motto for this school of adversarial reading. The idea that criticism should take the form of a fulsomely appreciative guided tour of a given work became increasingly unfashionable under the influence of feminist, Marxist and postcolonial studies in the 1970s and 1980s, and we can see the influence of all three of these theoretical schools in the attention Doan's article pays to issues of gender, class and race in her critique of Amis' novel.

*(See Chapter 3: Feminism; Chapter 6: Power)*

### Jean Baudrillard, *Simulations* (1983)

This would be the successive phases of the image:

– it is the reflection of a basic reality
– it masks and perverts a basic reality
– it masks the *absence* of a basic reality
– it bears no relation to any reality whatever: it is its own pure simulacrum.

In the first case, the image is a *good* appearance – the representation is of the order of sacrament. In the second, it is an *evil* appearance – of the order of malefice. In the third, it *plays at being* an appearance – it is of the order of sorcery. In the fourth, it is no longer the order of appearance at all, but of simulation. (Baudrillard 1983: pp. 11–12)

No theorist has written more provocatively on the fate of reality in the age of mechanical, digital and electronic reproduction than Jean Baudrillard. For Baudrillard, we live in a world in which 'reality' has somehow been absorbed by its own hi-tech self-representations; a world in which saturation media coverage shapes the course of current affairs, in which fly-on-the-wall documentaries seem to conjure up the events that they purport merely to represent, and in which museums are stocked with flawless replicas that are indistinguishable from the supposedly inimitable 'real' thing. If industrial modernity defined the real as *'that of which it is possible to give an equivalent reproduction'*, in the postmodern world, the real is *'that which is always already reproduced'* (p. 146). The story, possibly apocryphal, that Charlie Chaplin once came third in a Charlie Chaplin look-a-like competition, provides one useful indication of the paradoxically inverted relations between authentic reality and simulation in the modern world.

Crucially, Baudrillard does not argue that reality has been occluded or distorted by media simulation; he does not polemicize against spin doctors or media manipulators. Rather, his argument is that simulation has become, and perhaps always was, part of the very fabric of what he calls hyperreality. His most well-known illustration of hyperreality is given in his account of the enchanted crowds that flow through Disneyland. But it is not Walt Disney's fairytale theme park that Baudrillard labels as hyperreal; rather, it is the America that lies beyond its magical frontiers. Disneyland's function is to be such a delightfully artificial world of make-believe that the rest of non-Disneyfied America can only seem drably, reassuringly authentic by comparison. 'Disneyland exists', Baudrillard explains, 'in order to hide that it is the "real" country, all of "real" America that *is* Disneyland' (p. 25). According to this logic, it is the job of ostentatiously artificial constructs to try to 'contain' simulation by deflecting attention from the general simulatedness that surrounds them.

Baudrillard's theories have always been controversial, never more so than when he described on the first Gulf War of 1991 as a media-generated non-event (Norris 1992). His ideas have also acquired a certain currency in popular culture through being referenced in the Wachowski Brothers' *Matrix* films, though Baudrillard described these films as 'crude' and 'embarrassing' (Baudrillard 2005: p. 202). Baudrillardian notions of hyperreality have also been the subject of broadly satirical treatment in some recent British fiction, including Julian Barnes' *England, England* (1999), which deals with the Disneyfication of Englishness by the heritage industry, and A. N. Wilson's *A Jealous Ghost* (2005), in which the homicidal heroine is an obsessive Baudrillardian.

An area in which Baudrillard's ideas have been perhaps under-exploited is that of literary interpretation. It seems possible, for example, that his theories might help us think through the reality conundrums of a novel like Carter's *Nights at the Circus*, a text that resists traditional oppositions between authenticity and fakery. *Rosencrantz and Guildenstern are Dead*, in which the heroes seem trapped within multiple fictions, unable to make the transition from playful make-believe to 'real' life, also seems to invite a Baudrillardian interpretation. Though whether his theories will ever amount to a coherent interpretive method seems questionable, because we can never assume that Baudrillard's thought offers pure 'truth', untainted by simulation. As Tony Thwaites has remarked, 'Baudrillard's account of the simulacrum . . . has a quite indeterminate status as the simulation of a theory of simulation: it is the very simulacrum it fears' (Thwaites 2000: p. 273).

*(See Chapter 6: Aporia, Grand Narrative)*

### Andrzej Gasiorek, *Post-War British Fiction: Realism and After* (1995)

To deny that realism and experimentalism can easily be opposed is only a first step. A corollary of this view is the claim that neither term can be taken for granted. What it means to be an 'experimental' or 'realist' writer is very much up for grabs in the post-war context, partly because of the post-war avant-garde's failure to carry through on the political side of its aesthetic revolt, and partly because postmodernism has virtually turned the modernist impulse to 'make it new' into a contemporary orthodoxy.... [T]he distinction between experimentalism and realism should be seen as ambiguous and context-dependent.... The claim that experimental writing is inherently radical is as mistaken as the counter-claim that realism is a fundamentally conservative form.... The work of those writers who do not reject realism outright (Lamming, Naipaul, Berger, Lessing, Fowles, Wilson, Maitland, Rushdie) seeks in distinctive ways to retain realism's strengths, particularly its attention to the social and intersubjective nature of human life, while at the same time confronting the problem of representation. (Gasiorek 1995: pp. 181–2)

Andrzej Gasiorek's study of post-war British fiction deals persuasively with one of the major controversies to have bedevilled recent critical and theoretical debate on the novel: that is, the debate about the comparative virtues of traditional realism on the one hand, and of modernist and postmodernist experimentation on the other. The division of post-war British fiction into realist and experimental traditions is, on the face of it, an uncontroversially descriptive move. For example, no one would dispute that the realist novels of David Storey or Kinglsey Amis belong to a quite different wing of the house of fiction from that occupied by, say, experimental, anti-realist writers like Jeanette Winterson or Christine Brooke-Rose. However, the difference between realist and experimental writing is easier to recognize than to codify. If realist narrative is defined by its commitment to linguistic transparency and documentary verisimilitude, and experimental narrative is defined by its metafictional self-consciousness and/or outlandish content, then it would be hard to nominate a single text that belongs exclusively to one or other category. And this is not simply a problem of categorization: critics have also spilt a great deal of ink over the relative aesthetic and political merits of the two modes. A hugely influential text in this regard is Roland Barthes' *S/Z*, where he draws a well-known distinction between the traditional 'readerly' text (a closed system of secure meanings) and the experimental 'writerly' text (a fluid, open system that invites the reader to become co-author). What is less well-remembered about *S/Z*, is that the distinction between readerly and writerly texts ultimately comes to seem the function of the critic's ingenuity, and it is clear that Barthes is a critic who could make any text seem wildly writerly if he so chooses.

The faulty antithesis between realist and experimental writing has also formed the basis of some dubious assertions about the political affiliations and intellectual sophistication of modern fiction. Realism has long enjoyed kudos among Left-wing critics for its ability to represent the unfolding of history in complex social worlds. Experimental fiction, by contrast, cuts itself off from history and society, taking refuge in frivolous word-games or in the private mental worlds of idiosyncratic individuals. In recent years, however, many critics seem to have upended this comparative valuation. Realism, it has been alleged, tends to *naturalize* the status quo, which is to say that realist fiction invites us to recognize a certain version of reality as plausible and lifelike, and therefore as natural and inevitable. In its fidelity to the texture of day-to-day experience, realism seems to foreclose the possibility of radical change. Experimental fiction, on the other hand, has the power to defamiliarize the taken-for-granted, to shake up our ideas about what counts as 'normal', 'natural' or 'real', and for this reason it is arguable that metafiction and fantasy are more politically radical than realism.

Of course, when the argument is conducted at such an abstract level, it is all too easy to produce a falsely polarized map of post-war British fiction. The value of Gasiorek's study is that it returns us to the specifics of that body of writing, and forcibly reminds us that one of the hallmarks of recent fiction is its refusal to choose between hard-nosed realism and flamboyant experimentation. Gasiorek's canon of experimental realists in the quotation above (to which we could easily add such names as Muriel Spark, Kazuo Ishiguro, David Lodge, Jonathan Coe and Julian Barnes) provides a useful reminder that post-war British fiction has been more diverse and nuanced than some of its critics.

*(See Chapter 3: Experimental Novel)*

# Part III

# Critical Approaches

This section provides a guide to key critics, theorists, concepts and topics, focusing on their relevance for post-war literary studies. It concludes with five short essays outlining the most popular critical approaches to the field.

# 6 Key Critics, Concepts and Topics

*Claire Chambers, Katharine Cockin, Donna Cox, Katharine Cox, Julie Ellam, Jago Morrison and Jayne Murphy*

**Chapter Overview**

## Key Critics and Theorists

### Roland Barthes

Roland Barthes is a difficult writer to categorize. His wide-ranging writings stem from structuralist concerns evident in the system of codes he identifies in *S/Z* (1970) to the poststructuralist leanings of his essay, 'Death of the Author' (1968). The latter contribution is a core critical work that pithily outlines the desire to undermine the importance of the author in the act of interpretation and to consider the text as an intertextual assemblage of writings. Barthes' work has been an important influence on many critics of post-war literature.

### Homi K. Bhabha

Homi K. Bhabha has been one of the theorists whose work has most strongly affected critics' readings of postcolonial writing. His most influential texts in this field, *Nation and Narration* (1990) and *The Location of Culture* (1994) build upon the ideas of Edward Said, but also challenge them in significant ways, notably Said's notion of the power and pervasiveness of colonial discourse. Focusing on such themes as ambivalence and cultural hybridity, Bhabha stresses the gaps and contradictions within colonial discourse, arguing that it never fully manages to assert a fixed and stereotypical knowledge of the colonial Other as it sets out to do. In a British context, Bhabha's theories have been put to especially productive use by critics working on the changing, hybrid forms of writing produced by Black and Asian British writers of the post-war period.

*(See Hybridity)*

### Malcolm Bradbury

Malcolm Bradbury was a novelist, literary critic and Professor of American Studies at the University of East Anglia. The Creative Writing MA which he founded with Angus Wilson in 1970 has had its own effect on the literature scene as students such as Ian McEwan and Kazuo Ishiguro have since gone on to be internationally renowned authors. Bradbury also played an active role in the British Council's support of the study of British literature abroad.

Several of his criticisms have been influential in the study of contemporary British literature. *The Modern British Novel* (1993), for example, looks at the twentieth century and gives an overview of the development of the novel. *No, Not Bloomsbury* (1987) also has its focus on twentieth-century British fiction and examines the work of authors such as J. G. Ballard, John Fowles, Malcolm Lowry and Iris Murdoch. The eponymous essay discusses Kingsley Amis' comic fiction and this space is also used to trace the history of the genre in British fiction dating back to Henry Fielding. He argues that humour has been intrinsic to British writing and identity: 'Indeed, one of the things that has mediated social, political and intellectual life in Britain is its capacity for manifest humour' (p. 200). In 'The Novel No Longer Novel', he draws on *The Situation of the Novel* (1970) by Bernard Bergonzi to defend the state of literature. Bradbury looks back to the prominence of modernist writers in the first half of the twentieth century and considers the impact the Second World War has had on creativity both internationally and in Britain.

## Steven Connor

Steven Connor has written on literature, literary theory and cultural history, the latter in such texts as *Dumbstruck: A Cultural History of Ventriloquism* (2000) and *The Book of Skin* (2004). In post-war literary studies, his most influential works are *Postmodernist Culture: An Introduction to Theories of the Contemporary* (1989) and *The English Novel in History, 1950 to 1995* (1996).

*The English Novel in History, 1950 to 1995* explores key post-war novels in relation to the surrounding media culture as well as looking at the means of the novel's more recent production. The influence of history is remembered throughout and chapter five ('Origins and Reversions'), for example, examines how earlier novels have been rewritten in more recent decades, making reference to works such as *Frankenstein Unbound* (1973) by Brian Aldiss and *Indigo: Or, Mapping the Waters* (1992) by Marina Warner. He also discusses the work of other notable writers such as George Orwell, William Golding and Hanif Kureishi.

## Jacques Derrida

Derrida's three works entitled *Of Grammatology, Writing and Difference* (1967) and *Speech and Phenomena* (1967) were early works of poststructuralism and all attacked the philosophical presumptions of truth, knowledge and identity as knowable and stable. Derrida's writing is notoriously playful and elusive in keeping with his idea that there is no anchor or foundation to which the language system, discourse or text can fix itself. Language is a slippery thing and, in Derridean criticism, always says more than we intend it to.

*(See Deconstruction, Aporia)*

## Frantz Fanon

Frantz Fanon was a psychiatrist and political activist, who wrote illuminatingly on the psychological trauma experienced by black people due to their internalization of feelings of inferiority caused by colonialism. His two books, *Black Skin, White Masks* (1952) and *The Wretched of the Earth* (1961) argued that colonialism did not only ravage countries' economies and political structures, but also devastated the psychology of colonized people. In order to challenge colonialism, he argued, the formerly colonized countries would have to rebuild their own psychology, so that they became the subject, rather than the object, of their histories. He also maintained that in order to overturn the structures of colonialism, nationalists would have to do more than merely replace white leaders with black, but would have to rethink the very nature of institutions and methods of governance. It is worth noting that Fanon was not just an academic theorist, but also fought for his beliefs, joining with Algerian rebels to fight against the French occupation of the country.

*(See Mimicry, Negritude)*

## Michel Foucault

Michel Foucault's theories of circulating power and his radical interpretations of history are developed by cultural materialists and new historicists, but it is fair to say that new historicism is regarded as the one that is most clearly influenced by his ideas. *The Archaeology of Knowledge* (1972), *Discipline and Punish* (1977) and *The History of Sexuality Volume One* (1979) are some of the key texts that recur in new historicist readings. His conceptualizing of the seemingly monolithic powers of the state and institutions are further influences on both theories. A differentiation between the two approaches is made possible when one considers how they react to his work. Whereas new historicists tend to be charged with a pessimistic understanding of authority, cultural materialists are regarded as comparatively more optimistic in their search for subversion and dissidence.

*(See Power)*

## Dominic Head

Dominic Head's *The Cambridge Introduction to Modern British Fiction, 1950–2000* (2002) is to date his most influential contribution to this field of study, but some of his other works such as *Ian McEwan* (2007) and *The State of the Novel: Britain and Beyond* (2008) are also of considerable relevance to this period.

*The Cambridge Introduction to Modern British Fiction, 1950–2000* takes a comprehensive look over these 50 years by focusing on areas such as class, gender, national identity and multiculturalism. Because it takes a look at around two hundred works of fiction, the landscape of what constitutes post-war British fiction is given a broad remit and this is in keeping with the democratic way that the book has been devised. Numerous authors are focused upon and these include Iris Murdoch, Salman Rushdie and Angela Carter. Less well-known figures are also given space as with the analysis of Livi Michael's writing in chapter two ('Class and Social Change'). Head refers to her work *Under a Thin Moon* (1992) as an example of literature that 'encapsulates the broader social failure to re-think community' (p. 73). In his analysis of representations of national identity, he regards Englishness as having been reinvented and incorporating the legacy of imperialism into this study. This is comparable to chapter three ('Outside In') in *The English Novel in History, 1950 to 1995* by Stephen Connor.

## Jacques Lacan

Jacques Lacan was a practising French psychoanalyst who formed the contro-versial *École Freudienne*. He achieved notoriety for his unusual therapeutic practices and he continues to be a disruptive influence due to his theory's infamous resistance to full interpretation. His theories can be difficult to understand due to his deliberately cryptic and dense style of writing which, at times, resists being grounded in definite meaning due its use of word-play and syntactical difficulties. Lacan combined classic Freudian theory with structural linguistics to bring about a post-structuralist Freud which places language at the centre of its theory. Lacan offers a way out of what has been seen to be an essentialist or biological trap in Freud by reworking the scenarios and apparatus described by Freud into metaphoric representations of psychical formations. Among psychoanalytic critics, including in contemporary studies, his work is almost unparalleled in its depth of influence.

*(See Unconscious)*

### David Lodge

David Lodge is a renowned novelist, literary critic and academic. As with Malcolm Bradbury, he has also been influential as a writer of fiction and the trilogy of campus novels, which began with *Changing Places* (1975), are the most well known. His literary criticisms are numerous and include *The Art of Fiction* (1992) and *The Modes of Modern Writing: Metaphor, Metonymy and the Typology of Modern Literature* (1977). The latter is deemed to be one of his most influential texts and his edited collection of essays in *Modern Criticism and Theory: A Reader* (1988) brings together some of the most important theoretical writers for undergraduate students. *The Art of Fiction* is a collection of articles spanning British and American fiction of the nineteenth and twentieth centuries. Here Lodge addresses a non-academic audience and recommends it as a 'book to browse in' (xi). Martin Amis, John Barth and Graham Greene are among the contemporary writers that he discusses. *The Modes of Modern Writing* begins by asking 'What is Literature?' and looks to Roman Jakobson for a framework of explanation. Philip Larkin and British postmodern fiction are among the subjects singled out for analysis.

### Paulina Palmer

Paulina Palmer's work has been largely concerned with women's writing and representations of female sexuality in contemporary writing and draws on a feminist perspective. Her research also encompasses studies of the Gothic and has more recently been focusing on the work of Sarah Waters. Her publications include *Contemporary Women's Fiction: Narrative Practice and Feminist Theory* (1989), *Contemporary Lesbian Writing: Dreams, Desire, Difference* (1993) and *Lesbian Gothic: Transgressive Fictions* (1999).

*Contemporary Women's Fiction* studies British and American women writers from the 1960s onwards and examines the influence of different types of feminist frameworks that have become current since the 1970s and 1980s. *Contemporary Lesbian Writing* has a similar time frame and discusses literary theory and its uses in interpreting the fiction she targets. Fictions by writers such as Ellen Galford and Jeanette Winterson are critiqued as are the ideas of theorists such as Judith Butler, Adrienne Rich and Monique Wittig. In *Lesbian Gothic*, Palmer looks at contemporary fiction as well as works by writers from the past including Daphne du Maurier and Djuna Barnes, and in so doing allows for the relevance of historical context.

*(See Chapter 3: Feminism, Gothic)*

## Lorna Sage

Lorna Sage has made a significant impact on post-war literary studies, most notably with criticisms on writing by women. She edited *Flesh and the Mirror: Essays on the Art of Angela Carter* (1994), for instance, as well as *The Cambridge Guide to Women's Writing in English* (1999). She was also a prolific reviewer, for outlets such as the *Times Literary Supplement* and the *London Review of Books*, and her autobiographical work *Bad Blood: A Memoir* (2000) won the 2000 Whitbread Award for Biography. *Women in the House of Fiction: Post War Women Novelists* (1992) and the posthumous collection of her essays, *Moments of Truth: Twelve Twentieth Century Women Writers* (2001), are further examples of her insightful interpretations.

*Women in the House of Fiction* looks at the state of the novel as written by women in the West' after the Second World War. Although the content is largely dominated by English and American writers, it also includes analyses of work by Simone de Beauvoir and Doris Lessing. In the introduction, Sage explains her methodology: 'What this book tries to do is to characterise and celebrate what they've built. Of course, there's an orgy of demolition going on as well' (x). By looking at diversity and change in the role of women in the writings she examines, she refuses to limit this overview of the female novelist but does note some similarities: '. . . they pour back into the novel conviction, mockery and partisan passion' (xi).

*(See Chapter 3: Auto/Biography, Feminism)*

## Edward Said

Edward Said was one of the first people to draw attention to culture as an important part of empire-building. In his highly influential work, *Orientalism* (1978), he argues that colonization was not merely a physical act of territorial expansion. In order to achieve domination over colonized people, Said suggests that the Western colonizers had to convince the minds of both the rulers and the ruled that colonization was in everybody's best interest. Said demonstrates that scholarship and art are not culturally transcendent, but are often deeply dependent on the political and economic processes of colonialism. Even creative works, such as novels, are embedded in power structures. Said's work has been one of the most important influences on postcolonial studies from its inception in the late 1970s, inflecting many critics' interpretations of post-war texts.

*(See Power, Orientalism; Chapters 6 and 7: Postcolonial Theory)*

### Gayatry Chakravorty Spivak

Gayatry Chakravorty Spivak's writing has been one of the most influential oeuvres in postcolonial studies, influencing the reading of many post-war texts. Her readings of such iconic works as Salman Rushdie's *The Satanic Verses* have cemented her reputation as a critic as well as a theorist and cultural commentator. Spivak's theoretical work is challenging and often difficult to understand. However, perhaps her major contribution to postcolonial studies has been to alert us to the fact that many colonized people have had their voices utterly silenced by colonial processes, particularly colonized women, lower-class or -caste people, and indigenous groups such as the so-called 'tribal' people of India.

*(See History, Power; Chapters 6 and 7: Postcolonial Theory)*

### Randall Stevenson

Randall Stevenson's most significant contribution to the field of post-war literary studies is *The Oxford English Literary History vol 12, 1960–2000: The Last of England?* (2004). He has also edited *The Edinburgh Companion to Twentieth-Century Literatures in English* (2006) with Brian McHale and *Twentieth-Century Scottish Drama: An Anthology* (2001) with Cairns Craig.

*The Oxford English Literary History vol. 12, 1960–2000: The Last of England?* offers an overview of prose, poetry and drama and attempts the difficult task of surveying a still emerging era. Negative criticisms tended to focus on the perceived inattention to 'Movement' poets, Philip Larkin in particular, but as Stefan Collini notes in his review for the *Guardian*, this book gives 'a sense of the larger patterns found in the kaleidoscope of recent and contemporary writing' as well as an outline of the influence of 'formal experimentalism' (13 March 2004).

*(See History)*

### Philip Tew

Philip Tew's work focuses largely on contemporary British fiction. Among his list of publications, *The Contemporary British Novel* (2004) is of special interest for the purposes of this study, and he is also the co-editor of *Contemporary British Fiction* (2003) with Rod Mengham and Richard Lane, and *British Fiction Today* (2006) with Rod Mengham. *The Contemporary British Novel* discusses subjects such as the fall and rise of the middle-classes and the epilogue is an extended view of the teaching and study of the contemporary British novel. The problematic nature of British identity is also a current theme for debate.

*Contemporary British Fiction* has essays analysing the work of Martin Amis and Sarah Waters, among many others, and includes an essay by Dominic Head ('Julian Barnes and a Case of English Identity').

*(See Chapter 4)*

### Patricia Waugh

Patricia Waugh has been a prominent figure in the study of literary theory and British fiction for a number of years. The influence of modernism and postmodernism has been a central feature of her research in the past as is evidenced by works such as *Metafiction: The Theory and Practice of Self-Conscious Fiction* (1984), *Feminine Fictions: Revisiting the Postmodern* (1989) and *Practising Postmodernism: Reading Modernism* (1992). She has also edited numerous books and one of the most significant of these is *Modern Literary Theory: A Reader* (1989), which she co-edited with Philip Rice.

The first chapter of *Metafiction*, entitled 'What is Metafiction and Why Are They Saying Such Awful Things About It?' outlines the central thesis and explains how 'metafictional' writers 'explore a *theory* of fiction through the practice of *writing* fiction'. Writings by Malcolm Bradbury and David Lodge are just some of the many texts and authors studied.

*(See History; Chapter 3: Metafiction, Feminism)*

### Raymond Williams

Raymond Williams' use of the term cultural materialism and the ideas behind it were an important influence of critics working in post-war literary studies, particularly in the 1980s. Cultural Materialism is a late development of the Marxist critical tradition, in which literary works are systematically related to economic and social processes, and especially to the history of class struggle. Williams' own 1964 novel *Border Country* was an influential example of working-class Welsh fiction. Williams' ideas were also extensively used in early modern studies, for example by Dollimore and Sinfield in *Political Shakespeare: New Essays in Cultural Materialism* (1985). *Marxism and Literature* (1977), *Keywords* (1976) and *Problems in Materialism and Culture: Selected Essays* (1980) are three of his important studies.

*(See History, Power; Chapter 3: Education Act, Open University, Small Press Publishing, Regional Novel)*

## Key Concepts and Topics

### Abjection

Julia Kristeva outlines her concept of abjection in *Powers of Horror: An Essay on Abjection* (1980). In this work, Kristeva draws upon the anthropological work of Mary Douglas. In *Purity and Danger*, Douglas describes the cultural meaning of the notion of pollution in primitive societies. Kristeva re-defines this by connecting pollution with abjection as that which disturbs order or that which transgresses borders of the clean and proper body. While its literal sense means 'cast out', the position of 'otherness' connected to the abject is understood to be integral to the formation of a sense of self. Kristeva's explanation of the maternal body as abject has been utilized by Barbara Creed in her notion of the 'monstrous feminine'.

### Ambivalence

Even in the most confident colonial text, Bhabha suggests that there are moments of ambivalence, moments when it is possible to divine that the argument is contradictory. Colonial discourse is predicated on the assumptions that the colonized subject is alien, dangerous and essentially different from the colonizer, while at the same time he is seen as educable, capable of being remade in the colonizer's image. Furthermore Bhabha suggests that the very basis of colonialism was to deny most of the world's people liberty, under the pretense of bringing liberty, equality and social advance to colonized countries. Colonial texts anxiously seek to hide or disavow these mutually exclusive suppositions. Bhabha has therefore put his finger on worrying paradoxes that are implicit in the colonial enterprise, and he suggests that many colonial texts contain internal tensions that arise from these ambivalences.

*(See Homi K. Bhabha)*

### Aporia

This term is associated with the practice of deconstruction and refers to a site of contradiction and conflict within a text that cannot be overcome or deciphered. It is a type of textual knot or problem that the text is unable to explain and which the critic draws attention to.

*(See Jacques Derrida, Deconstruction)*

### Avant-garde

The innovation and experimentalism associated with the avant-garde is uncompromising, forceful and risk-taking, exemplified by the military roots of the phrase 'avant-garde' as the front line of the army in warfare. Thus the driving force is one of constant revolution and reaction especially in relation to the popular or mainstream culture and tradition. Key theorists of the avant-garde include Renato Poggioli, Peter Burger, Clement Greenberg and Theodor Adorno.

*(See Chapter 3: Experimental Novel)*

## Deconstruction

Deconstruction is a term that was coined by, and is primarily associated with, Derrida. His reluctance to explain directly what deconstruction actually is adds to its ambiguity and difficulty, but is also indicative of the elusive tendencies of the deconstructive act. Deconstruction addresses the meaning-rich text, directing critical work into unravelling binary oppositions, etymologies and other linguistic games thereby demonstrating implicit textual conflict.

*(See Jacques Derrida)*

## Écriture Féminine

Écriture Féminine is a way of using language that is said to be associated with femininity and may disrupt or subvert formal language associated with masculine use and patriarchal control.

## Essentialism

Essentialism is the belief in an innate difference, for instance, between the way that male and female think and write. Anti-essentialism suggests that any differences are produced by culture and socialization and are contextual.

## Grand Narrative

Lyotard directly addressed the grand, master or meta-narratives that he identified as pervasive structures that had traditionally underpinned Western thought. In *The Postmodern Condition* (1979), he questioned the validity of these universal stories, thereby directly challenging the legacy of the Enlightenment as a means of legitimizing knowledge. Accordingly, postmodernism regards such master narratives critically, referring to their 'natural' relationship as receptacles for knowledge and truth as arbitrary and flawed.

## Gynocritics

Gynocritics is a concept established by Elaine Showalter, a prominent Anglo-American critic. This term refers to the study of women's writing and literary tradition including genre, common themes, development of aesthetic criteria and study of specific writers and texts.

*(See Feminism)*

## Hybridity

According to Homi K. Bhabha, the colonial enterprise causes hybridity, or cultural and social mixing in at least three ways. Firstly, an imposed colonial education means that colonized subjects increasingly begin to resemble the colonizer, and differences between the two are reduced. Secondly, knowledge is changed when it is transplanted to another country or context. Geographical dislocation undercuts the voice of authority, and its original message is destabilized and transformed. When missionaries brought the Bible to a receptive group of 'natives' in Meerut, India, for instance, they found that it was 'repeated, translated, misread, displaced' (Bhabha 1994: p. 102). Thirdly, the mass migration caused by European colonization has also led to the creation of a 'third space' that is neither colonial nor colonized, but a mixture of both. This space, Bhabha suggests, is productive and enabling. However, some thinkers have criticized this positive depiction of hybridity, pointing out that the kind of cultural mixing which Bhabha discusses is often based on traumatic and oppressive experiences (see Young 1995). For example, in colonial Jamaica, hybridity in the sense of racial mixing was often the result of white plantation owners raping black slaves.

*(See Mimicry; Chapters 6 and 7: Postcolonial Theory)*

### History

Both new historicism and cultural materialism have played a part in bringing the historical context back into literary studies. This development may be understood as a reaction against the excesses of new criticism, structuralism and poststructuralism which tend to offer text-based and synchronic readings and, therefore, have distanced the text from its context. Both new historicism and cultural materialism challenge the older and more traditional historicist interpretations of the past and consider history as fragmented rather than unified. Because of this, history is not recognized as a coherent list of facts. Instead, the past is interpreted through texts as these are seen as the only available way to understand it.

*(See Raymond Williams)*

### Ideology

Ideology is a system of unconsciously held beliefs. In its more general usage, references to the dominant ideology denote the more powerful and prevailing set of ideas in a society. Its use is strongly connected to (but not limited by) Marxist thinking as this approach has given the term a wider currency; even here, its definition varies slightly. Marxist Louis Althusser in his concept of Ideological State Apparatus explains the way a state controls and divides its society by producing apparent agreement through ideas and systems of belief. Education, for example, is regarded by Althusser as an ISA.

*(See Raymond Williams)*

### Intertextuality

The echoes or traces of other texts unconsciously layer and interact to form the text under analysis. By its very nature, intertextuality refutes notions of closure. Intertextuality is not to be reduced primarily to conscious authorial allusions nor to the critical practice of returning to a prior text. For example, Jean Rhys' achievements in her novel *Wide Sargasso Sea* (1966), with its allusions to Charlotte Brontë's *Jane Eyre* (1847), constructs a narrative of madness, colonialism and the 'other' about which Brontë is largely silent.

## Irony

Irony results from the juxtaposition of layers of meaning within a text, offering multiple readings and often situating a superior, privileged meaning alongside a more direct, limited meaning. The reader is therefore invited to appreciate the disjunction between the available meanings, including those provided by the context or circumstances, and to acknowledge (if not relish) the ulterior meaning. Irony can depend, as it does in the novels of Evelyn Waugh, on the omission of the relevant frame of reference or system of values which makes sense of the narrative. In Muriel Spark's *The Driver's Seat* (1970), irony works to devastating effect in a critique of masochism, which gradually becomes apparent in a developing insight into the motives of the main character, who ultimately seeks her own murder.

*(See Chapter 3: The Movement, Feminism, Metafiction)*

## Mimicry

Homi K. Bhabha's theory of mimicry came in response to what he saw as Edward Said's failure to examine resistance by colonized people in his study of Orientalism. One major weakness of *Orientalism* is the overwhelming attention it pays to the one-way transfer of knowledge and representations from the West to the East. This is problematic because it allows no room for resistance by non-Western people. Bhabha's theory of mimicry is also a response to Thomas Macaulay's *Minute on Indian Education* (1835), which suggests that in order to rule India, the British needed to create a class of Indians who took on Western tastes, attitudes and education, becoming intermediaries between the colonized masses and the British colonial rulers. In this process, Bhabha argues that the colonizers became *menaced* by these same 'mimic men'. These mimic men were 'almost the same but not quite' (Bhabha 1994: p. 86) as the colonizers. The very fact that these supposedly inferior people could assume English manners, speak the English language fluently and dress in Western dress could undermine Orientalist assumptions about the 'differences' between West and East.

*(See Homi K. Bhabha; Chapters 6 and 7: Postcolonial Theory)*

## Myth

Myth especially involves the retelling of traditional stories and generates a different level of understanding. Notable examples include Angela Carter's prolific reworkings of fairy tales such as Little Red Riding Hood in *The Bloody*

*Chamber and Other Stories* (1979). The mythopoeic and the construction of myths can be seen in Alasdair Gray's *Lanark* (1981) and John Crace's *Arcadia* (2004). The operation of myth in a text lends itself to a complex, multi-layered set of possible meanings, drawing on a wider system of meanings beyond the text with the weight of authority, history or association with what Carl Jung (1875–1961) identified as a collective unconscious.

*(See Freud; Unconscious; Chapter 3: Gothic, Magic Realism)*

## Négritude

Négritude was a literary movement developed by such thinkers as Léopold Sédar Senghor (Senegal) and Aimé Césaire (Martinique) in the immediate pre- and post-war period. They argued that Africa and its diaspora have distinct characteristics that set them apart from other groups of people. The négritude movement amounted to a celebration of black identity and a rejection of Western ideals and values. Its proponents maintained that art being made by artists of African descent requires a separate evaluation than that being made by the rest of the world. Négritude is open to charges that it essentializes the African 'race', but it was a necessary movement in order to overturn the crushing effects of colonialism on the black psyche.

*(See Frantz Fanon; Chapters 6 and 7: Postcolonial Theory)*

## Oedipal Crisis

Based on the model presented in Sophocles, *Oedipus Rex*, the Oedipal drama can be understood as the definitive triadic model of family life upon which Western culture is founded. The incest taboo is seen as central to such a social model. The Oedipal crisis describes the entry into the cultural order and the 'normal' socialization process of the human animal. The path is described as different for girls and boys. The girls' pathway is notoriously more fraught with difficulties due to her necessary rejection of her first love object which is the same sex as herself and her development of penis envy. Because of her difficult path through such a formative apparatus, the female subject is described by Freud as inherently weaker with a lowered sense of justice and heightened jealousy. Due to his more straightforward path through the Oedipal crisis, it is posited that the boy is able to form a much stronger ego.

*(See Freud, Unconscious)*

## Orientalism

Edward W. Said asserts that Western scholarship and art produced an image of the 'Orient'. Our ideas about non-Western people are invented; shaped by centuries of what he terms 'Orientalism': both academic and more popular forms of representation of the East. Said argues that this European discourse about the East is a way of legitimizing colonial rule and justifying Europe's expansion into non-Western countries. Said argues that Orientalist texts define the Orient in terms of everything that the West, allegedly, is not. They achieve this through binary oppositions, so that if the East is stereotyped as being irrational, primitive and tyrannical, then it allows the West to define itself as rational, modern and democratic. It is worth noticing that such binaries always mean that the East is positioned as the weaker partner in binary stereotypes.

*(See Chapters 6 and 7: Postcolonial Theory)*

## Performativity

Performativity is the process by which the constant reproduction of a particular set of mannerisms, or gestures which give the semblance of femininity or masculinity, for instance, actually constitutes the gender itself.

*(See Chapter 3: Feminism)*

## Phallogocentrism

Phallogocentrism is a way of thinking and writing that seeks to fix meaning and is associated with masculinity and rational intellectualism. This concept is often referred to and challenged by advocates of *écriture féminine*.

*(See Chapter 3: Feminism)*

## Postcolonial Theory

Unlike critics such as Boehmer, postcolonial theorists, particularly Bhabha and Spivak, tend to discuss postcolonial issues in a general, philosophical way, and do not examine specific literary texts as often as postcolonial *critics* do. Edward Said, Homi K. Bhabha and Gayatri Spivak are regarded as the most important postcolonial theorists. They are often known as the 'Big Three' or 'the Holy Trinity', signalling the great attention that (perhaps unfairly) has been concentrated on their work in the field.

*(See Homi K. Bhabha, Gayatry Chakravorty Spivak, Edward Said, Frantz Fanon)*

## Power

The role of State power and control and the marginalizing effects of dominant ideologies are negotiated by new historicists and cultural materialists. The ability of the marginalized to respond and destabilize the dominant powers is also of concern, but the fine difference between the two positions becomes highlighted when the question of resistance comes into play. Comparatively speaking, cultural materialism is more optimistic than new historicism in the possibility of challenging oppression.

*(See Michel Foucault, Raymond Williams)*

## Semiotic

The Kristevan notion of the semiotic is not to be understood in the traditional sense of the study of a system of signs although it does carry such connotations. Described in *Revolution in Poetic Language* (1974), the Kristevan notion of the semiotic roughly corresponds to the pre-Oedipal state of the Freudian infant or the Lacan's Imaginary realm. As a pre-linguistic state, it both counters the symbolic and provides the foundation for it. The symbiotic connection to the maternal body is emphasized so that bodily pulses and rhythms act as a foundation upon which the symbolic is overlaid. The semiotic thereby acts as the precondition of culture and language. In Kristevan theory, the domain of the semiotic is identified as the *chora*, with deliberate reference being made to Plato's cave in *Timaeus*. The semiotic may act to disrupt the symbolic. This has been identified as taking place in some *avant-garde* experimental writing. In this sense, the semiotic may be viewed as the unconscious of language itself.

(*See Unconscious, Freud, Jacques Lacan, Symbolic; Chapter 3: Feminism*)

## Social Realism

The social realism of the 1950s, exemplified by the work of Alan Sillitoe and John Braine, is related to earlier aesthetic modes of representation which attempted to record a shared reality and appeal to the reader's experience, expecting a recognition of the familiar world depicted in the novel or play. To some extent the support of a realist mode by a wider political movement derived from a collective experience is less apparent in the 1950s than in the socialist realism promoted from 1934 by the Soviet State, demonstrated in Lewis Grassic Gibbon's trilogy *A Scot's Quair* (1934), depicted the underlying truths of life in a direct and accessible mode, emphasizing action and causality and the determining links to wider social circumstances and environment. To some extent, a similar approach is seen in Pat Barker's *The Century's Daughter* (1986).

(*See Chapter 3: Regional Novel*)

## Subaltern

Spivak calls subordinated people, particularly third-world women and so-called tribal people, 'subalterns', taking a term originally used by the Marxist philosopher Antonio Gramsci to refer to the working classes. She raises doubt about academic enterprises to try to give these subalterns a voice in history. The idea that an intellectual can restore the voice of a subaltern accords too much transparency and a lack of bias to the scholar. However well-intentioned, the intellectual will actually slot the subaltern into certain theories and discourses. So Spivak famously concludes that the subaltern cannot speak, not in the sense that she does not attempt to articulate feelings, desires etc., but that we can never see this subaltern undistorted by power structures and discourses.

*(See Gayatry Chakravorty Spivak; Chapters 6 and 7: Postcolonial Theory)*

## Symbolic

The Symbolic is understood by Lacanian theory to represent the order of language and culture. It is associated with paternal law and prohibition. In a typical Lacanian pun, the *non du père* is understood to be instilled in the *nom du père*. The symbolic breaks up the dyadic relation between the mother and child and thereby performs a necessary cut from the maternal body so that the infant may differentiate itself from the other in order to form its own sense of self. It must be understood, however, that at the same time as this initiation into the beginnings of subjectivity takes place, the infant undergoes a radical loss in its separation from its first object. It is due to such a formative loss that the child must learn to sign; in other words, the child must use the symbolic order of language to represent what it formerly possessed. The symbolic can therefore be seen to be a reaction to such loss and the very constitution of the human subject is instilled in a compensatory reaction to lack.

*(See Jacques Lacan, Unconscious, Semiotic; Kristeva)*

## Unconscious

Freud's concept of the unconscious remains a radical one. It is understood to be a repository of the repressed. The repressed may surface at times to disrupt conscious life; it does so in the forms of slips of the tongue ('para-praxes'), jokes, memory failure, misinterpretations and misplacements. The unconscious is formed through the acceptance of the Oedipal prohibition whereby the infant must relinquish its pleasure-seeking existence, what Freud terms the 'pleasure principle' and accept the restrictions of reality. Due to such repression which is necessary to the social organism, the formation of its ego, the infant becomes radically split in the very formation of its ego. The unconscious is radically other yet carried within the human subject. For Freud, the 'royal road' to the unconscious is through dreams which offer themselves as coded representations for interpretation by the analyst.

*(See Freud, Jacques Lacan, Gayatry Chakravorty Spivak, Kristeva)*

# 7 Changes in Critical Responses and Approaches

## Donna Cox, Katharine Cox, Julie Ellam, Jayne Murphy and Claire Chambers

The period covered by this book extends over sixty years. During this period there have been major and rapid changes in every area of life, not least the literary and artistic worlds. Even the technological contexts for any act of reading and writing have fundamentally changed. Print culture now occupies a place alongside cyberspace where anyone may become an author reaching an unknown, international and potentially interactive readership. How these contexts have influenced authors in this period and how this has affected narrative form is one major concern. Another is the range of experiences which readers of post-war British literature bring to bear on their literary criticism. This chapter explores some of the most significant theoretical and critical approaches to post-war British literature. Each section begins with a summary of some of the relevance of these ideas to specific literary texts and is then followed by a detailed examination of the key ideas.

## Introduction to Poststructuralism and Postmodernism

If literature is made up of language, the workings of language should provide an insight into the literary text. In the post-war period, insights from linguistics and philosophy have been applied to the analysis of the novel, such as those which explore metafiction and revisionist history. Especially in the post-war period, novelists were concerned to respond to the terrors of totalitarianism and explored this in bizarre worlds and dystopias, as demonstrated by Anthony Burgess in *A Clockwork Orange* (1962) and George Orwell, *1984* (1949). The questioning of master narratives, whether religious, philosophical, scientific or political, has led to a scepticism which insists on the relative value of different positions rather than any overarching claim for universal truth. If all belief systems were misguided in attempting completeness in their account of the world where does that leave the modern reader or author? One celebrated literary engagement with these ideas is Salman Rushdie's magic realist novel, *The Satanic Verses* (1988). Such a critique of master narratives was posed by poststructuralism, a development from structural linguistics.

When literary studies was developing in the early twentieth century, literary critics attempted to construct a specialism for the study of literature as distinct from philology, history and any of the new social sciences, so the idea that linguistic methodologies should be used in literary studies was especially threatening. Although the major impact of structuralism was felt in the 1960s, the seminal work from which these ideas derived, Saussure's *General Course in Linguistics*, had been published in 1916. The production of meaning through relationships within a given structure rather than directly, causally or in any determining way arising from the world outside the text, challenged literary critics who regarded the text as author-centred or determined by the author's social circumstances. For those formalist critics who had seen literature as relatively autonomous and consisting of an interplay of devices and functions, the structuralist revolution came as less of a shock. Undoubtedly, structuralism, poststructuralism and postmodernism have had a major impact on the assumptions all critics bring to their readings of post-war British literature.

*(See Chapter 3: Metafiction; Chapter 6: Patricia Waugh)*

## Poststructuralism and Postmodernism (Katharine Cox)

Twentieth-century literary criticism has been dominated by a succession of prominent theoretical discourses which has inevitably led to increased complexity for students introduced to these concepts during their analysis of English and Cultural studies. As Jonathan Culler wryly notes: '[i]f the observers and belligerents of recent critical debates could agree on anything, it would be that contemporary critical theory is confusing and confused' (Culler 1998: p. 17). It is the intention of this handbook to dispel some of these confusions, and to demonstrate, in the critical approaches section, that critical practice is informed by theory. However, it should be remembered that some theoretical standpoints can be very complex indeed, and this is most evident in an encounter with postmodernism. This hotly contested concept will be briefly introduced in order to effectively situate ideas of poststructuralism. The purpose of this chapter is to illustrate the radical change in academic thought initiated by the birth of poststructuralism, through encounter with key theorists, and to assess the impact upon literary analysis caused by the use of poststructuralist thinking as a means of examining post-war British literature. This will be approached by surveying key works and thinkers in this theoretical area and by assessing their impact upon the study of literature.

It is often the experience of students to feel distanced from the literature in question and even to feel bewilderment when employing theoretical ideas. Reactions of alienation come in part from the fashion of adopting literary and cultural theory to interpret text as a 'bolt-on' to thinking. The challenge is to engage in a reading of literature without becoming bogged down in the theoretical mire and moving towards recognizing the theories that reside at the heart of critical practice.

Post-war literary and cultural criticism has been subject to a raft of different theoretical focalizers often collected under the umbrella heading of post-modern approaches. This chapter will firstly consider the contested term 'postmodernism' as applied to changing societal and philosophical emphases, before concentrating on the critical stance of poststructuralism and its literary application via methods of deconstruction.

The term 'postmodernism' is used liberally by critics and media alike, and has been applied to all fields of the arts and humanities. It has also been used to refer to society itself as a way of commenting on the contemporary experience. Postmodernism's diverse presence in critical works creates problems as critics contradict one another, in effect confirming Steven Connor's stance that '[t]he difficulties of knowing the contemporary are well known. Knowledge, it is often claimed, can only be gained and enjoyed about what is in some sense over and done with' (Connor 1989: p. 3). The problem here is whether modernism (the precursor to postmodernism) can even be considered to be 'over and done with'. To clarify, postmodern features in literature such as plurality, linguistic play and heterogeneity have been variably treated by critics either to indicate a continuation of modernist concerns (as a type of 'high modernism') or to demonstrate a break with earlier writing; critics have even identified key features of postmodern game-playing as early as the eighteenth century with Lawrence Sterne's novel *The Life and Opinions of Tristram Shandy* (1767).

Although the idea of postmodernism and its application are not unproblematic it seems appropriate to locate this concept with a period of societal change coinciding with World War II and its aftermath. Accordingly, earlier examples of writing that display postmodern features can be identified as exhibiting proto-postmodern techniques (such as the case of Sterne's writing or elements of James Joyce's *Ulysses* (1922)). Again, this does not represent a consensus on the timing of postmodernism but rather indicates dominant thinking on the subject. This era of global conflict was typified as a time of pessimism and negativity exemplified by such factors as the legacy of Nazi and Soviet totalitarianism, the revelation of systematic atrocities committed in the Holocaust, and the continued threat of annihilation through nuclear war. Rapid technological expansion and advancement also drew attention to the 'developing' nations of the world, the shifting of world power evident in the Cold War, fears for the environment as well as concerns relating to over-population. In the face of such turmoil, postmodern writing is typified by a tendency towards self-referential play, pastiche and fragmentation. These resultant societal upheavals are mirrored in art and literature where the juxtaposition and clash of genre undermine prior conventions; this is especially evident in the visual art of Richard Hamilton (*Just What Is It That Makes Today's Homes So Different, So Appealing?* (1956)), where 'high' and 'mass' culture meet. Accordingly, postmodern literature has demonstrated a propensity for self-reflexivity while its subversive examination of power and structures of ideology have made it a vehicle for postcolonial and meta-historical discourses exemplified by Salman Rushdie's *Midnight's Children* (1981).

Having briefly examined some of the cultural changes leading to a climate of postmodernism it seems appropriate to address the concept directly. The most prominent definition of postmodernism is offered by Jean-Françoise Lyotard in his seminal essay 'The Post-Modern Condition: A Report on Knowledge' (1979), which is often cited by commentators on the postmodern.

In this work Lyotard addresses the changing value of different types of knowledge in the post-industrial (postmodern) age. On a practical level, his arguments address power and knowledge. In terms of implications for literature, he breaks down the monopoly on the author as primary source of textual meaning through the implications of his statement of postmodernism as: '[s]implifying to the extreme, I define *postmodern* as an incredulity towards metanarratives' (Lyotard 1984: xxiv). There have been various translations of this phrase and numerous commentaries upon the concept, but Lyotard is here attacking the existence and implied supremacy of master narratives upon which society bases itself. These include, for example, the dominant systems of capitalism, Marxism, religion, science and, to extend further, the role and function of the author; in fact, any totalizing system that appears to offer stable meanings of identity, truth and knowledge. This is an assault on the tenets of liberal humanist criticism which advocated the moral truth and potential 'good' offered by literature. Through a rejection of these universal systems, all positions and criticism become relative: there is no truth to be found, and no fundamental or absolute identity. Without these founding narratives or myths, generalization becomes impossible and so gives way to the margin and the plural.

Like postmodernism, poststructuralism shares this assault on systems of meaning and in particular treats language with distrust. In theoretical books on the subject the boundaries between postmodernism and poststructuralism may seem rather blurred. It can be argued that the postmodern rather supplanted poststructuralism as the more fashionable term and one that entered popular consciousness via the media. Additionally, commentators on theory such as M. H. Abrams (1999: p. 238) prefer to consider poststructuralism to be the theoretical branch of postmodernism, with the act of deconstruction functioning as one of the tools of poststructural critical practice upon the text.

The influence of poststructuralism has been crucial to the effect of literary criticism upon the study of post-war British fiction. Poststructuralism, as the name suggests, is seen as coming 'after' but also is a reaction to the theories of structuralism, and it is a discipline that revolutionized our manner of approaching literature. Key theorists associated with poststructuralism include: Jacques Lacan, Roland Barthes, Jacques Derrida and Julia Kristeva, Michel Foucault and Gilles Deleuze. This is in itself a controversial area as many of the critics cited as structuralists are also claimed to be poststructuralists (such as Barthes and Kristeva). Frank Lentricchia recalls the academic responses to the theories of Jacques Derrida as being akin to being roused from a 'dogmatic slumber' (Culler 1998: p. 12). Poststructuralists argue that they are merely pushing the logic of structuralism to its natural conclusions, so poststructuralism can be viewed as an extension of structuralism, but one that is a critique leading to a transgression of structuralism. In this way poststructuralist criticism often takes structuralist processes as its starting point before undermining them and causing them to collapse (cf. Eagleton 1985: p. 133). The movement of structuralists to poststructuralism is one arguably based on the principles of the earlier theory. This is partly due to the logic of structuralism, which called for the grammars of texts to be exposed, which is then undermined by poststructuralists who point to the text's conflict and inability to confirm to order and containable patterning.

The birth of poststructuralism can be found in the early 1960s in Foucault's *Madness and Civilization* (1961), which points to the concept of madness as being a constructed notion, and Deleuze's *Nietzsche and Philosophy* (1963) that sought to challenge dominant philosophical thought. Despite these rebuttals to contemporaneous critical practice, these texts were fairly marginal and did not offer a serious threat to dominant thinking. The key period for this type of theory came later and can be positioned from 1967 onwards with the publication of Derrida's lecture, 'Structure, Sign and Play in the Discourse of the Human Sciences', delivered a year earlier, and his body of work *Of Grammatology, Writing and Difference, and Speech and Phenomenon* (all 1967) along with the writings of Barthes ('The Death of Author' 1968) and Foucault 'What is an Author?' (1969). Derrida's writings expressly denied the organization or agency of a central model of language implicit in the work of structuralists; in doing so, the scientific master narrative proposed by structuralist linguistics was undermined. By applying this to literature, Barthes and Foucault argued that there is no overall vantage point from which to view the text. Accordingly, the notion of author as central determiner of meaning is destabilized. Literature is viewed as text which derives its meaning from being read and interpreted by the reader/critic and so decentres the liberal humanist model of the figure of the author. The reference point of the author is now undermined and her/his importance is decentred.

Poststructuralist concerns include a philosophical shift away from the primacy of the author towards the birth of reader/critic, as evidenced above, while the act of interpreting a text is largely indebted to the process of deconstruction, termed by Derrida. Before addressing the process of deconstruction it is advantageous to encounter an explication of Kristeva's term, intertextuality, and its implications for textual analysis. Her idea of the intertext was to point to a series of meanings and inferences that are generated by the text. Kristeva's essay 'Word, Dialogue and Novel' (1969), addressed the text as being made up of a network of unconscious meanings and allusions. In her further work, *Desire in Language: A Semiotic Approach to Literature and Art* (1969) and *Revolution in Poetic Language* (1974) she expanded this idea, arguing that meaning is produced outside of the text. Kristeva and Barthes share some common ground in their meditations upon intertextuality, as Barthes notes: '[the text offers] a multi-dimensional space in which a variety of writings, none of them original, blend and clash' (Barthes 1968: p. 146). It is the analysis of these fragments and intertexts that makes problematic structuralism's illustrations of order and system. In turn, poststructuralist analysis subverts the paired oppositions so favoured by structuralists and instead identifies a covert hierarchy to these binary couplings; focused and intensive readings make prominent the inferior binary pairings or 'other' and so decentre the text. The poststructuralist reading of text participates in the act of deconstruction as the reader probes the limitations of the text, focusing on areas of etymology, absence or marginality, in a manner of undoing the text (Eagleton 1983). The result of this practice causes acute textual difficulty which is termed *aporia*. Derridean analysis of literature is typified by a playfulness and circularity that revels in exposing the labyrinthine technique of chasing the trace meanings of words and phrases, in search of an unstable, unknowable origin. There is a rejection of the 'centre' and an emphasis placed on that which is peripheral, where that which cannot be easily contained is relegated.

The appearance of poststructuralism at the end of the 1960s radically challenged previously held assumptions about the nature of knowledge, which had wide-reaching implications for the study of literature. These critical works and their theories of poststructuralism revolutionized literary criticism as critics could no longer claim to look for a stable truth and had a wide-reaching effect on both the criticism of literature and also its production. Both our reading of texts and the creation of these texts has been deeply influenced by changes in critical approaches. A text may both be produced deconstructively and/or deconstructed through critical analysis. The Czech born playwright Tom Stoppard's drama *Rosencrantz and Guildenstern are Dead* (1966) famously takes the peripheral figures from Shakespeare's *Hamlet* and thrusts their untold story onto centre stage, while John Fowles' *The French Lieutenant's Woman* (1969) draws attention in the later stages to its own fictiveness and the author as construct. What is fascinating about these examples is that they appear concurrently with the theoretical thinking about authorship by Barthes and Derrida.

The application of poststructuralism continues to have relevance as the high point of postmodernism in the 1980s saw contemporary writers whose work was theoretically informed. Knowledge of key theoretical directions is therefore instrumental in the analysis of post-war literature. The changing theoretical landscape has also changed the nature of some of the texts being produced. The rise of theoretically knowledgeable writers such as Julian Barnes, Jeanette Winterson, Salman Rushdie, Martin Amis and others, calls for the critic to be aware of the theories that inform their writing and thinking. To focus purely on the literary text would be to ignore the effect of literary criticism upon its production.

*(See Chapter 6: Lacan, Derrida, Kristeva, Foucault, Barthes, Deconstruction, Intertextuality, Unconscious; Chapter 3: Experimental Novel, Magic Realism)*

## Introduction to New Historicism and Cultural Materialism

If a literary text has a context which is inescapable and determines the form and shape of that text, the task of the literary critic inevitably involves reading which is wider than the literary words on the page. Those words are weighted with historical resonance and value, with traces of the conflict and fantasy which their author experienced in a specific time and place. What information might the literary critic need to understand post-war British literature? An appreciation of the experiments in the *nouveau roman* in France could be used to illuminate the work of Ann Quin, B. S. Johnson and Christine Brooke-Rose. How do their very different life stories impinge on, or even determine, the kinds of experimental novel they produced? Evelyn Waugh's style, his use of irony and omissions could be related to the treatment in his novels of morality, relative values and sexual propriety. Perhaps he needs to create a sense of distance from his material because it is so closely shaped by his own religious convictions, sexual anguish and self-consciousness about social class in a period of social crisis.

This kind of literary analysis tends to explore why a text is written in the way it is, as much as how it is written. The imperative to reveal the ideological force of literature and the determining effects of the social framework on the literary text was central to Raymond Williams' literary criticism, which was at once attentive to literary form and insistent on the social and cultural context of literature and its significant place in the interplay of power relations in society. His book *The Country and the City* (1973) has been particularly influential in the study of the regional novel. However, the searching eye that New Historicism and Cultural Materialism each brings to the question of historical representation has had an appreciable impact on the way we read post-war literatures of all kinds.

*(See Chapter 3: Experimental Novel, Regional Novel; Chapter 6: Irony, History, Williams, Foucault)*

## New Historicism and Cultural Materialism (Julie Ellam)

Both the new historicism and cultural materialism came into prominence as emerging literary theories in the 1980s. These critical approaches signalled a re-vitalized attempt to contextualize the literary text, and the reader, in a historical framework: 'For new historicism and cultural materialism the object of study is not the text and its context, not literature and its history, but rather literature *in* history' (Brannigan 1998: p. 3). This use of history as context is distinct from the text-focused new criticism and elements of structuralist and poststructuralist thinking that have either eschewed historicity or relegated it to a secondary position.

These theories have been used largely in relation to Renaissance Studies, particularly in their use in the 1980s and have questioned the traditional liberal humanist view of interpretations of history. Both critique the traditional understanding of history, and so question the idea that history is a unified coherent subject. Both interpret the past as only knowable through texts. There are many other convergences between new historicism and cultural materialism as, for example, they refuse to accept the notion of canonicity unquestioningly and their criticisms of abuses of power are central themes. It is worthwhile remembering that these theories are not in opposition to each other; however, the differences between their methodologies and influences are notable and, therefore, become the focus of this section.

## New Historicism

New historicism, which is also known as cultural poetics, evolved from scholarship based in the United States and is defined by its analysis of literary texts alongside non-literary texts that are contemporary to the time of writing. This attempt at giving equal weighting to the literary and non-literary is bound up in the reasoning that avoids privileging the literary. Stephen Greenblatt is often given credit for giving the term 'new historicism' credence and his *Renaissance Self-Fashioning: From More to Shakespeare* (1980) is now regarded as a defining text. Here, Greenblatt examines the construction of identities in the sixteenth century.

The work of Michel Foucault has been extremely influential on this theory and an understanding of his theoretical position helps to differentiate it from cultural materialism. His conceptualization of power circulating in society, rather than coming from the top straight down to the bottom of the hierarchy, is engaged with, as is the drawing on a radical thinking of historicism. His understanding of the role of institutions in maintaining power and the effects of internalized forms of control, which are brought to light most notably in *Discipline and Punish* (1975, France), are also part of the new historicist framework for interpretation. Kiernan Ryan's *New Historicism and Cultural Materialism: A Reader* (1996) points out that cultural materialists are also inspired by Foucault, 'but its stress tends to fall on the conflicts rather than the rules' when compared to new historicist readings (1996: p. 1).

Historicist, rather than historical, approaches accept the textuality of history; that is historicism is self-conscious of only being able to know the past through language. The term new historicism shows an independence from former historicist accounts in that theories of subjectivity, rather than individuality, are used. In new historicism (and cultural materialism), the liberal humanist belief in essential identity is deconstructed and traditional readings of history as unified and coherent are contested.

## Cultural Materialism

In contrast with new historicism, cultural materialism has been historically understood as British-based and has been notably influenced by feminism and poststructuralism and the work of Marxists such as Louis Althusser and Raymond Williams. Jeremy Hawthorn, in *A Glossary of Contemporary Literary Theory* (2000), argues that cultural materialism is indebted to Williams for much of its thinking and for the name, which appears in 'Notes on Marxism in Britain Since 1945' (2000: p. 237). This essay is included in *Problems in Materialism and Culture: Selected Essays* (1980). Cultural materialists also understand the import of Foucault (and poststructuralism), but their position tends to be less accepting of the power of the state in comparison to new historicists. Conversely, cultural materialists may be seen as overly optimistic about changing the dominant order. This belief in change, or progress, is influenced by the theoretical underpinning of Marxism.

In the introduction to *Political Shakespeare* (1985), Jonathan Dollimore highlights his understanding of the differences between cultural materialism and new historicism and argues that the former, 'allows much to human agency', whereas the latter is generally concerned with the interaction, 'between State power and cultural forms' in the Renaissance period (at the time of writing) (1985: p. 3). Expanding on this definition, cultural materialists also interpret literature in its context, but do so in a way that allows more for autonomy and subversiveness than new historicist theorists.

The influence of Foucault has been seen to lend new historicism a pessimistic tone, as subversion and dissension is noted but is considered contained once more by the dominant ideology. By contrast, cultural materialism tends to regard the gaps in the text and disruptions to this ideology as positive challenges to the dominant order. This is exemplified in Alan Sinfield's essay, 'Cultural Materialism, *Othello* and the Politics of Plausibility', which is included in *Faultlines: Cultural Materialism and the Politics of Dissident Reading* (1992). In this essay, Sinfield outlines how the, 'inter-involvement of resistance and control' in a text means that dissidence is incorporated, but it also follows that the opposite is possible: that the subordinate is not always subordinated (p. 47).

Another useful example of cultural materialism being used in practice is evident in *Shakespeare Recycled: The Making of Historical Drama* (1992) by Graham Holderness. His analysis of E. M. W. Tillyard's *Shakespeare's History Plays* (1944) is understood by Hawthorn as exemplifying how for cultural materialists, 'the focus of study is not the text, but the birth and life of the text in culture and history' (Hawthorn 2000: p. 239). Tillyard's work is examined and criticized for its unified view of history and for its adherence to the dominant ideologies that require such unity.

Although new historicism and cultural materialism have come to be seen as specific to Renaissance studies, this view is no longer tenable. These are, after all, theoretical positions and are not restricted by a particular time frame. Essays such as 'The Third World of Criticism: From Aeschylus to Ezra Pound' by Jerome McGann and Nancy Armstrong's 'The Politics of Domestic Fiction: Dickens, Thackeray and the Brontës', which are both included in Ryan's *New Historicism and Cultural Materialism*, demonstrate this movement away from the Renaissance period.

## In Practice

In this section, *Money: A Suicide Note* (1984), written by Martin Amis, and *Trainspotting* (1993) by Irvine Welsh are examined using new historicism and cultural materialism, respectively, in order to demonstrate the different uses of these approaches.

## New Historicism

In *Money*, the main protagonist and wholly unreliable narrator John Self is a darkly comic figure that disintegrates through the course of the novel as he fails to succeed in any aspect of his life. This has been regarded as a representative novel of the 1980s as it reflects the greed and individualism made fashionable in Thatcher's Britain. It also draws on postmodern techniques, such as introducing the author as a character, to remind the readers this is a work of fiction.

Using a new historicist approach, and when reading *Money* alongside the infamous 'Gotcha' headline in the *Sun*, which appeared after the sinking of the Argentine ship Belgrano in the Falklands War in 1982, John Self comes to stand for this time of self-concern and the selfishness of the individual. This headline has become representative of all that is patriotic and xenophobic about Britain's most popular newspaper. It is thought approximately 1,200 men were killed and 'Gotcha' symbolizes a dominant culture's means for glorifying war and hate. The portrayal of John Self's search for hedonistic pleasures and descent into wretchedness in a late capitalist society is the flipside to this arrogant jingoism that demands a winner and loser.

The humour inspired by his losses acts as a safety valve that allows for laughter in a rivalry-fuelled society. This safety valve is switched off, however, when the jokes end and the containment of the individual in a society of winners and losers continues. John Self considers the power of money at the end of the novel and compares the desire to attain it to addiction to heroin: 'Maybe money is the great conspiracy, the great fiction. The great addiction too: we're all addicted and we can't break the habit now. There's not even anything very twentieth century about it, except the disposition. You just can't kick it, that junk, even if you want to. You can't get the money monkey off your back' (1984: p. 384). According to this novel, capitalism appears to be inescapable.

Louis Montrose famously argues that new historicism focuses on the historicity of the texts and the textuality of history. When using this framework, *Money* and its comic portrayal of a disintegrating failure feeds into the textuality of its own history and comes to symbolize the 'greed is good' (and bad) motif of the 1987 film *Wall Street*. In these cultural representations, whether good or bad, greed has become inevitable in this climate of reactionary politics.

## Cultural Materialism

*Trainspotting* is set in Edinburgh at the time of the AIDS outbreak in the late 1980s. It is narrated by various voices, but Renton dominates with his take on heroin and politics: 'Society invents a spurious convoluted logic tae absorb and change people whae's behaviour is outside its mainstream. Suppose that ah ken aw the pros and cons, know that ah'm gunnae huv a short life, am ay sound mind etcetera, etcetera, but still want tae use smack? They won't let ye dae it. They won't let ye dae it, because it's seen as a sign ay thir ain failure' (1993: p. 187). Renton goes on to declare he chooses to reject the terms of the Coca Cola advertisement and chooses not to choose life, that is, not the conventional consumer-driven one. His nihilistic sentiments appear to submit to late capitalism as he inverts his own logic, which criticizes alienation, and chooses self-destruction instead.

On the surface, this quotation and the novel as a whole refuse to submit to political engagement. In this light, the novel submits to Walter Benjamin's view in 'The Storyteller' (1936) where the oral tradition of storytelling is preferred over the bourgeois, individualistic novel and the act of novel reading. Renton thus becomes a symbol of the selfish reader who turns away from the collective shared experience.

Renton will not engage with political opposition to the dominant ideology, but by stepping back from his claims, and by avoiding the trap of understanding this narrator at face value only, this novel gives a damning critique of late twentieth-century Britain. It has the cumulative effect of depicting a society of abject souls that are as individualistic as the capitalist society desires. Through the descriptions of violence and drug-fuelled disasters, capitalism and conservative values are attacked. Renton's nihilism is a wonderful testament to and indictment of the outcome of Thatcher's desire for 'no society'. In addition, the continued relevance of *Trainspotting* into the early part of the twenty-first century invites one to question the viability of democracy and points up the similarities between new Labour and Thatcher's rule.

By refusing to write for the literary establishment, Welsh has produced a work that has been accepted on his terms. *Trainspotting* has helped to broaden the scope of the contemporary novel with its Scottish working-class backdrop, rather than middle-class London. It has also reached a wide-reading public, which has no doubt been assisted by its popular reputation (whether justified or not) as the most shop-lifted book of the 1990s.

(*See Chapter 6: Williams, History, Ideology, Irony; Chapter 3: Experimental Novel, Regional Novel*)

## Introduction to Gender and Sexuality

Some literary critics, especially those influenced by Practical Criticism and New Criticism, rejected the sex of the author as an irrelevant piece of bio-graphical information. The quality of the writing rather than facts about the author's life were the aspects considered of interest to literary criticism. It is not surprising, therefore, that the dominance of male authors in the post-war literary scene, and especially in the influential group of writers known as The Movement is often overlooked. Feminist scholarship, aiming at the recovery of a long tradition of women's writing, has demonstrated the extent to which the sex of the author does affect the use of language and literary form, even if some distinguished female authors such as Muriel Spark and Iris Murdoch have made clear that they do not write with their sex in mind. On the other hand, literature provides the potential for authors to adopt a persona in their work and to explore some imaginative cross-dressing, something with which Philip Larkin experimented under the pseudonym Brunette Coleman. A liter-ary criticism concerned with images of women inevitably includes the con-trast presented with male characterization and in recent years critics have addressed masculinity as well as femininity when considering gender. The question of whether experimentation in literary form is gendered has fascin-ated many recent theorists who have speculated as to whether a challenging mode of writing, l'écriture féminine, might be designated feminine even if authored by men as well as women.

(*See Chapter 3: The Movement; Chapter 6: Écriture Féminine*)

## Gender and Sexuality (Jayne Murphy)

Critical approaches based on gender have effectively transformed the study of post-war literature, modifying the positions from which we read texts and questioning the aesthetic standards we apply to them. While there is now a range of critical positions from which to assess a work, including radical feminist, black feminist, lesbian or queer, these perspectives have all grown from the early feminist criticism which emerged from the women's move-ment of the 1970s and 1980s.

Central to feminism, and to feminist literary criticism, is the belief that women are marginalized within patriarchal society which privileges the male while attributing to the female, and to femininity, all those qualities despised by men. Simone de Beauvoir's 1949 work *The Second Sex* pioneered this concept, stating that 'One is not born, but rather becomes, a woman' (cited in Gamble 2001: p. 34). Many contemporary feminists follow de Beauvoir in maintaining the sex/gender separation. While sex refers to a biological category, gender is seen as a cultural construction. From this anti-essentialist perspective femininity or masculinity are considered cultural constructions rather than innate essences, while qualities which might conventionally be said to define femininity, such as gentleness or passivity, are seen as products of socialization along with women's marginalization. Literature, as a medium through which socialization and therefore gendering take effect, is consequently of paramount importance to feminists. While feminist literary criticism is multi-faceted, encompassing many subtle distinctions, the political implications of gender will be the core of any reading.

Feminist critics of the 1960s and early seventies were hampered by an academic canon containing few women writers. Early feminists therefore focused on the critique of disempowering depictions of women found in texts by male authors. Feminist criticism then turned to the rediscovery of neglected women's works, questioning what 'aesthetic criteria' (LeBihan cited in Gamble 2001: p. 130) should be applied to them, moving away from the androcentric aesthetics which remained unquestioned in earlier criticism. The critic Elaine Showalter was instrumental in pioneering this approach, known as 'gynocritics', in works such as *A Literature of Their Own: British Women Novelists from Bronte to Lessing* (1978) and *The New Feminist Criticism* (1986).

Both academia and the publishing industry kept pace with continuing changes in the women's movement; women's writing modules appeared in university prospectuses while within the publishing industry the development of houses such as The Women's Press and Virago and the introduction of institutions such as the Orange Prize have further promoted both women's writing and feminist literary criticism. The development of a new aesthetics of female writing has meant that topics, themes and genres previously viewed as less prestigious because they were written or read predominantly by women are now legitimate areas of study in academia and critics of post-war fiction have an abundant supply of women's writing to study and a variety of feminist perspectives from which texts may be read. Other marginalized groups also now have their own canons and critical techniques to use.

Readings based on gender may take a number of different approaches. Those commonly referred to as Anglo-American feminism have often tended 'to be more sceptical about recent critical theory' (Barry 2002: p. 124), taking a more traditional, liberal humanist approach to literature, although some

British and American critics have made use of Marxist or psychoanalytic theories. Readings based on French Feminism will often take considerably more theoretical approaches, drawing heavily on psychoanalysis or post-structuralist theories of language.

So how would a critic approach a post-war text from one of the above perspectives? The text's representation of gender – including both masculinity and femininity – may be critiqued, with discussion of whether gender is depicted as a natural 'essence' or as culturally constructed, how characters conform to or subvert conventions of gender and the implications of such compliance or defiance. Questions asked might include whether the text represents 'woman' or 'man' as single, universal concepts or shows differences at play within these terms. How do protagonists' cultural origins or ethnicity impact on their gendering within the text and what assumptions are readers invited to make? The balance of power between different characters may be discussed, with comment on the interaction between factors such as class and capital and the representation of gender, while an increased awareness and interest in genres or themes commonly used and read by women may lead critics to focus on the use of a particular genre and its subversive potential.

Early feminism's insistence that biology need not determine destiny was modified during the 1980s and 1990s by a reclamation of the female body; and an exploration of the role of cultural conventions in sculpting female and male bodies. This theoretical return to the body has led to a corresponding critical interest in the representation of the 'sexed' body in literature. However, the knowledge and use of gender theory has become so widespread in both creative and critical processes that certain topics, such as menstruation, motherhood, madness and eating disorders have become staples of women's fiction causing critics, including Showalter, to question whether women's writing should remain a genre on its own, a debate which in turn reflects the development of postfeminism. Feminist theory and criticism itself has therefore been instrumental in shaping women's fiction.

While Anglo-American feminist critics have traditionally concerned themselves with the political representation of women in texts, those drawing on French feminist theory may be more interested in the use of language in a text. Toril Moi in *Sexual/Textual Politics* (2002) suggests that the work of Hélène Cixous, Luce Irigaray and Julia Kristeva is 'most representative of the main trends in French feminist theory', (p. 95). These three figures draw on psychoanalytic theory and linguistics to address language itself. Cixous and Irigaray are most associated with the concept of *écriture féminine*, or feminine language; a style of writing that they suggest offers a challenge to patriarchal authority. Moi comments, 'One of Cixous's most accessible ideas is her analysis of what one might call 'patriarchal binary thought' (2002: p. 103). In works such as *The Laugh of The Medusa* published in 1975 and other subsequent texts

Cixous suggests that Western philosophers have always thought in terms of binary oppositions which reflect a male/female opposition that underlies traditional Western thought and which always privileges the masculine term at the expense of the feminine. Cixous proposes a new use of language that will not equate the feminine with negativity and will allow meaning to flow freely from word to word. A similar new use of language is proposed by Luce Irigaray in works such as *Speculum of The Other Woman* (1974) and *This Sex Which Is Not One* (1977). Irigaray terms this new usage 'le parler femme' or 'womanspeak' (Moi: p. 143) suggesting that this is a form of language that 'emerges spontaneously when women speak together' (Moi: p. 143).

Irigaray's version of feminine writing resists patriarchal language by use of parody and mimicry and by 'writing from within the white space between men's lines' (LeBihan, cited in Gamble 2001: p. 135). However, both Cixous and Irigaray link *écriture féminine* with the female body; an association which links the concept of feminine writing with essentialism. Julia Kristeva has also theorized on the disruptive and subversive potential of language, but her work may be read as anti-essentialist. In *Revolution in Poetic Language* (1974) she draws on psychoanalysis and linguistics to suggest that language consists of the symbolic, which is the formal, structured and grammatical use of language, and the *semiotic*, an emotional, aspect of language linked to the bodily sensations and drives of pre-Oedipal infancy. While the symbolic is associated with rules, laws and patriarchal society, the semiotic represents the eruption into formal language of a more instinctive force linked to sounds and rhythm and which, like femininity in patriarchal society, is repressed and marginalized in formal language use. Kristeva suggests that semiotic eruptions can disrupt symbolic or formal language and also the patriarchal order that it reflects and supports. Again *Sexual/Textual Politics* provides a comprehensive but accessible introduction to Kristeva's work discussing its anti-essentialism along with the arguably more essentialist theories of Cixous and Irigaray. Whether *écriture féminine* and the semiotic are potentially subversive is a topic still open to discussion, but both approaches have been influential, offering critics the opportunity to focus extensively on the use of language in a text and to consider just how language itself might be used subversively by a feminist writer. Conversely, the writers of fiction who have been influenced by such theories and previous critical readings may themselves choose to experiment with syntax and sentence structure in their own work.

While feminist criticism may focus mainly on the representation of gender, lesbian and gay readings will also study a text from a position of self-conscious marginality. Developing out of 'mainstream' feminism, the lesbian feminist movement has given rise to an increasing market for lesbian fiction, which has become a sub-genre in itself, with many large bookstores having a lesbian and gay section. Literary canons and critical techniques have emerged correspondingly. Critics of lesbian and gay fiction may foreground the sexuality of characters, focus on non-sexual same-sex relationships within a text or discuss why a particular work may be read as 'lesbian' or 'gay'. Queer criticism, a more recent development, will often focus on the transgression of sexual 'norms' and the contradictions to be found in conventional sexual identities. In queer criticism particularly, the fluidity of subjectivity may be foregrounded. While feminist or lesbian feminist readings may adopt a 'woman-centred' perspective, critics, whether male or female, utilizing queer approaches draw on poststructuralist and psychoanalytic theories of subjectivity that suggest that there is no fixed and stable identity but rather fluctuating subjectivities created contextually. Critics using queer theory expand the exploration of gender begun by feminist criticism. One such theorist is Judith Butler, whose *Gender Trouble: Feminism and the Subversion of Identity* (1990, 1999) suggests that gender, rather than being indicative of any internal essence, is an effect produced by the constant repetition of a set of stylized acts. Butler states,

> In other words, acts and gestures, articulated and enacted desires create the illusion of an interior and organizing gender core, an illusion discursively maintained for the purposes of the regulation of sexuality within the obligatory frame of reproductive heterosexuality. (1999: p. 173)

Butler's anti-essentialism therefore critiques the concept of gender identity suggesting that this has no natural basis. In *Gender Trouble* and later works such as *Bodies That Matter: On The Discursive Limits of 'Sex'* (1993), Butler goes on to challenge the concept of the 'sexed' body itself, suggesting that this is a cultural construction imposed to maintain the dominance of heterosexuality. The sexed body is therefore a product of discourse, constructed culturally and contextually. For Butler, acts of parody such as drag are potentially subversive in that they may expose the constructed nature of the 'original' that is being copied. It may be seen therefore that queer theory places more emphasis on acts, or what is done with a body, than on physical characteristics which may be used to categorize and unify male or female. Queer critiques will draw out and examine those facets of characterization which appear to contradict the concept of fixed identity. Similarly, queer readings tend to emphasize and celebrate the transgression of all boundaries, even those adopted by conventional lesbian or gay characters in a text. A further focus is on the bodies of characters, examining physical attributes and uses and questioning whether these conform to or subvert conventional ideas of the 'sexed' body. While queer critiques may seem to reject the concept of fixed and gendered identities, they are, like feminist critiques, based on the adoption of marginalized position from which to study a text. In this sense, they owe much to the feminist theory which pioneered this strategic approach.

In conclusion, critical approaches based on gender or sexuality, while appearing to differ, share common roots in the second wave feminism of the 1960s and 1970s. By making acceptable the taking up of marginalized or minority positions from which to read texts gender theory has influenced literary criticism itself, being instrumental in the development of new aesthetics to be applied to fictions of the marginalized. It has led to the development of specific canons and the growth of new genre, although the separation of 'marginal' fictions from those considered 'mainstream' is now itself a contentious topic.

*(See Chapter 6: Gynocritics, Écriture Féminine, Symbolic, Semiotic, Kristeva; Chapter 3: Feminism)*

## Introduction to Postcolonialism

The relationship between literature and politics comes to the fore when the issue of colonialism is considered. The invasion of one country by another, the appropriation of land and the imposition of the language and cultural practices of the dominating people, clearly, comprise some of the defining events in many national histories. Literature, on the other hand, has provided a powerful means to challenge such acts of cultural invasion and domination. For some writers this takes the form of a very deliberate response; for others writing is centred on personal experience, refusing to reinforce the power of the dominant forces by entering into a dialogue. Writings of both kinds explore ideas of affiliation and hybridity, memory and imaginative speculation. The latter takes an experimental turn in the novels of Wilson Harris, such as *Jonestown* (1996), where he explores difference by bringing together different cultural forms, traditions and communities, using dream to access a communal history which must be told. An investigation of place becomes of central importance, especially the relationship between places which have founded the postcolonial situation. Similarly the examination of historical context and the traces of history which make a mark on the literary text provide the necessary means of interpretation in postcolonial approaches to literature. Accounts of the end of the British Empire and the effects of decolonization, independence, international trade and migration all become relevant for analyses of the post-war British novel since it is in this period that many former colonies have gained independence. Caryl Philips' *A State of Independence* (1986) concerns the protagonist's journey from St Kitt's to England. The impact of migration to England in the 1950s is given close attention in Andrea Levy's *Small Island* (2004), which details the experiences of those who arrived on SS Windrush, the community they settled in and its transformation.

Whether set in a former colony or somewhere less expected, such as the suburbs in Hanif Kureishi's *The Buddha of Suburbia* (1990), questions of identity are always bound up with location and movement in postcolonial literature.

## Postcolonialism (Claire Chambers)

Postcolonialism is a notoriously difficult term to define. Critics have debated every aspect of the term, from minutiae such as whether it should be hyphenated, to broader issues, such as its relationship to the theories of poststructuralism and postmodernism, and its uneasy position within the academy. This section considers postcolonialism in its various forms: as a historical period, a type of literature, a strategy of reading, and a literary theory, and concludes by outlining key postcolonial concepts.

The first, most obvious definition of the term 'postcolonial' is of course that it signifies the historical period that comes after the moment of formal decolonization. In terms of European empires in the modern period, there were two main periods of decolonization: firstly in the late eighteenth to early nineteenth centuries in North America, Haiti and Latin America, which involved the largely violent decolonization of mostly white settlers. The second period ran from approximately the mid-1940s to the 1960s, and concerned the rapid dissolution of European empires. This period of decolonization was ostensibly less violent than the earlier American process of decolonization and mostly affected non-white communities. The terms 'postcolonial' and 'postcolonialism' almost always refer to the second, more recent period of the decolonization.

Stephen Howe, along with some other historians, is critical of the term postcolonialism. He writes:

> To some people, [postcolonialism is] an all-purpose label for the entire state
> of the contemporary world. To others, it's just the tag for a few Professors
> of English Literature, their books, and courses. Like most 'post' words,
> it seems to involve coming after something – so some view its use as
> dangerously misguided, for implying that colonialism is utterly dead and
> done with. (Howe 2002: pp. 25–26)

There is some truth in each of Howe's three main criticisms here. The term 'postcolonialism' is sometimes used in a loose, un-illuminating way, denoting a whole range of phenomena in the modern world; it can also be a self-perpetuating demarcation designed to promote individual academics' careers and with little basis in the 'real' world; and finally the term 'postcolonialism' can be misleading, because it implies that colonialism is safely in the past when in fact the impact of European colonization continues to shape the modern world. Taking an opposite view, other critics have argued that the very term postcolonialism is Eurocentric, making the impact of European colonialism loom too large. Finally, some scholars have pointed out that there is a major difference between settled colonies like Australia and Canada, whose white inhabitants negotiated their independence peacefully and maintained relatively cordial relations with the colonial metropole, and non-settled colonies like those of the Indian subcontinent, the Caribbean, and Africa, where the process of decolonization was far more traumatic. Examples of critics who contest the term include Dirlik, McClintock and Zeleza. However, despite his reservations, Howe himself uses the term 'postcolonial' at several moments in his book on the history of empire. This suggests that, notwithstanding the problems he has with it, he nonetheless finds it useful in denoting the situation of formerly colonized countries.

The remainder of this section addresses the term 'postcolonial' as it is used within literary studies. As we have seen, Howe (and other historians) are somewhat hostile and dismissive about what is seen as the densely theoretical and historically unaware work of 'Literature Professors'. However, I will argue that, when it is combined with a clear sense of historical context, the 'postcolonial' literary endeavour is very helpful in allowing us to understand both colonization and decolonization as cultural phenomena. In literary studies, 'postcolonial' denotes three areas: an umbrella term that enables us to group together writing, a critical approach to this writing, and a literary theory, and these are what this essay will interrogate.

## Literature

Postcolonialism is an umbrella term that has been used to group together texts written in countries once colonized by Europe and literature written by migrants from these countries (who are now based in the former colonial centre). Thus it embraces writing by authors living in former colonies, such as India, as well as writers living in Britain. Of course, this encompasses literature produced in all sorts of locations across the globe. But it can be divided into two broad categories: (1) settler nations, such as Canada and Australia, which gained independence from Britain in the late nineteenth and early twentieth century and (2) second-phase colonies from the post-WWII era: colonies in the Caribbean, South Asia and Africa gained the right to govern their own affairs.

To clarify this definition of the term 'postcolonial literature', John McLeod's definition is useful:

> Very basically, and in a literary context, postcolonialism involves one or more of the following:

- Reading texts produced by writers from countries with a history of colonialism, primarily those texts concerned with the workings and legacy of colonialism in either the past or the present.
- Reading texts produced by those that have migrated from countries with a history of colonialism, or those descended from migrant families, which deal in the main with diaspora experience and its many consequences. (John McLeod 2000: p. 33)

This is a concise but elastic definition of postcolonialism. What is obvious straight away is the broad scope of the term. In literature, the field of post-colonialism embraces writers as diverse as literary celebrities like Nigerian novelist Chinua Achebe, Margaret Atwood and Salman Rushdie, along with Kenyan novelist Ngugi wa Thiong'o (who has made a conscious decision to write only in his native tongue Gĩkũyũ) and Bessie Head, a South-African writer who lived in Botswana. These writers may share a history of colonialism, but it goes without saying that colonialism was not the same thing in India and Canada, in Botswana and Kenya.

Postcolonial literature is extremely diverse. It incorporates the literatures and cultural practices of all countries with a history of colonialism, both settled and non-settled colonies, which have had very different experiences of colonialism. And we could take this further. Even within individual nations, people's experiences are divergent. Australia is a good example: two critics suggest that Australia today may be seen as at once 'coloniser, colonised, and postcolonial' (Childs and Williams 1997: p. 2). Australian aboriginal people are marginalized and impoverished in modern Australian society, and some people argue that they are 'internally colonized' by white Australians. However, we can also see Australia as a postcolonial nation, given that it is no longer governed by the British centre. Even this is open to dispute, because the Queen of England is still the head of state in Australia; thus colonialism continues in a new guise: neo-colonialism. This example shows just how complex it is to speak of 'postcolonial' literature. Should white Australian and aboriginal Australian writing both be termed 'postcolonial'?

Within the formerly colonized countries there are also two other major divisions: class and gender. As is well-known, many of the nationalist leaders who replaced the British colonizers were actually similar to the people they replaced, in every area except their race. Leaders such as Jaharwalal Nehru and Mohandas Gandhi in India, Norman Manley and Arthur Chung in the Caribbean, and Jomo Kenyatta and Kwame Nkrumah in Africa were all middle-class, well-educated males. It has been argued that the colonies' working classes and women were doubly or even triply colonized (see Petersen and Rutherford 1986). The withdrawal of European administrators may have meant the end of their racial colonization, but they continue to be oppressed for their gender and social class. As we shall see, the postcolonial theorist Gayatri Spivak argues that many of these people are 'silenced', unable to write about their experiences because they are denied access to education. It is important to realize that 'postcolonial literature' tends to be produced by an elite: upper- and middle-class men (and some women); sometimes working-class men, but rarely by people who are triply colonized on the basis of race, class and gender.

## Colonial Literary Practices

Empires are rarely successful unless they encourage a certain amount of consent from the people they govern. One of the most important tools that British (and other) colonizers used in order to persuade their subject peoples of the legitimacy of their rule was literature. In fact, one scholar has described empire as a 'textual undertaking' (Boehmer 1995: p. 5). Novelists and poets including H. Rider Haggard and G. A. Henty wrote imaginative works extolling the rationality and fair play of empire-builders. To take just one example, Rudyard Kipling, who lived most of his days in India and increasingly became seen as a mouthpiece for the British empire, wrote a famous poem entitled 'The White Man's Burden' (1899). The poem opens as follows:

> Take up the White Man's burden –
> Send forth the best ye breed –
> Go bind your sons to exile
> To serve your captives' need;
> To wait in heavy harness
> On fluttered folk and wild –
> Your new caught, sullen peoples,
> Half devil and half child [. . .]
>
> Take up the White Man's burden –
> The savage wars of peace –
> Fill full the mouth of Famine
> And bid the sickness cease. (In Cochrane 1977: p. 128)

Kipling portrays colonization as a noble enterprise, carried out by the 'best' men from European nations. These men are portrayed as being motivated by the selfless desire to improve the 'native's' lot: he describes them as fighting for peace and stability in the colonized nations. These are noble men who want to eradicate hunger, and cure disease. Yet he suggests that the colonizer's work is a thankless task, a 'burden', because irrational colonized people are not grateful for the 'help' and are instead rebellious and 'sullen'.

Of course, novels, poems and plays were not the only types of colonial writing that propagated such notions of the colonizers' superiority to the people whose land they occupied. Other kinds of writing, like legal reports, scientific tracts and histories, were written – in apparently objective language – to justify the rational benefits of empire. This context is important because it shows that colonialism was not only shaped by military conflict and economic pursuit of profit. Importantly, literature and culture were also implicated in the unequal power dynamics of colonialism. And one of the ways that colonial writers reinforced their power was through colonial education. What is really striking about the colonial education system is that pupils in the colonies did not learn about their own cultural traditions, geography and history. Instead, the syllabus was based on English literature. Pupils were taught English classics, such as Dickens and Wordsworth. Children learnt about Wordsworth's daffodils when they had never actually seen such flowers. One important African writer, Ngugi wa Thiong'o, has described this process, whereby children were taught about the superiority of English culture over what was presented as their own backward and degraded language and culture, as 'colonizing the mind'. Such an education had a great impact on the psychologies of colonized peoples. As well as having their countries physically occupied by Europeans, an attempt was made to create a colonial mindset, persuading colonized people that European culture was superior.

## Postcolonial Literary Practices

Postcolonialism is not simply a historical term that names a period which comes after empire. It refers to particular modes of representation and even gives us a set of reading practices that we can apply to texts, a kind of literary criticism toolkit, to put it somewhat bluntly. To sharpen up our definition, I want to turn to a helpful definition from the critic Elleke Boehmer's excellent book, *Colonial and Postcolonial Literature:*

> Rather than simply being the writing which 'came after' empire,
> *postcolonial* literature is that which critically scrutinizes the colonial
> relationship. It is writing that sets out in one way or another to resist
> colonialist perspectives. As well as a change in power, decolonization
> demanded symbolic overhaul, a reshaping of dominant meanings.
> Postcolonial literature formed part of that overhaul. To give expression
> to colonized experience, postcolonial writers sought to undercut
> thematically and formally the discourses which supported colonization –
> the myths of power, the race classifications, the imagery of subordination.
> (Boehmer 1995: p. 3)

According to this definition, writing may sometimes be considered 'postcolonial' when it precedes decolonization, but nonetheless resists and opposes colonialism. A postcolonial approach requires us to read with an awareness that literature and culture were often implicated in the unequal power dynamics of colonialism. Empires were of course shaped by military conflict and economic pursuit of profit, but literary texts helped to sustain the colonial vision, to reinforce hierarchies that set European culture above all others. With this in mind, a postcolonial approach asks us to be attentive to such power dynamics when we read literature. Postcolonial criticism offers us strategies of reading, emphasizing a need to be aware of how colonialism affected modes of representation, and then to consider how postcolonial writers challenge colonialist assumptions (such as race classifications and postulations about the superiority of European culture) through their literary texts.

One of the main ways in which colonized people challenged colonial assumptions was to take their colonizers' literary forms – biographies, novels, poems, essays – and reshape them in order to challenge colonial values. Alternatively, writers could look for indigenous literary forms, such as oral story-telling, folk songs, written poetic forms such as the *ghazal* (Urdu) and use these as vehicles for the expression of anti-colonial feeling. Finally, many writers took the two things – colonial and indigenous literary forms – and created new texts which contained elements of both. Postcolonial writing is often interpreted as being hybridized and multifarious, incorporating influences from both East and West.

Yet it would be a mistake to assume that postcolonial literature is always stridently confident in its opposition to colonial values. In fact, postcolonial writers often recognize that certain benefits can be derived from the colonial encounter. The very fact that many postcolonial writers choose (or are compelled) to write in English, even though it may not be their mother tongue, and use arguably Western literary forms such as the novel, shows that they are not wholly opposed to everything associated with their colonizers. Many postcolonial writers express the pain experienced by formerly colonized people, who struggle to define their identity, caught as they are between ideas emanating from the overlapping categories of the West and the non-West. Howe argues:

> the theme of feeling culturally divided, even schizophrenic, torn between
> local tradition and colonial – then global – modernity became perhaps
> the most constantly recurring preoccupation of African, Asian, and other
> 'postcolonial' writers and artists. (Howe 2002: p. 20)

Identity is a recurring concern in postcolonial writing. The desire to be independent of colonial ways of thinking can lead to writers celebrating and at times idealizing local traditions, but others express anxiety that some of these traditions can be oppressive or backward-looking. For instance, in *Things Fall Apart*, Chinua Achebe presents us with the richness of Ibo culture, but questions some of its traditions, such as twin infanticide and wife beating.

## Postcolonial Literary Criticism

In the 1940s, 1950s and 1960s, the British Empire rapidly unravelled in a process of decolonization. Many of the nations that had newly become independent from the British empire decided to join the new Commonwealth, which was designed to be a decentralized and loose association of the countries that used to be part of the British empire.

In response to this process, and to the increasing wealth of national literatures being produced in formerly colonized countries, certain academics from within English literature began to turn their attention towards literature from Commonwealth countries. 'Commonwealth literature' as an area of serious study began at Leeds University, under the tutelage of such critics as William Walsh and Norman Jeffares.

The work of the Commonwealth literature critics was extremely important as they allowed new voices from non-Western countries to enter the literary canon. This entry on 'postcolonialism' might not have been written if it were not for their efforts to get writers such as Chinua Achebe, R. K. Narayan and George Lamming, from Nigeria, India and Barbados, respectively, to be recognized as great artists.

However, there were certain problems with their approach to non-Western literatures. Firstly, they judged the literature being produced by non-Western writers by the standards that English Literature deemed appropriate to define 'great literature'. Thus, they looked for evidence of universal themes, aesthetic merit and linguistic excellence, but unlike later postcolonial critics they did not think to challenge the Eurocentric bias with which these judgements were passed. Secondly, as a result of their preoccupation with universal, liberal themes, the Commonwealth critics often overlooked the nationalist and local concerns of the writers they were studying. For example, when examining the work of the Indian writer R. K. Narayan, who was writing from the 1930s, they would argue that his writing evoked images of a universal humanity, but would neglect his arguments about India's struggle for national self-definition.

Commonwealth literature clearly did not go far enough in challenging colonial discourse, but arguably later postcolonial literary critics went further. After 1978, which saw the publication of Edward Said's highly influential text *Orientalism*, to be discussed shortly, there was an outpouring of works about colonial discourse and the 'postcolonial condition'.

Four types of postcolonial critical practice came into currency in the 1980s.

1   Reading classic English literary texts for evidence about imperial atti-
    tudes. Novels such as Joseph Conrad's *Heart of Darkness* (1899) and E. M.
    Forster's *A Passage to India* (1924), which explicitly dealt with imperial-
    ism, were examined in the new light of Said's theory of Orientalism.
    Also, texts such as William Shakespeare's *The Tempest* (1611), Charlotte
    Brontë's *Jane Eyre* (1847) and Jane Austen's *Mansfield Park* (1814), which
    on the surface had very little to do with the colonial project, were also
    examined for their latent assumptions.

2   Reading colonial texts for ways in which colonial discourse is unstable.
    This is the kind of reading inspired in particular by the theorist Homi K.
    Bhabha. Using this approach, critics look for moments when colonial
    discourse is ambivalent; looking for slippages in argument, when colo-
    nial discourse contradicts itself.

3   Reading texts by writers from formerly colonized countries. This kind
    of study was particularly inspired by one text, *The Empire Writes Back*,
    written in 1989 by the Australian critics Bill Ashcroft, Gareth Griffiths
    and Helen Tiffin. They argued that literature from formerly colonized
    countries attempts to question and parody colonial discourses, 'writing
    back' to the centre to contest accepted truths. These postcolonial writers,
    they argue, remake the English language and the novel form to chal-
    lenge the assumptions of colonialism. Although very influential, and a
    brave attempt to make theoretical connections between literatures from
    differently colonized countries, *The Empire Writes Back* has been rightly
    criticized for its homogenizing tendencies. Problems with the book
    include the fact that it ignores historical differences, so America is seen
    as a postcolonial nation, because it was colonized by Britain.

According to Ashcroft *et al.*, even Britain has some claim to 'postcolonial status', as it was once colonized by the Romans and Normans.
Famously, the writers of *The Empire Writes Back* argue:

> We use the term 'post-colonial' [. . .] to cover all of the culture affected
> by imperial process from the moment of colonisation to the present
> day. This is because there is a continuity of preoccupations through-
> out the historical process initiated by European imperial aggression'.
> (Ashcroft et al. 1989: p. 2)

It can be argued that the writers are far too totalizing about history,
collapsing different experiences of colonialism under much too expan-
sive an umbrella term.

Furthermore, several commentators have pointed out that postcolonial writers are not merely 'writing back' to the centre. Critics such
as Anne McClintock observe that this notion that postcolonial writers
simply seek to challenge colonial discourse, actually reinserts European

ideas at the centre. She writes that 'colonialism returns at the moment of its disappearance' (McClintock 1995: p. 11), suggesting that too much attention is still being accorded to the West, even if critics now seek to challenge its assumptions.

4  Reading texts by migrant or diasporic writers. The final undertaking of postcolonial scholars is to examine literature being produced by what are often termed 'migrant' or 'diasporic' writers. One of the main legacies of decolonization has been immigration by formerly colonized peoples to the colonial metropole and to other Western countries. Among postcolonial criticism's most pressing concerns, therefore, has been to examine texts produced by these migrants, their children, and their grandchildren.

## Postcolonial Theory

Unlike critics such as Boehmer, postcolonial theorists, particularly Bhabha and Spivak, tend to discuss postcolonial issues in a general, philosophical way, and do not examine specific literary texts as often as postcolonial *critics* do. Edward Said, Homi K. Bhabha and Gayatri Spivak are regarded as the most important postcolonial theorists. They are often known as the 'Big Three' or 'the Holy Trinity', signalling the great attention that (perhaps unfairly) has been concentrated on their work in the field.

Postcolonialism has often been subject to criticism. Some of the charges against it have already been discussed. These criticisms are not always fair and often simplify the very subtle arguments of postcolonial theorists. Spivak, for example, is often at pains to complicate and question her own complicity in the very colonial structures she seeks to challenge. In an autobiographical essay (1992) she is the first to point out her own privileged position as a rich Bengali Brahmin educated in the West. The title of her 1993 book, *Outside in the Teaching Machine*, also interrogates her paradoxical position both within and outside of the academic institutions of the West. Furthermore, the charge that postcolonialism ignores the issue of neo-colonialism in today's world is not entirely justified; for example, Said looks at American imperialism in some detail in *Orientalism* and has written extensively on current events such as 9/11 (see Said 2005).

Ultimately, I would argue that it is reasonable to be suspicious of the term 'postcolonialism'. However, if we are wary of its limitations, 'postcolonialism' can be a useful term. It has the strength of indicating both a historical period (after colonialism) and an aesthetic discourse. One of the most important things about postcolonialism is that we now routinely ask questions about the legacy of empire when we read literary texts. But reading postcolonial texts requires us to immerse ourselves in specific cultural contexts and time periods. It also makes us rethink 'knowledge' as a product of colonialism. As long as we realize that the term is not supposed to indicate the end of the colonial legacy or unequal power relations, the term can highlight the extent to which colonialism has shaped our worldview without us even realizing it. As Gyan Prakash has commented:

> One of the distinct effects of the recent emergence of postcolonial criticism has been to force a radical re-thinking of forms of knowledge and social identities authored and authorized by colonialism and western domination. (Prakash 1992: p. 8)

## Introduction to Psychoanalysis

Story-telling takes on a different meaning for psychoanalytic critics. In the post-war British novel, the story-telling process and the creation of myths and symbols is often a self-conscious matter. The idea that the self is not entirely rational – that there is another realm at work and apparent in the use of language, in dream and in bodily manifestations – is a principle concern of psychoanalytic criticism although it informs other approaches. In this regard, the myth criticism of Northrop Frye and the work of Carl Jung in the exploration of recurring symbols and archetypes in literature are relevant.

Rather than communicating directly and coherently, the literary text is assumed to have an unconscious, another dimension which is not immediately apparent but susceptible to a close examination. The therapeutic context shows us that stories tell more about us than we are aware of or in control of. Pat Barker's novel, *Regeneration* (1981), returns to the beginnings of the famous 'talking-cure' when it was put into practice, in treating the damaged veterans of the First World War, and explores the effects of trauma by tracing cause to symptoms in a range of patients. The exploration of the power of the unconscious, and the need to control it, is a principle concern of Aldous Huxley in *Brave New World* (1932) where there is state regulation of sex, violence and fantasy. Huxley also addresses the fundamental ideas of psychoanalysis, that child development has a determining effect on the self, by creating a world in which humans are reproduced asexually in a laboratory and natural childbirth and motherhood is perceived to be primitive. This novel has influenced later science fiction novels such as Marge Piercy, *Woman on the Edge of Time* (1976) and Margaret Atwood, *The Handmaid's Tale* (1985), as well as the work of a wide range of post-war and contemporary writers whose work engages self-consciously with ideas drawn from psychoanalysis.

## Psychoanalysis (Donna Cox)

Now accepted as a major strand of poststructuralist analytical theory, psychoanalysis was originally a theory which, in its application, offered relief to patients suffering from the after-affects of psychical trauma. The originator of this theory is recognized as the Austrian physician, Sigmund Freud (1856–1939), who first coined the term 'psycho-analysis' in one of his early papers which refers to it as a 'new method'. The practitioner of this new technique was required to work with the patient's presentation of their story to work back to recover the embedded trauma and thereby release the knots which held the symptom in place. Freud describes this process:

> Travelling backwards into the patient's past, step by step, and always guided by the organic train of symptoms and memories and thoughts aroused, I finally reached the starting-point of the pathological process. (Freud 1999 [1896]: p. 151)

The nascent principles of the technique were discovered in Freud's treatment of his early patients for hysteria. The first patient of the new therapy, named as 'Anna O.' by the case history, referred to the technique as 'the talking cure'. The act of telling directed towards another person is a central feature of the treatment. Such linguistic representation can therefore be seen to be pivotal to the presentation of illness, to the therapeutic application and to the 'cure' itself. That this theory is now utilized as an aspect of literary analysis through a poststructuralist perspective raises questions about principles held in common by the two techniques. Both techniques have a linguistic focus and apply a systematic pressure to the object of their enquiry. Central to human understanding of the self in the psychoanalytical scenario is the unfolding of personal story in a presentation of narrative. Freud noted the role of story in human representation and how the self is projected in the production of such narrative; he termed this the 'compulsion to tell'. His first patients told incessant stories in order to alleviate their suffering; it was deemed to be a process which offered relief through catharsis so that the act of telling was very clearly linked with unloading and working out trauma in words.

So much Freudian theory has become culturally embedded in the Western world that it is now difficult to think outside psychoanalysis. We are familiar with such terms as 'anal' or 'repressed' while the interpretation of dreams, Freudian slips, the Oedipal complex, and penis envy are concepts which have become common currency to the extent of being employed in a humorous manner or as jokes. Perhaps the most radical concept posited by Freud was his concept of the unconscious. Once it is accepted that each of us carries within us a repository for repressed desires, impulses, thoughts and fears which is termed 'the unconscious', we can no longer posit that the human organism is fully known to itself or central to the production of knowledge. Psychoanalysis thereby offers a reading where the human subject is decentred as the producer of meaning and the seeming stability of 'I' is troubled. The existence of a repressed repository known as the unconscious means that no human subject is known completely to itself, let alone to others. Freud's thinking did for the psychical dimension what Copernicus did for the planetary system; it overturned accepted lore and revolutionized thinking by decentring the human as the pivot of the world. The unconscious is an unknown place where the subject cannot consciously travel; it presents an 'other' which is carried within the domain of the normal human being. While the unconscious must remain radically unknown, it may surface in dreams, free association and slips of the tongue and in analysis itself. It is the concept of the unconscious which offers readers of literary texts the option of analysing the 'unsaid' of the text which becomes implicit in its telling. Psychoanalysis then can offer a useful literary tool with which to prise open the 'other' of the text. Instead of reading the text for its conscious meaning, the reader may choose to examine the repressed meaning of the text. It may be used to analyse an area of 'unsaid' in a text, an area which does not become manifest and remains unconscious although its influence is still felt through its unrepresentability which remains somehow central to the story. A good example of such a reading might be produced in considering the presentation of the moors by Emily Brontë in *Wuthering Heights*. The moors can be considered to represent an area of repressed desire as the reader never accompanies Cathy and Heathcliff when they escape to play in this area; it remains 'unsaid' and therefore 'other' to the dominant storyline yet central to its movement.

Linguistic interest forms the basis of Freud's new science. His early work very much entailed the problems of linguistic access and moved on to become interested primarily in the interpretative process as it is involved in analysing the patient's spoken story. After using the technique of hypnotism with his early patients, Freud moved quickly to his 'pressure technique' to work on the suggestible mind. It was discovered by Freud that the patient could 'resist' analysis and that this 'resistance' could be a useful tool in therapy as it allowed the analyst to view the patient's processes of defence which conversely could reveal what was being hidden. It was also discovered that an interspace between the patient (analysand) and the doctor (analyst) existed as a kind of space into which the patient could 'project' feelings, such as love, anger or hatred. This projection is called 'transference' and exists as an arena into which desire is projected. Transference becomes Freud's key tool in the psychotherapeutic relation as it reveals a manifestation which may be manipulated. Due to its linguistic base, Freud himself applied his technique to literary analysis in order to produce readings of texts, including dramatic works and paintings. He also commented on the act of writing itself in his paper 'Creative writers and day-dreaming' (1908). His famous Oedipal Complex is itself based on a literary model of the triadic family relation presented in the ancient Greek tragedy by Sophocles, *Oedipus Rex*.

Freud describes a family-based drama as a reiterative process which forms the basis of the socially produced subject in Western society; the stages through which the subject is required to pass may be retarded or flawed in some manner and therefore traumatic material may be repressed which can cause psychosomatic disorder or psychosis in later life. The triadic relationship in Sophocles' drama is used to explain relationships which are formative upon the social subject. The incest taboo is seen to be central to the mechanism of social order while the marks of sexual identity such as the possession or lack of a penis are impressed upon the body in society. The paternal principal is seen to be connected with the pressures of moral law and acts as the prohibitive threat which separates the infant from its first love object. This scenario is often replicated in textual presentations or analytical readings. In Toni Morrison's novel *Beloved*, it might be posited that Paul D. signifies the intrusion of the prohibitive third term into the dyadic relationship of Sethe and Beloved. Psychoanalysis places stress on developmental factors which affect the human organism, thereby placing emphasis on the role of childhood and repressed memory in the formation of the adult. From a narrative of personal chronology, it offers a view of the subject as one which carries with it a complex layering of developmental strands or strata. Such a presentation was extremely suggestive to modernist writers, such as James Joyce or Virginia Woolf, who were deeply influenced by the work of Freud.

Continuing Freud's work on ego theory, Melanie Klein (1882–1960) reformulates the Freudian idea of 'penis envy' as a response to the first signifier of visual difference and desire. The infant's envy and desire is instead entwined with its regard for the first object which Klein regards as the breast. In this scenario, therefore, the male organism would have 'breast envy'. Klein's theory is termed 'object relations' theory. The infant is in a state of envy and gratitude in relation to its first object, the breast, and may harbour phantasies of identification which cause it to fragment in terms of ego formation, thus creating a disturbance in object relations. This process is described in 'Envy and Gratitude' (1957). In 'Early Stages of the Oedipus Conflict and of Super-ego Formation' (1928), Klein describes the little boy's fear of the mother as the primary castrator due to her powerful role as first love object. Klein's theories have proved useful to those theorists of 'maternal thinking'. It may also be utilized in analyses of literary representations of maternal power.

How has psychoanalytical theory been utilized in literary analysis? Psychoanalytical theory was used during the 1950s and 1960s to analyse characters as if they were real people instead of textual functions. Such readings became uniform in considering the character of Holden Caulfield in J. D. Salinger's *The Catcher in the Rye* or in readings of Alice in Lewis Carroll's *Alice's Adventures in Wonderland*. Its application has since evolved and became much more sophisticated through its alliance with poststructuralist thought, so much so that it has itself become a major strand of poststructuralist theory. In its meeting with postructuralism, Freudian theory becomes filtered through Saussurian linguistics, and Lacanian and Derridean theory to become a cogent agent of sophisticated linguistic analysis. In his structuralist readings of narrative, for example, Jean Genette presents us with a scenario where the signified can be regarded as the 'unconscious' of the signifier. Central to the poststructuralist acquisition of Freudian theory is the somewhat arcane work of French psychoanalyst Jacques Lacan (1901–81). Lacan reworks Freud in such a way that language becomes central to psychoanalytical theory; he gives a metaphorical consideration of the mechanical processes described by Freud so that the biological is reformulated into the metaphoric to escape the essentialist trap. The penis so central to Freudian theories of sexual difference becomes transmuted in Lacanian theory into the phallus, a totem of power which is not possessed by subjects of either sex or gender. The phallus simply becomes a symbol of absolute power, a cultural signifier. While it may be believed that another subject is in possession of the phallus, for example, the mother may appear to be 'phallic' to the infant, it is impossible for anyone to possess the phallus or to wield absolute power. This does not mean, however, that it is not possible to form the illusion that an other or one holds absolute power.

As with Freudian theory, there are certain elements of Lacanian theory which are utilized by literary analysis due to their redolence and the suggestive readings they enable. Lacan's earliest work was on aspects of paranoia and he moved on to produce his famous paper on the 'mirror stage' which describes what is posited as a radical split which takes place in the subject at the very moment it takes up its position in the social order. He states that this splitting takes places in a *stadium du miroir* so that the split unfolds as a never-ending drama which is replayed within each human organism as it seeks autonomy. As the infant recognizes itself for the first time as an organism discrete from its mother, it breaks out of the mother-child dyad. At the same time as this happens, the child becomes radically split in itself as the reflection it identifies with is not itself but a reflection. There are therefore two places of 'I'; the 'I' which is represented in the mirror and the 'I' which recognizes the 'I' in the mirror. Such splitting at the very basis of subject formation is considered to be a normal phase in human development by Lacan. It is at this moment that the child enters the social order as it is instilled in language, termed the Symbolic by Lacan. From this moment on, the child will not be caught up in the image or the Imaginary realm but will be subject to the Symbolic. Such a scenario may easily be utilized in literary readings and has been applied, for example, to analysis of Tennyson's 'The Lady of Shallot'. Lacan goes on to identify the Symbolic with the paternal function as the third term which intrudes upon the mother–child dyad; he states that the child must learn to accept the prohibitions placed upon it by the paternal threat and puns that in the child must simultaneously accept the *nom-du-pere* and the *non-due-pere*. From this point onwards, the child is separated from its first object and is in a state of lack; it is this lack that constitutes the mechanics of desire; the new human subject must subsequently fill the gap between itself and others with words which act as compensation.

Lacan's most famous dictum is that 'the unconscious is structured like a language' which seems to posit that the unconscious is subject to its syntactical logic, formed from the repression of the symbolic as it is represented in conscious thought. Lacan posited that there are points of meaning in the signifying chain where the signifier and signified become tied together in a type of quilting of different semiotic layers; he uses the term *points de capiton* to denote these areas of catchment. While he accepts that there is slippage (*glissement*) of meaning, meaning usually becomes fixed in relation to a central reference point which forms the pinion; that central reference point is the phallus which has been termed the 'transcendental signifier'. The centrality of the phallus to Lacanian theory remains contentious and is a feature of Lacanian theory to which Derrida gives special attention in order to deconstruct what he sees as binarist logic. Due to his sometimes playful and/or inflammatory statements on femininity, Lacan has also been the subject of much feminist challenge.

French feminist theorists rework Freud and Lacan in order to reformulate gender concepts or accept and negotiate new ones which serve a feminist purpose. There is an acceptance of and negotiation with the main terminology and concepts of psychoanalysis in order to re-work and posit new theories on gendered positions which the human subject is required to take up as it enters the symbolic order and takes its place in the social world. Hélène Cixous propounds the ideal project of *écriture féminine* or feminine writing which works to disrupt received notions of power instilled in language, a challenge which extends to the production of academic writing itself. Her puns and word play work to decentre semantic meaning and disrupt symbolic logos into a proliferation of multiple meaning which challenges the notion of what Derrida terms 'phallogocentricism'. Julia Kristeva reworks the concept of the 'symbolic' and the 'semiotic' to offer a theoretical semiotic shift. She considers that the realm of the 'semiotic' precedes that of the 'symbolic' order and represents a pre-linguistic dimension which exists in the dyadic relation of mother and infant. This is a place of pulsions and drives within a realm which Kristeva, with reference to Plato's cave, terms the 'chora'. The symbolic is understood to overlay the semiotic realm which it seeks to suppress although it is simultaneously dependent upon it. The concept of semiotic can be used convincingly in textual analyses. The concept of the semiotic can easily be applied, for example, to Michèle Roberts' *Daughters of the House* in which we see the character Léonie crossing the channel from Britain to France. Her transition between languages is presented at mid-point between territories where the subterranean flow would seem to present us with a semiotic pre-linguistic state. Kristeva's notion of abjection put forward in *Powers of Horror* has been utilized by many feminist theorists working with concepts drawn from psychoanalysis, most notably Barbara Creed who formulated her concept of the 'monstrous feminine' through reference to Kristeva's development of the concept. The notion of abjection, however, is taken from Mary Douglas' work on anthropology and here some connection can be made with Freud's work on civilization and its discontents, anthropological theory and structuralist practice.

Due to Freud's interest in femininity and his famous essays on sexuality, psychoanalytical theory is also utilized by contemporary theorists to think about gender construction. Judith Butler makes extensive use of psychoanalytical concepts drawn from Freudian theory and combines them with Foucauldian thinking to examine gender as a culturally produced discourse which reproduces itself through dissemination. Such discourse becomes, it is argued, naturalized through performance to the extent that it becomes self-perpetuating and performative. J. L. Austin's notion of the performative in linguistics becomes allied with Riviere's notion of 'masquerade' in relation to gender. Butler also utilizes Freudian theory in her earlier work on psychic subjection to explain the linguistic subjection of the subject. To do this, she draws on the work of Hegel and Althusser to theorize the mechanism of power as it is instilled in the human social organism. Althusser artfully merges Marxist ideas with those of psychoanalysis in order to formulate thinking on human 'subjection'. His concept of 'interpellation' is close to the performative imperative of J. L. Austin as it is formulated by Butler. His system of ISAs (Ideological State Apparatuses) point to a psychical state of oppression whereby a political system is internalized and psychically invested in as it is perpetuated by the state. Within these terms, the capitalist perpetuation of the family-orientated drama is an example of such an ideological apparatus. The 'phallus' and problems of power would, therefore, seem to shift the notion of oppression away from the possession of a penis towards the problem of power itself which seeks to create an other in order to maintain its position in power. It is such a notion that is central to Butler's seminal work in *Gender Trouble* (1990) and *The Psychic Life of Power* (1977).

As a body of thought, psychoanalytical theory can be used to elucidate structure and mechanical processes in texts. It is a theory which may be utilized with any number of approaches to offer a sophisticated analysis of texts and textual production.

# Part IV

# Mapping the Field

# 8 Issues of Gender and Sexuality

## *Susan Watkins*

---

**Chapter Overview**

---

The latter half of the twentieth century saw significant changes in ideas about gender and sexuality. Some of the legal milestones that chart the evolution of attitudes are well known; others less so. The Equal Pay Act of 1970 and the Sex Discrimination Act of 1975 are arguably of less significance for women than the Abortion Act of 1967 and the increasing availability of the contraceptive pill from 1961 onwards. The gradual decriminalization of male homosexuality in this period can be traced back to the Wolfenden Report of 1957, which recommended the legalization of male homosexual sexual behaviour between consenting adults in private. It was not until 1967, however, that the Sexual Offences Act received royal assent and only in 1994 that the age of consent for male homosexual sex was reduced from 21 to 18 and finally, in 2000, to 16. Gay men and women are still not able to marry, although civil partnerships, which came into being in December 2005, now offer legal recognition of same-sex relationships and allow civil partners to share many of the same rights as heterosexual married couples. In 2002 a judgement by the European Court of Human Rights found that the United Kingdom had breached Article 8 and Article 12 of the European Convention on Human Rights (the right to respect for private life and the right to marry) in relation to transsexual people. As a result, The Gender Recognition Act of 2004 enabled transsexual people to change their legal gender, acquire a new birth certificate (if the birth was registered in the United Kingdom) and marry in the reassigned gender.

My phrase 'the evolution of attitudes' encompasses a metaphor not merely of change but also, implicitly, of progress, but is it appropriate to see the post-war period as demonstrating a 'whiggish' version of the history of gender and sexuality; i.e. as embodying a gradual progressive development towards more enlightened and liberal beliefs? The absence of any juridical reference to lesbian sexuality complicates a simple notion of law reform as the embodiment of relaxing social attitudes. Female same-sex sexuality has never been penalized in law, a fact that could suggest both a tolerant, or prejudiced response to lesbianism. What Terry Castle (1993) calls the 'apparitional' (not quite visible) nature of lesbian sexuality may imply that women who desired other women had freedoms that homosexual men did not, or it may suggest that lesbianism was considered so threatening to the social fabric that legislation on the subject was avoided for fear of increasing its visibility. In 1921 the Director of Public Prosecutions advised Parliament not to legislate against lesbianism in order to avoid 'bring[ing] it to the notice of women who have never heard of it, never thought of it, never dreamed of it' (Sinfield 1994: p. 49).

The French philosopher and theorist Michel Foucault was the first to challenge a number of common assumptions about the history of sexuality. According to Foucault's key work *The History of Sexuality* (1979), it is commonly assumed that the Victorian period can be characterized by its repressive, prohibitive attitude to sexuality (what Foucault terms the *repressive hypothesis*); by extension, most histories of sexuality claim that the twentieth-century is marked by an increasingly open and liberal conception of sexuality. Foucault's quarrel is with the idea that the repressive hypothesis can ever be efficacious. In fact, he suggests that while attempting to regulate and prohibit sexuality and confine it to a marital, reproductive context, Victorian pseudo-scientific medical discourse actually becomes productive and generative of 'illicit' sexuality. Writing about sex, ostensibly to control it, actually makes readers more knowing and curious and gives them access to ideas about sex that they might not otherwise have had: 'far from being repressed in [nineteenth-century] society [sexuality] was constantly aroused' (Stoler 1995: p. 3). It is almost certainly the case that the ostensibly enlightened relaxation of repressive legislation and liberalization of the law around sexuality in the post-war period can also be seen as an attempt to control and circumscribe threatening sexual behaviour. For example, male homosexual sexual acts are only permissible in certain strictly defined contexts, between men of certain ages and the 'sanctity of *marriage*' is actually confined to heterosexual couples by the creation of civil partnerships.

## Gender, Sexuality and Post-War Literature

The relationship between changes in attitudes to sexuality and gender and post-war British literary production is complex. One obvious issue to consider is the relaxation in censorship laws in this period, evident in the famous trials that accompany and in some cases generate those changes. In 1960 the trial brought against Penguin Books for publishing D. H. Lawrence's *Lady Chatterley's Lover* was the first prosecution under the Obscene Publications Act of 1959. The Act allowed publication if a text could be proved to be 'for the public good'. It also insisted that the work had to be judged as a whole and allowed expert witnesses to be heard in the novel's defence. The defence therefore focused on arguing that the novel's treatment of sexuality and adultery was morally serious (though explicit) and in fact was part of a deeply considered Lawrentian philosophy that Richard Hoggart (one expert witness for the defence) even described as 'Puritan' (Rolph 1961: p. 102). Penguin was acquitted and queues developed to purchase the book.

The story of the Lady Chatterley trial may suggest that the post-war period inaugurated a gradual liberalization of the censorship of literature. In 'Annus Mirabilis', Philip Larkin famously claimed that the year 1963 marked the beginning of sexual freedom. He mentions the end of the ban on Lawrence's novel and the appearance of the Beatles first album *Please Please Me*. John Sutherland, writing about censorship in the period, claims that: 'The road to freedom from censorship over the period 1960–77 is best conceived as a series of rushing advances, encountered by stubborn rearguard and backlash actions' (Sutherland 1982: p. 4). Yet, as Herbert Marcuse suggests in his essay, 'Repressive Tolerance' (1965), the idea that the loosening of restrictions brings complete freedom to publish is a fiction: the apparently 'free' market brings restrictions of its own. In the increasingly commercial world of publishing and book-selling, narrow definitions of genre and niche markets create their own kinds of invisible censorship. Equally, an author writing with an internalized censor in mind may have to exercise (consciously or unconsciously) a certain kind of 'creative ingenuity' (Morrison and Watkins 2006: p. 21) that can produce interesting work. In the immediate post-war period, 'coded' references to illicit sexuality were common. Of necessity, these avoided the clichéd representations of sexual behaviour and desire that circulate now in much writing about sex. Larkin's poem makes use of hyperbole and irony in its specific dating of sexual liberalization to one particular year: sexual intercourse itself of course does not begin in 1963. At most, the speaker suggests that disapproval of pre-marital sex disappeared at that precise point in history. The suggestion that '[e]veryone' shared in these more liberal attitudes; that 'every life' was transformed and that it was impossible to lose out in the new permissive climate is qualified by the sorrowful phrase 'which was rather late for me' (p. 3), which modulates into 'just too late for me' (p. 18) in the final stanza. Larkin suggests here not only the speaker's woeful awareness of a misfit between the discourses around him and his own experience, but also therefore the limitations of views of cultural history which see change in sweeping and absolute terms and disregard complexity, difference and subjective experience. He also makes clear that such changes can be less about individuals' experience of their lives and more about cultural shifts, which include a move towards the increasing significance of *popular* as well as elite cultural forms, though these may be more or less available to particular individuals.

If the post-war period and its literature did not mark an entirely straight-forward development from repression to tolerance of gender and sexual difference, what kinds of changes were significant in the period? One import-ant transition is the move from the *identity* politics of opposition in literature of the 1960s and 1970s to the more fluid, 'performative', queer conceptions of gendered and sexual *subjectivity* in late twentieth- and twenty-first-century literature and cultural politics. If the Lady Chatterley trial stood for anything it stood for the association of sexuality with authentic identity and the notion that sexual authenticity could challenge political orthodoxy (Dollimore in Sinfield 1983: pp. 52–3). These beliefs were dear to the early women's liberation and gay rights movements and can be seen in the literature of the period 1960–80. This period saw the flowering in the west of what has come to be known as second-wave feminism (to distinguish it from the first-wave feminism of the late-nineteenth and early twentieth centuries which focused on the struggle for the vote, the legal rights of married women to own prop-erty, divorce and retain custody of their children and access to employment and educational opportunities).

Second-wave feminism in the United Kingdom (unlike in the United States) was marked by a radical rather than a liberal, reformist agenda, whether that was framed in relation to Marxism and the 'class struggle' and linked with the British Left, or in connection with a newly politicized understanding of the female body as the site of a contestatory 'politics of the personal'. Marxist feminism was interested in transforming society rather than (as liberal feminism attempted) seeking equality within existing economic and social structures. For Marxist feminists, it is the complex intersections between cap-italism and patriarchy that explain the oppression of women. Issues that had been considered politically insignificant or invisible now became the subject of serious discussion and campaigning, for example, women's domestic labour in the home and the relationship between that work and their role in the public sphere in the wage-labour force. The 'Wages for Housework' campaign is a case in point. Founded in 1972, the Wages for Housework Campaign has consistently argued that housework should be counted as part of a country's Gross National Product (GNP). In doing so, the campaign drew attention to the issues of how we value and reward different kinds of labour and determine the 'cost' of housework, whether we pay someone else to do it or do it ourselves.

*Take Back the Night* (or *Reclaim the Night*) is another key campaign of this period that derives from the radical feminist redefinition of politics to encompass personal, emotional and sexual issues. *Reclaim the Night* marches, which usually cross areas in a particular community that are widely perceived to be unsafe for local women, focus on women's rights to dress as they please, and walk wherever they like at night without fear of sexual violence. The campaign highlights the issues of women's sexual autonomy and control over their bodies and was one of the first high-profile movements to make apparent the gendered nature of space and place. The gay liberation movement in the 1960s and 1970s also made use of ideas about sexuality, space and place, which is apparent in one of its central metaphors: 'coming out of the closet'. The implications of this metaphor, now common parlance, are manifold. 'Coming out' is about authenticity, honesty and confession; it defines identity primarily in terms of sexuality. It also suggests that in being honest about one's sexual identity, one can gain freedom from, even a place from which to challenge, the restrictions of a homophobic, heteronormative society. The women's and gay liberation movements were both keen to adopt a stance that opposed conventional patriarchal and heterosexual norms (such as marriage and the nuclear family) and rejected liberal, assimilationist policies. Instead, they attempted to work with a stable understanding of 'difference' which could be used to establish a consistent definition of alternative gendered or sexual identity capable of challenging the status quo.

Some of the key tropes and modes of the literature written in this era allude to the notion of women's and gay men's oppression by a patriarchal, heterosexist society. Women's writing of this period questions the prominence of domestic labour, the focus on appearance and body image (what has more recently been referred to as the 'beauty myth' [Wolf, 1990]) and childcare in women's lives; it often constructs narratives that move the heroine away from confinement in domestic space towards a role in the public sphere or an epiphanic moment of intense, if transient, spiritual enlightenment. Jane Dowson and Alice Entwistle suggest that women's poetry in the post-war period is marked by 'the tensions between women's enlarging public lives and unchanging private commitments', which appear in their 'ambivalent treatment of domesticity and motherhood' (Dowson and Entwistle 2005: p. 6). One writer whose early fiction makes use of such ideas and yet also challenges them is Doris Lessing. In a number of novels, short stories and other work published in the 1950s, 1960s and early 1970s such as *In Pursuit of the English* (1960), *The Golden Notebook* (1962), the 'Children of Violence' sequence (1952–1969), 'To Room Nineteen' (1963) and *The Summer Before the Dark* (1973) she is concerned with women's position in society, the work that they do (particularly as housewives, carers and mothers), their role within the family and outside it and their attempts to move outside marital and familial structures. *In Pursuit of the English* is a memoir recounting Lessing's arrival in England after the Second World War. It is set in the immediate post-war period, evoking the atmosphere of 'austerity Britain' and the housing crisis in London at the time. However, the narrator's position as a single mother who also has to work for a living means that she is very conscious of the situation of other women renting rooms in the house where she is living. Mrs Skeffington, for example, is a victim of domestic violence who is exhausted by her daughter's night-time crying and is desperate enough to try and abort her unwanted pregnancy. The landlady Flo also has a fraught relationship with her daughter Aurora that verges on neglect. The narrator forms a significant friendship with Rose, who has an unsatisfactory on-off relationship with Flo's brother-in-law Dickie and is uncertain about the impact of agreeing to pre-marital sex on her chances of marriage. This friendship is threatened by the narrator's willingness to befriend Miss Privet, a prostitute. The narrator never really finds the English working class that she is in pursuit of; instead she finds a community of women who are all, in their different ways, trying to make sense of the economics of emotional, sexual and domestic labour. The era Lessing represents here is a transitional one: the war-time nurseries are starting to close and expectations about women's roles are altering. As the narrator tells us:

> Once, she [Flo] asked Welfare if Aurora could go to a council nursery. But the reply was that Flo had a nice home and it was better for small children to be with their mothers. Besides, the council nurseries were closing down. 'Women marry to have children', said the official when Flo said she was trained for restaurant work and wanted to go back to it. (Lessing 1993: p. 125)

The elevation of women's role in the home in the 1950s is clearly alluded to here and the memoir closes with the arrival of television and several tenants leaving, including the narrator.

In her later short story, 'To Room Nineteen', Lessing gives an account of Susan and Matthew Rawlings' failing marriage and Susan's increasingly desperate attempts to escape from family and home. The atmosphere here is different from 'In Pursuit of the English'. Unlike the narrator of 'In Pursuit', Susan Rawlings leads a privileged, middle-class lifestyle with a big house, five children, an attractive (although intermittently adulterous) husband, a cleaner and an au pair. The gender ideology of the era has shifted firmly towards women's association with children and home: 'Children needed their mother to a certain age, that both parents knew and agreed on, and when these four healthy, wisely brought-up children were of the right age, Susan would work again' (Lessing 1994: p. 355). Susan's malaise is difficult for her to define. She feels she ought to be happy with her lot in life and yet the text uses increasingly violent imagery to describe her emotional ties to her family: on one occasion she holidays alone and keeps in regular telephone contact: 'Susan prowled over wild country with the telephone wire holding her to her duty like a leash. The next time she must telephone, or wait to be telephoned, nailed her to her cross' (Lessing 1994: p. 371).

The story generates an intense hope in the reader that Susan will escape from the oppressive structures around her and clearly alludes to the liberation narratives that were dear to the second-wave feminist movement. However, Lessing is sceptical about many of the metaphors and narrative patterns of liberation, empowerment, consciousness raising and escape that were prevalent in this period. Not for Susan a moment of epiphany or spiritual communion with nature. Instead, the relentless pressure leads to her experiencing occasional freakish visions of a malevolent ginger demon – an energetic masculine alter ego that I have elsewhere argued represents the control and self-determination that Susan's life as mother and home worker lacks (Watkins 2001: p. 18). The idea that women need a private female-centred space and place in which they can access their creative powers has been dear to feminists since the publication of Virginia Woolf's essay *A Room of One's Own* (1929). However, in 'To Room Nineteen' Lessing shows that a space outside patriarchal society is next to impossible. Susan begins by turning one of the rooms in her house into 'Mother's Room', with the intention that this will be a sacrosanct space for her, but gradually it is invaded by other family members. Eventually she is so desperate that she hires a room in a dingy hotel (the 'room nineteen' of the title). Although initially she feels that in this room she will be able to recover the 'essential Susan' from 'cold storage' (Lessing 1994: p. 359), her husband becomes suspicious and has her followed. The only way she can explain her need for the room in terms he will understand is to pretend that she is having an affair, but when this leads to questions she cannot answer she commits suicide by gassing herself in the room.

Lessing's use of the room metaphor is by no means unique. Marilyn French's *The Women's Room* was first published in the United States in 1977 and Lynn Reid-Banks' *The L-Shaped Room* appeared in 1960. In different ways women writers of the late 1950s, 1960s and 1970s were using this image in their fiction in order to think through the issues of women's difference and their place in society. As well as alluding to the idea that the room provides a space for creative opposition to patriarchal culture, they considered whether it can also be a prison, where those who challenge social conventions are 'othered', still occupying a place within society but securely subordinated. Lesbian writers of this period were also preoccupied by similar questions about sexuality: to what extent can people attracted to those of the same sex place themselves outside patriarchal, heterosexist culture in order to challenge it?

## Lesbian Feminist Writing

Lesbian feminism of the 1960s, 1970s and early 1980s attacks patriarchal control of women's sexuality and reproduction and argues for the importance of what Adrienne Rich calls the 'lesbian continuum' in women's experience and writing. In her essay, 'Compulsory Heterosexuality and Lesbian Existence' (1980), Rich suggests that heterosexuality is not something people can freely choose; nor is it an innate 'orientation'. Heterosexuality needs to be understood as a powerful institution allied to patriarchy that oppresses women by making it almost impossible to be anything other than heterosexual without severe disapproval. Rich argues that most women's primary orientation is lesbian because of the primacy of the mother-daughter bond; she redefines lesbianism as a continuum of experience which includes much more than sexual behaviour or desire. Rich's understanding of lesbianism as a woman-centred challenge to patriarchal, heterosexist culture was important because it questioned the assumptions of earlier lesbian fiction such as Radclyffe Hall's *The Well of Loneliness* (1928), which presented lesbianism as a tragedy of birth which should be the object of pity and sympathy. Many other novels throughout the twentieth century relied on what Patricia Juliana Smith terms 'lesbian panic': 'the disruptive action or reaction that occurs when a character – or, conceivably, an author – is either unable or unwilling to confront or reveal her own lesbianism or lesbian desire' (Smith 1997: p. 2). Smith discusses how the figure of the lesbian in such texts tends to represent an alluring threat which has to be neutralized by the end of the novel.

Many of these ideas are alluded to but only partly shared by Jeanette Winterson in her influential first novel *Oranges are not the Only Fruit* (1985). The striking thing about the book is the way it refuses to focus on providing an explanation for the central character's sexuality. Jeannette rehearses others' explanations for her relationship with Melanie with puzzlement. Whereas some in the church forgave her 'on the admittedly dubious grounds that they had read Havelock Ellis and knew about Inversion' (Winterson 1991: p. 126) her mother stresses making the right moral choices: 'you made people and yourself what you wanted. Anyone could be saved and anyone could fall to the Devil, it was their choice' (p. 126). Jeannette has never thought about her sexuality as a wicked choice (despite her strict upbringing in a fundamentalist evangelical church) and she has never perceived herself to have an innate sexual 'orientation'. She describes her love for Melanie as 'an accident' (p. 126) and refuses to separate this love from her love for God and the church until she is forced to undergo an exorcism for what her church assumes is demonic possession. A number of women in the novel seem to have conscious or unconscious lesbian tendencies, including Jeannette's fearsomely authoritarian mother: many women characters attempt to support her against the patriarchal, heterosexist power of the church, led by Pastor Spratt; men in the novel (with the exception of the Pastor) are almost invisible. However, although the idea of the lesbian continuum is being suggested here, it is also questioned by the fact that Jeannette's mother frequently betrays her and is herself an agent of the church's power. Some critics have suggested that Jeannette's sexual initiation is described in childlike, innocent terms that focus on emotional response rather than desire. While this may be seen as an attempt to redefine lesbianism in Rich's terms as a continuum of experience rather than solely focused on sexual behaviour, others have complained that this 'vanilla' version of lesbian experience avoids the aspects that are most threatening to heterosexist, patriarchal culture: women desiring and having sex with other women. However, the scene of Jeannette's sexual initiation with Melanie is subtle and far more suggestive than it may first appear to be: 'she stroked my head for a long time, and then we hugged and it felt like drowning. Then I was frightened but couldn't stop. There was something crawling in my belly. I had an octopus inside me' (p. 86). A uterine, fluid female morphology is certainly present in this imagery, which surely requires only minimal decoding or imagination to understand.

## Realism and Experimentalism

The styles and forms of writing of this period are often described as realist or confessional in order to distinguish them from the more experimental writing of later twentieth-century, postmodernist literature. Where post-war poetry is concerned, a similar functional opposition tends to appear between confessionalism and formal experimentalism, so that confessional poetry, as represented in Al Alvarez's anthology, *The New Poetry* (1962) stands for the authentic expression of the poet's intimate and sometimes painful experience (which may often include sexual experience) and formalism is read as the exhibition of a concern with technical virtuosity. Such oppositions never function perfectly, however. In the Movement poets of the 1950s, as represented in the *New Lines* anthology (1956), the use of traditional metrical and rhyme forms does not 'engage notions of finish, of the polished object'; rather, such forms 'define the space in which the self can act with poetic authority' (Crozier in Sinfield 1983: p. 206). The conflation of a concern with both subjectivity *and* form here is striking. Both self-revelation and formal innovation in poetry can be selected as indicators of development or progress from what went before; however, neither necessarily implies an alteration or development in terms of content. Crozier claims, for example, that 'the Movement's ideological characteristics . . . imply a social matrix largely made up of males. Certainly, the Movement provoked a number of squeamish reactions to what was felt as its posture of tough and aggressive philistinism' (p. 208).

Both fictional and poetic modes certainly do evoke authenticity and verisimilitude, but often in ways that are much more experimental and troubled than might at first glance appear to be the case. Lessing's 'In Pursuit of the English' is partly a memoir, partly an autobiographical essay. The narrator is referred to as 'Doris' and many of the events described are based on what happened to Lessing on arriving in England. Jeanette Winterson's *Oranges are not the Only Fruit* is also semi-autobiographical, but when asked whether the novel was autobiographical, Winterson replied:

> Yes and no. All writers draw on their experience but experience isn't what makes a good book. As the stand-up comics say, 'It's the way you tell 'em'. Oranges is written in the first person, it's direct and uninhibited, but it isn't autobiography in the real sense. I have noticed that when women writers put themselves into their fiction, it's called autobiography. When men do it, such as Paul Auster or Milan Kundera it is called meta-fiction.

The semi-autobiographical 'coming out' *bildungsroman* is obviously an important reference point in *Oranges* and yet Winterson is keen for readers to recognize the novel's challenges to linear developmental narratives, or 'straight thinking', which rely on an understanding of sexual identity as coherent and stable and assume a trajectory that gradually allows more open expression of that self. In the introduction to the novel she writes that: 'Oranges is an experimental novel: its interests are anti-linear . . . I really don't see the point of reading in straight lines. We don't think like that and we don't live like that' (xiii).

A story like 'To Room Nineteen' also acknowledges the appeal of realism's claims to represent authentic experience. When reading the story we encounter the third-person narrator as a world-weary character who is tired of the foresight that omniscience provides. The ironies that result are present in the very first lines: 'This is a story, I suppose, about a failure in intelligence. The Rawlings's marriage was grounded in intelligence' (Lessing 1994: p. 352). The parallel syntactic structures here evoke the sense that there is almost no purpose in continuing: it seems obvious that the story will be about the failure of a marriage. The realist mode therefore seems deliberately oppressive, tired, dry and redundant; much like the gender ideologies of the period in question. Lessing has been termed an 'experimental realist' (Gasiorek 1995: p. 93) and an ironic or self-conscious realist (King 1989: pp. 14–25). She is a writer whose use of realism (much like her own and Winterson's use of autobiography) can at best be described as partial and may better be characterized as attempting to heighten our awareness of the *provisional* status of literary forms. In drawing our attention to this she also alerts readers to the fact that both dominant and oppositional gender and sexual ideologies can only ever be provisional.

## Play and Performativity

In contrast to the decades of the 1960s, 1970s and early 1980s, late-twentieth- and early twenty-first-century culture appears to crack apart any consensus about definitions of patriarchy, oppression, sexuality and gender and reconceives sexual politics in terms styled by notions of coalition rather than essence. Narratives about empowering women, which aimed to substitute socially constructed notions of the 'feminine' with 'authentic' feminist consciousness, are replaced with ideas of the gendered self as palimpsest or performance, fragmented and overwritten by multiple, hybrid conceptions of gendered identity as difference. Rather than providing an entire 'technology' of the self (Foucault, 1988) in order to (em)power a 'coming-out' narrative, sexuality is reconceived as performance, invoking pleasurable metaphors of cross-dressing and transvestism rather than a dour 'epistemology of the closet' (Kosofsky Sedgwick 1990). A key thinker here is Judith Butler, whose *Gender Trouble* (1990) was enormously influential. Butler avoids thinking of gender as something you *are* and instead suggests that gender is something you *do*. Moving away from 'being' to 'doing' gender allows her to argue that it is best understood as *performance* rather than essence. Those performances that are socially acceptable and legitimized are those that accord most closely with our society's tendency to think of gender and sexuality in binary terms (for example, straight/gay; male/female); socially accepted gender performances tend also to be perceived as 'natural' and 'authentic'. Lesbian and gay subculture, however, often celebrates explicitly 'fake', theatrical constructions of sexuality such as cross-dressing, drag and the adoption of 'butch' and 'femme' sexual identities. For Butler, these aspects of lesbian and gay identity create trouble both for a patriarchal, heterosexist culture and also for second-wave feminist and lesbian-feminist politics. They do so because they suggest that *all* gender and sexual identities, whether straight, gay, bisexual, feminine or masculine are constructed. In other words, there is no identity position that exists outside culture. This argument is problematic for patriarchy, which tends to make claims about women's natural orientation towards home and family using socio-biological definitions about femininity that are fundamentally essentialist. It is also problematic for second-wave feminism and lesbian feminism, which has often relied on the idea of recovering women's

171

authentic identities (such as a continuum of woman-identified or lesbian experience) from beneath the surface of socially imposed patriarchal, hetero-sexist norms.

Rather than using the idea of moving outside culture to find an uncon-taminated source for an authentic feminist politics, Butler argues that the constructedness of gender and sexual identities also allows creative possi-bilities for challenging the status quo. Gender performances can never be perfect because they have to be repeated in different contexts and alter over time. Butler terms this imperfect repetition the '*contingency* of that [gender] construction' (Butler 1990: p. 38). The contingency of gender performances means that they can alter; that there may be a 'variation on that repetition' (p. 145) that allows for a creative transformation and rewriting of previous conventional gender constructions.

It may be argued that Butler's ideas represent a more sustained intellectual move in the wider culture away from second-wave feminism towards what has been variously referred to as third-wave feminism, or postfeminsm. Gillis, Howie and Munford (2004) explore many different, historically specific manifestations of the term 'third wave', acknowledging that it represents a move away from stable, transhistorical definitions of gender. Second-wave feminism often ignored those differences of race, sexuality, class and age that fracture women's shared experience and complicate both simple accounts of women's oppression and simple political solutions to that oppression. The term postfeminism has been far more problematic, because it can often be used to suggest the redundancy of feminism and backlash against it (Faludi 1991), rather than acknowledging that feminism is evolving and diverse. What is clear is that at the end of the twentieth century lesbian sexuality is far less likely to be understood in relation to feminism and gender and far more likely to become a part of queer theory's broader focus on *sexualities*, includ-ing gay male, bisexual and transgender as well as lesbian.

Literature of this period begins to make more use of fantasy, science fiction, magic realism and gothic. Partly this suggests a postmodernist impulse away from the elitism and difficulty of modernism towards the recognition that all art forms (even 'lowbrow' ones) are of equal value, but it also acknowledges the challenge that 'minor' or 'genre' forms can offer to the implicit values and hierarchies of realism. The recognition that gender performances are often scripted in popular as well as elite culture is key in the work of Angela Carter. Indeed, Judith Butler's ideas about gender as performative have been used so frequently in relation to Carter's novels that Bristow and Broughton write of the rather repetitive critical 'Butlerification' of her work (1997: p. 19). Clearly Carter is interested in metaphors of gender as theatrical, camp, performed, cross-dressed and elaborately constructed. In novels like *The Magic Toyshop* (1967), *The Passion of New Eve* (1977), *Nights at the Circus* (1984) and *Wise*

*Children* (1991), as well as in the short story collection *The Bloody Chamber* (1979), she acknowledges that inauthenticity is pleasurable and that the artifice of attempting to match patriarchal gender norms can be masochistically pleasing. She also makes claims for the disruptive power that can reside within what Luce Irigaray would term *mimesis* of the feminine role.

Irigaray's understanding of mimesis as containing a 'resistant surplus' that avoids the less subversive 'masquerade' of gender norms (1985, 1991) has suggestive parallels with Butler's idea of gender as performative. What is apparent is the growing prevalence in literature and culture of metaphors of the stage, mirrors, puppets and ventriloquism to explain gender as opposed to the 'room' analogy that was significant earlier in the century. In one sense, however, the metaphors of performance are still 'troubled' by the question of agency. How exactly does repetitive gender performance become subversive without recourse to a notion of the 'real' self in the wings? Joanne Trevenna claims that Carter's use of these metaphors actually has less in common with Butler's radical constructionist position and has more affiliations with the views of Simone de Beauvoir, whose notion that 'one is not born but becomes a woman' suggests that 'a pre-gendered subject position exists' (Trevenna 2002: p. 275). However, *The Passion of New Eve*, one of the texts she analyses in order to make this point, is a very slippery example. In this novel the transsexual Eve/Evelyn is trained in the performance of appropriately feminine gender traits after her male to female operation by the community of Beulah women. However, this programming seems to be only partially successful: 'the cock in my head, still, twitched at the sight of myself' (Carter 1982: p. 75). The most effective performer of femininity is actually the transvestite Tristessa. Although the residual maleness lying beneath the superficial accoutrements of femininity may imply, as Trevenna suggests, 'a pre-existing subject position, conditionally linked to original sexual biology' (Trevenna 2002: p. 272), Carter could equally be implying that all performances of femininity rely on an introjected fantasy of masculine desire and agency that may be experienced as primary or authentic but is similarly constructed, or, in Butler's terms contingent. In other words, Carter's vision of femininity as a flagrantly assumed, transvestite or transsexual surface that superficially overlays a masculine subject position holds true for those whose biology is female. Joan Riviere's essay, 'Womanliness as a Masquerade' (1929) is extremely important to Carter and to Judith Butler and Luce Irigaray's understanding of gender as performance or mimesis. In her essay, Riviere discusses the case of a woman who was extremely successful professionally and intellectually and yet after speaking in public felt a compulsive need to seek reassurance from men by excessively 'feminine' flirtatious behaviour. Riviere suggests that:

Womanliness therefore could be assumed and worn as a mask, both to hide the possession of masculinity and to avert the reprisals expected if she was found to possess it – much as a thief will turn out his pockets and ask to be searched to prove that he has not the stolen goods. The reader may now ask how I define womanliness or where I draw the line between genuine womanliness and the 'masquerade'. My suggestion is not, however, that there is any such difference; whether radical or superficial. They are the same thing. (Riviere 1966: p. 213)

One reading of Carter's work, then, is that it seeks to make apparent not merely the theatricality of femininity but also the artifice of masculinity, 'fictionalizing' the primacy of masculinity for both genders.

## Herstories

Carter's *Nights at the Circus* (1984) is another text interested in questions of origin. Set at the turn of the nineteenth to the twentieth century, the novel rewrites the *fin de siecle* concerns with reality and fantasy, objectivity and illusion, progress and degeneration in the story of Fevvers, the winged aerialist whose wings just may be real. This interest in rewriting, particularly in rewriting Victorian literature or revisiting the Victorian period in fiction, is apparent in the work of many British contemporary women writers, including Sarah Waters and A. S. Byatt as well as Carter. In *The Victorian Woman Question in Contemporary Feminist Fiction* (2005), Jeannette King claims that 'by making female experience central to their narratives, such novels gave women back their place in history, not just as victims but as agents' (King 2005: p. 3). What might certainly be termed 'historiographic metafiction' (Hutcheon 1988) is used by these writers as a device to rewrite the experience of women and make present the lesbian experience in fiction and culture of this era. The attractions of rewriting or writing back are manifold. As Steven Connor puts it:

> In engaging with their literary precedents, such novels engage with the history of beliefs and attitudes to which those originals belonged and which they have helped to shape. In reworking their precedents, such novels both acknowledge the continuing force of the novelistic past in the present and investigate the capacity of novels to intervene in that present. (Connor 1996)

Frequently, novelists like Carter question beliefs about his-story as progressive (in relation to issues of gender and sexuality) and in creating a presence for lesbian experience in the Victorian period (in the case of Waters) demand that we rethink assumptions about the 'absent' or 'apparitional' lesbian. In an essay jointly written with Laura Doan, Waters refers to this as 'making up lost time' (Doan and Waters in Alderson and Anderson 2000: p. 12). In her most recent novel, *The Night Watch* (2006), Waters shifts from the Victorian period to the late 1940s and adopts the structural device of moving backwards from the post-war era to events during the Second World War. This allows a far more complex relation to ideas about nostalgia and revisiting the past to function at the level of character and plot. Most (though not all) of the characters in the novel are nostalgic for the war and the greater freedoms it allowed both sexually and in terms of roles for women. Yet this period of comparative licence is heavily ironized by its position in the text, which follows on from the more austere and conservative post-war years that begin the novel. In the '1944' section of the novel, Julia and Helen, in the first stages of undeclared attraction to each other, notice flowers emerging through some split sandbags around a bomb-damaged office building:

> Julia pulled on a broken stalk. 'Nature triumphant over war,' she said, in a wireless voice; for it was the sort of thing people were always writing about to the radio – the new variety of wildflower they had spotted on the bomb-sites, the new species of bird, all of that – it had got terribly boring. (Waters 2006: p. 209)

The final '1941' section of the novel, set during the Blitz, concludes with Kay, an ambulance driver, finding Helen, who will become her lover but will later betray her with Julia, half buried under rubble. The image the reader is left with is of Helen emerging from the earth like a flower:

> The dust fell away. The skin beneath was pink, plump, astonishingly smooth. Key brushed a little longer, then moved her hand to the curve of Helen's jaw and cupped it with her palm – not wanting to leave her, after all; gazing at her in a sort of wonder; unable to believe that something so fresh and so unmarked could have emerged from so much chaos. (p. 470)

The optimistic sense of life amid chaos refers both back (in terms of the reader's reading experience or plot) and forward (in terms of the character's lives and story) to the 'Nature triumphant over war' episode. The temporalities here are dizzying and the implicit comment on ideas of progress is interesting. Rather than merely 'filling in the gaps' of his-story or 'making up for lost time', Waters here suggests something more complex. At both the level of the individual's subjective experience and in terms of wider social and cultural mores, changes in attitudes to gender and sexuality during the twentieth century cannot be understood simply in terms of progress towards more liberal attitudes.

Narratives of change in literary criticism and cultural politics, as well as in history, make use of vocabularies of maturation and progress versus degeneration and decline which often tend to invoke patriarchal and hetero-sexist patterns of critical thought. Readers and critics have on occasion been too quick to associate late twentieth-century stylistic and generic experimentalism with subversion of established ways of thinking about gender and sexuality and have often perceived 'outmoded' early twentieth-century realism as the home of 'old-fashioned' identity politics. In the current climate much recent fiction suggests that we need to re-evaluate the important role that identity politics continues to play for readers and writers in contemporary British literature and culture, especially in the context of debates about 'race', ethnicity, diaspora and national identity and their multiple connections with gender and sexuality.

# Changes in the Canon: After Windrush

## Ruvani Ranasinha

---

**Chapter Overview**

---

In the popular imagination, the arrival of 492 predominantly black Caribbean migrants on the *SS Empire Windrush* at Tilbury docks in 1948 has become both *the* story of post-war immigration, and the point at which Britain became a multi-cultural society. In the wake of Indian independence, the Nationality Act of 1948 gave citizens of the African and Caribbean colonies, and of the former colonies in the Indian subcontinent rights of residence in Britain. Perceived links to the 'mother country', the pinnacle of civilization in the colonial imagination, made Britain with its open door policy, fuelled by its need for labour, the most natural destination for black and South Asian migrants. However, while the focus on 'the Windrush generation' in the media retrieves an important 'hidden' history, it also – albeit unwittingly – fuels the misconception that black and Asian immigration to Britain is largely a post-war phenomenon. This in turn erases the historical, political and literary impact of the embryonic South Asian, South East Asian and Black diasporic communities on British culture prior to the better known post-1945 period. Literary critics and historians have begun to challenge this misperception drawing upon evidence of continuous black presence since the sixteenth century, imbricated with histories of slavery and imperialism, notably the increasing stream of letters, memoirs, autobiographies and fiction by black and Asian authors since the late eighteenth century (Fryer 1984; Sandhu 2003; Visram 1986).

Nevertheless, the *mass* post-war migration as a consequence of Britain's imperial legacy since the end of the Second World War, and later related modes of civil oppression and neo-colonialism, profoundly transformed Britain demographically and imaginatively. It radically changed the critical climate for the appreciation and consumption of minority culture in Britain. Successive waves of Asian, African and Caribbean immigrants and their descendants, emerging from distinct historic and cultural circumstances, initiated the shifting reconstruction of the 'expatriate' or 'migrant' writer into 'minority' writer. Individual expatriate or migrant writers do not constitute a category. Minority literature is, however, a matter of mass: it becomes a *phenomenon* when substantial numbers of writers constitute the literary scene, if their work has an impact, and is regarded as significant. Gaining symbolic legitimacy is entwined with its increasing commercial viability.

This essay explores the ways in which 'new' writers have emerged in the second half of the twentieth century, in the aftermath of Empire and the dismantling of received attitudes towards race, nationality and citizenship. It considers the role some of these writers have played in broader, shifting debates on race and multiculturalism in Britain. In what ways have these texts shaped the British literary scene and critical climate in terms of the development of the critical perspectives that are now seen as legitimate and necessary? To what extent have these texts brought issues of cultural identity, race, ethnicity and hybridity to the fore and uncovered the question of 'Englishness' or 'Britishness' as a central problem underlying British politics?

The emergence of the postcolonial novel as a recognized category in the British literary scene, and in the predominantly metropolitan stronghold of English Language publishing has been well-charted (Huggan 2001; Procter 2003; Israel 2006). And for all its problems, the category 'Black British writing' (and increasingly 'British Asian') has generated much fruitful literary criticism and anthologizing. Discussions of Black British or more accurately perhaps Black Atlantic culture and a 'Black British Canon' continue to provoke important debate (Low & Wynne Davies 2006). But rather than trace the rise of the postcolonial canon, the essay considers how British writers of African, Caribbean and South Asian and South–East Asian origin have shifted expectations of what constitutes *contemporary British fiction*. In what ways have for example, Salman Rushdie, Ben Okri, Chimamanda Ngozi Adichie or Andrea Levy's individual stories with wider resonance sometimes (but not always) overlaid with larger postcolonial histories changed the way we think about contemporary British literature? For black and Asian writing is often discussed, as a genre in itself, so this essay attempts to re-direct perceptions of these black or Asian writers and situate them not as part of an isolated, separate tradition but within the developing context of the local milieux in which they found themselves, such as the more recent inventive qualities of contemporary British fiction. These writers have developed in relation to, and not separate from mainstream British (and American) culture. Not that they were simply assimilated by the mainstream, but many worked and lived in a fundamentally dialogic relation to it.

## 1950s: Caribbean Voices and Metropolitan Modernism

In an extraordinary burst of literary productivity, it was the Caribbean writers George Lamming, Andrew Salkey, Sylvia Wynter and the Indo-Caribbean writers Sam Selvon and V. S. Naipaul who emerged on the literary scene of the post-war era with novels about their Caribbean environments and new London homes. Most of these writers first worked on BBC Colonial Service as broadcast journalists before publishing their first novels, and later contributed to a BBC radio programme 'Caribbean Voices'. Published by Longman and Faber, as well as newly established presses keen to attract new voices in the context of a post-war publishing boom, Caribbean writers were reviewed to critical acclaim by leading periodicals and the mainstream press. Their South Asian contemporaries, Kamala Markandaya and Attia Hosain also published their first novels in 1950s Britain, achieving quieter critical success. In the immediate aftermath of Britain's withdrawal from India in 1947 and Sri Lanka in 1948, there was not a wide constituency or readership for writing on India or empire, which was no longer an immediate concern. In contrast Caribbean writers became important figures in London's literary scene by translating post-war, urban themes of migration, race-relations and the waning of empire into high culture.

The 1950s marked an important shift in Britain's identity. In the context of the new socialism of the post-war Labour government and the Welfare State, the working class was identified as a new and significant area of the literary map. The 1950s and early 1960s saw the rise of white working-class culture as a legitimate subject for middle-class art. This period marked the establishment of a 'black' British population resisted by the 'Keep Britain White' campaigns. Riots in London, Liverpool and Birmingham against the newly arrived 'coloured' immigrants followed. Black migration is constructed as the problem in increasingly racialized debates about immigration and in racialized constructions of 'Britishness' which frame the action of Sam Selvon's novel *The Lonely Londoners* (1956): 'when the English people starting to make rab about how much too West Indians coming into the country . . . big discussion going on in Parliament about the situation' (p. 24). Selvon himself arrived on the same boat as George Lamming in 1950. His novel is pivotal in its representation of a London characterized by racism, segregation and fear. Writers followed in his footsteps notably Colin MacInnes with *City of Spades* (1957) and *Absolute Beginners* (1959).

Selvon's complex engagement with 1950s London dramatizes the colonized subjects' 'voyage in' to the idealized heart of the empire – the site of culture, history and privilege – and articulates the myth of the centre in different ways. The key to *The Lonely Londoners* is the actual moment of arrival; Galahad's anticipation of arrival and his performance of bravado, inclusion and self-sufficiency. Under veteran Moses' guidance, Galahad learns about survival and exile in the racialized spaces of post-war London, where to find work and restaurants that will serve him: 'They don't tell you outright that they don't want coloured fellars, they just say sorry the vacancy get filled'. Yet the pull of the metropolis is not fully countered by the racism endured. Galahad describes Piccadilly as a magnet, as the 'beginning and end of the world . . . to have said Piccadilly is my playground . . . to say these things, to have lived these things, to have lived in the great city of London, centre of the world' (p. 137). The 'boys' are determined to claim their piece of London's greatness despite constantly being told they do not belong. Galahad's sexual adventures transform the city into a place of pleasure. Selvon's use of a modified form of Trinidadian Creole in terms of diction and syntax in both narrative and descriptive passages enacts the recolonization of the city through language, and the re-appropriation of space. The novel represents the concrete ways in which a black population impacts on London:

> before Jamaicans start to invade Britain, it was hell of thing to pick up a piece of saltfish anywhere, or to get a thing like pepper sauce or dashneen or even garlic . . . But now papa! Shop all around start to take in stocks of foodstuffs what West Indians like and today is no trouble at all to get saltfish. (p. 77)

While the question of language asserts a distinct cultural identity, *The Lonely Londoners* simultaneously signals its close dialogue with modernist fiction. It plays with the conventions of modernist urban thematics from its first sentence: 'One grim winter evening, when it had a kind of unrealness about London, with a fog sleeping restlessly over the city and the lights showing in the blur as if is not London at all but some strange place on another planet' echoing of course, Eliot's 'unreal city' and the representation of a modern metropolis (p. 23). The novel recalls modernist story-telling in its use of metropolitan geography, its loose, episodic structure as a collection of stories, mini biographies and sketches of a city of alienating crowds, and in the free associative style in the celebrated lyrical passage describing Hyde Park in the summer that recalls the stream of conscious techniques of James Joyce and Virginia Woolf. *The Lonely Londoners* foregrounds London not as one city, but as a compendium of little cities, another modernist trope:

> It have people in London who don't know what happening in the room next to them, far more the street, or how other people living. London is a place like that. It divide up in little worlds, and you stay in the world you belong to and you don't know anything about what happening in the other ones except what you read in the papers. (p. 74)

The novel ends on a modernist note of irresolution rather than closure: Moses Aloetta stands before the Thames pondering his future, with a sense of foreboding: 'the forlorn shadow of doom fall on all the spades in the country' (p. 141). *The Lonely Londoners* anticipates the conflicts such as the Notting Hill race riots in 1958 that became a central issue of political and social life in Britain.

We can see how in Simon Gikandi's formulation Selvon's text both appropriates and rejects 'the hegemonic European idea of the modern' by thematizing both the colonial's admiration for celebrated metropolitan places while staking a postcolonial claim of possession (Gikandi 1992: x). Similarly, the alienation of city and idea of loneliness in urban environment, the 'feeling of loneliness and fright [that] come on [Galahad] all of a sudden' (p. 41) takes on different meaning to the alienation of metropolitan modernists. Echoing Frantz Fanon, Galahad's estrangement from the self stems from his visible signifier of difference:

> 'And Galahad watch the colour of his hand, and talk to it, saying, "Colour, is you that causing all this, you know. Look at you so black and innocent . . . So Galahad talking to the colour Black, as if is a person'. (p. 88)

Indo-Caribbean writer V. S. Naipaul's self-consciously experimental fiction intersects even more closely with the typologies of modernist fiction. Naipaul's experimentation with language stemmed from the need to discover a literary form for the psychic and symbolic sense of homelessness emblematized in his study of colonial displacement in *A House for Mr Biswas* (1961), and in the dislocated, transnational homeless protagonist of his novel *The Mimic Men* (1967): the 'spectral, disintegrating, pointless, fluid' figure of Ralph Singh exiled in London (p. 61). Both *The Mimic Men* (1967) and the Booker-winning *In a Free State* (1971) dwelt on 'mimic men of the New World' absurdly imitating their former colonial masters, and on the anxiety of displaced individuals (p. 175). Naipaul remains a remarkable forerunner of displacement, alienation and migrancy as key late twentieth-century predicaments. His studies of both

181

local and global homelessness and insecurity are increasingly accepted as perceptive examinations of the preoccupations of our time. *The Mimic Men* mournfully chronicles the profound transformation Britain, particularly London, was undergoing. This is juxtaposed with the author-narrator's own poignant desire to 'find the centre', the London of his literary dreams:

> Here was the city, the world. I waited for the flowering to come to me. Excitement! Its heart must have lain somewhere. But the god of the city was elusive. The tram was filled with individuals, each man returning to his own cell. (p. 23)

Ralph describes the imaginary island Isabella as a place of disorder as though he was escaping disorder by coming to Britain: 'To be born on an Island like Isabella, an obscure new world plantation, second-hand and barbarous was to be born to disorder' (p. 141). But on arrival in London he finds England to be the 'greater disorder, the final emptiness' (p. 11). The novel exposes the colonial fantasy surrounding the centre and mother country.

## 1960s: Commonwealth Literature

Although Naipaul seeks to separate himself, he, as one of the group of writers of the receding British Empire published in London in the 1950s and 1960s, was part of the emergence of what became Commonwealth Literature. This group included Sam Selvon, George Lamming and Edgar Mittelholzer, but also Nigerian Chinua Achebe (*Things Fall Apart* (1958) published on the eve of Nigeria's independence), and Kenyan Ngugi (*Weep Not, Child* (1964) and *Grain of Wheat* (1967)), who pioneered the African novel in English, as well as Indian writers R. K. Narayan and Raja Rao. Many of these authors were engaged in building a national literature in the context of decolonization, and in countering Europe's fictions by telling their own stories: the 'Empire writes back' in Salman Rushdie's later formulation. Dominica-born Jean Rhys' *Wide Sargasso Sea* (1966) deconstructs and rewrites *Jane Eyre* using the voice of the white Creole heiress Bertha/Antoinette marginalized in Brontë's text. In this regard, Naipaul became the anomaly as the apocalyptic, spokesperson for revisionist accounts of imperial history. In his *A Bend in the River* (1979) (and as well as in his non-fiction *A Congo Diary* 1980) Conrad's Mr Kurtz from *A Heart of Darkness* is reincarnated as a despotic Mobutu figure, the 'Big Man'. Yet, in their different ways all these pioneers helped re-shape literature in the English-speaking world.

The 1960s saw the development of an interest in liberal universities in these writers, coinciding with the questioning of the cultural assumptions of the imperial era. This interest was characterized by the promotion of

'Commonwealth Literature' in higher education, particularly at the Universities of Kent and Leeds, where it was taught as a subject from the early 1960s. The emergence of a critical apparatus to examine these texts in relation to each other, rather than against English Literature marks a concretized shift from expectations of assimilation to European literary conventions to an acknowledgment of a diversity of cultural and literary practices. At the same time, such a paradigm reinvigorated critical assumptions about an 'Indian' or 'African' worldview versus an English one and unwittingly facilitated a false separation between postcolonial and British writings, particularly in relation to diasporic writers who could be productively examined in relation to British cultural contexts.

## 1970s and 1980s: 'Raj Fictions' and the Radicalization of Minorities

Paradoxically, despite the dismantling of imperial ideologies in some Commonwealth writing, the 1970s saw a renewed interest in empire literature, and nostalgia for the British Raj. In the first decade of its inception, three Eurocentric novels on the Raj won the Booker Prize: J. G. Farrell's *The Siege of Krishnapur* (1973), Ruth Prawer Jhabvala's *Heat and Dust* (1975) and Paul Scott's *Staying On* (1977). This literary revival prefigured the cult of Merchant Ivory films and documentaries on India in the 1980s.

Salman Rushdie argued that this spate of films on India (*Gandhi* (1982), *A Passage to India* (1984) and the re-popularizing of the 1970s Raj novels with TV screenings) were the 'artistic counterpart of the rise of conservative ideologies' (p. 92). In an important essay in 1984 that marked his emergence as an influential political and cultural commentator, Rushdie cites Thatcher's speech justifying white British fears of being 'swamped' by 'people of other cultures' made on television in 1978, as a prime example of the relation of the rise of the new conservatism to issues of race and immigration (p. 171). This kind of xenophobia was translated in political terms into the flurry of new anti-immigration legislation passed in the 1980s. (The 1981 British Nationality Act removed the automatic right of all children born in the United Kingdom to be citizens. Subsequently, in 1987, The Carriers' Liability Act cut the number seeking asylum by half. In the same year, visa requirements were introduced for visitors from five Asian and African countries. Most controversial was the new bill introduced to restrict family reunion.) Rushdie noted that the 'continuing decline, the growing poverty and the meanness of spirit of much of Thatcherite Britain encourages many Britons to turn their eyes nostalgically to the lost hour of their precedence', and that this has led to 'refurbishment of the Empire's tarnished image' (Rushdie 1991: pp. 91–2).

In the context of Raj nostalgia, Rushdie sought to break with a series of traditional, monolithic tropes about the Indian subcontinent, and present a newer and fresher picture in his novel *Midnight's Children* (1981). Analogously Kureishi suggests his rough, wild films on race, sex and class in contemporary London, *My Beautiful Laundrette* (1986) and *Sammy and Rosie Get Laid* (1988), were consciously formulated against both Raj-revival, 'lavish films in exotic settings' and genteel Merchant Ivory representations of Thatcherite heritage culture evoking an image of Englishness that encapsulated the identity only of its elite, ruling class (Kureishi 1996: p. 5). For Kureishi, the latter's recreations of England's past embody '. . . an effete quality that has nothing to with the England I know, I mean England is horrible and full of drugs' and forms part of his project of revising and disrupting 'Englishness' and 'Britishness' (Singer 1991: p. 109). Although Kureishi brings to the fore questions of race and cultural displacement, mining territories unavailable to his white British contemporaries, he shares other preoccupations with urban decay, extremes of wealth and Thatcherite individualism with contemporary writers such as (Martin Amis' *Money*). Kureishi (whose own screenplay *My Beautiful Laundrette* (1986) made the surprising move from minority art-house to mainstream) explains his resistance to the limitations of 'minority' art:

> What we need is imaginative writing that gives us a sense of the shifts and difficulties within a whole society. If contemporary writing which emerges from oppressed groups ignores the central concerns and major conflicts of the larger society, it will automatically designate itself as minor, as a sub-genre. And it must not allow itself to be rendered invisible and marginalized in this way (Kureishi 1985: pp. 25–6).

At the same time, as Kureishi was quick to observe, 'one plus of the repressive eighties has been a cultural interest in marginalized and excluded groups', (*Sammy and Rosie*, p. 63). The rise of the new conservatism, alongside the radicalization of blacks and Asians in London and other inner cities is captured in Tariq Mehmood's novel *Hand on the Sun* (1983) and revisited in Syed Manzurul Islam's comic-fantastical short stories in *The Mapmakers of Spitalfields* (1997).

Jamaican Linton Kwesi Johnson (*Mi Revalueshanary Fren* 2002) and Benjamin Zephaniah's poetry revitalized the British poetry scene, fusing their commitment to global black politics with local urban protest against British SUS laws, discrimination and high unemployment in a highly charged, radical new form of performance or Dub Poetry, drawing on Jamaican speech rhythms and dialects. They influenced a range of performance poets and a new generation of rappers, and further popularized poetry with their poems for children.

The relations between individual, artistic and collective identity in the context of racism, Third Worldism, and the struggle for Black and Asian visibility and recognition in 1970s and 1980s Britain, were also explored in Rasheed Araeen's performance art. Black and Asian feminists, Amrit Wilson and Hazel Carby brought feminist perspectives to the anti-racist struggles. While Beryl Gilroy from Guyana (*Black Teacher* 1976) and Nigerian-born Buchi Emecheta's (*Second-Class Citizen* 1976) semi-autobiographical novels explore sexual politics and racial prejudice drawing on their own earlier experiences of isolation and 'fight for dignity and survival' in Britain.) The radicalization of black and Asians in the inner cities and the subsequent Scarman Enquiry and Report was accompanied by a shift from commercial to state funding, which promoted their work on their own terms as could never have happened before, and increased minority artists' access, although unevenly, to a national literary and cultural apparatus. The creation of Channel 4 (which produced Kureishi's and later Meera Syal's first films) was partly in response to the Scarman report. Certain institutions such as GLC and BFI had already begun to respond to ethnic and sexual minorities and their demand for representation, and this support resulted in a flowering of writing by ethnic minority authors in the 1980s with the creation of the several black and Asian theatre and films collectives, and the Asian Women Writers' Workshop and later Women Against Fundamentalism (1990). The Asian Women Writer's Workshop (AWWW) (1984–97), founded by writer-activist Ravinder Randhawa, provided a platform for several Asian women writers Leena Dhingra, Rukhasana Ahmad and Meera Syal, went on to become established writers. Black and Asian women's writing in Britain came to the fore in the mid-1980s: a body of writing provoked by the politics of Thatcherism and the need to articulate not only race but gender politics, and supported by the newly established feminist publishing houses Virago and The Women's Press who published several black and Asian women writers, such as Grace Nichols' *The Fat Black Woman's Poems* (1984), Leena Dhingra's *Amritvela* (1986), Ravinder Randhawa's *A Wicked Old Woman* (1987), Suniti Namjoshi's *The Blue Donkey Fables* (1988), alongside important creative anthologies such as *Rights of Way* and *Watchers and Seekers* (1987). Some of these diverse writers formed their own publishing co-operatives and brought gendered questions of cultural identity to the fore, developing feminist themes, and challenging Eurocentric models of feminism by reformulating gendered ethnicities in their writings. As Merle Collins' poem 'Same but Different' illustrates:

> My friend and I
> Travelled home together by night bus
> My friend is white
> As we parted at the station-stop
> she said
> that her fears
> were of rapists and robbers
> for me

that too
But as I walked the distance home
on pounding tiptoe
Each sudden shadow
Was the threat of the National Front. (Collins 1987: p. 32)

In the early 1980s, the phenomenal success and award of the Booker Prize (1981) to Rushdie's *Midnight's Children* had a huge impact on the literary spheres he straddles: postcolonial/Indian writing in English *and* contemporary British fiction. Likewise Kureishi's hugely successful screenplay *My Beautiful Laundrette* (1986) made the unexpected move into mainstream culture and commercial audiences. Kureishi articulated and popularized British Asian experiences that had previously received marginal cultural representation and asserted their place in the nation. These were just some of texts that propelled issues of race, colonial histories and the historicity of black British experiences (previously thought of as marginal) into the mainstream. This continued to be an important trend in the 1990s and beyond, exemplified by David Dabydeen's *The Intended* (1991) and *Disappearance* (1993), Caryl Philips' *Cambridge* (1991), Vikram Seth's *A Suitable Boy* (1993), Zadie Smith's *White Teeth* (2000), Hari Kunzru's *The Impressionist* (2002), Monica Ali's *Brick Lane* (2003) and Andrea Levy's *Small Island* (2004). With the spate of critical writings that followed in their wake – partly as a result of the growth and increasing influence of postcolonial theory from the 1980s and 1990s, but also because Rushdie's work influenced Homi K. Bhabha's theorizing of migration and hybridity, while Caryl Philips' novels produced a poetics of migration akin to Paul Gilroy's conceptualizing of the Black Atlantic – these texts and their successors gained wider currency. The last two decades have seen not only the proliferation of postcolonial literatures in English as such, but also the rapid growth within universities of postcolonial literary studies as both a scholarly, critical and a pedagogical field.

Rushdie's magic realist, digressive, anarchic, inventive novel revived the British literary novel, *alongside* the formally experimental works of his contemporaries Ian McEwan (1948–), Martin Amis (1949–) and Julian Barnes (1946–). Angela Carter (*Nights at the Circus* 1984), Martin Amis (alongside African-American writer Toni Morrison) and Rushdie were all influenced by Latin American magical realism, primarily in the translations of Gabriel García Márquez's *One Hundred Years of Solitude* that began to filter into Britain's Anglocentric culture. Angela Carter's mining of traditional fairy tales to create new hybrid tales in highly charged prose from the late 1960s influenced Rushdie's own re-shaping of the literary landscape in his *Midnight's Children* and *Shame*, and reverberates in the later lyrical work of Bernadine Evaristo. These British postmodernists challenged the realist novel of the 1950s, 1960s and early 1970s, and eclipsed parochial novels about infidelity in Hampstead, in the context of a new market for the literary novel, and the hype generated by the Booker Prize televised from 1980. The mixture of fictional and historical narratives in the work of Rushdie, Barnes (*Flaubert's Parrot* (1984) and *A History of the World in 10½ Chapters* (1989), and Graham Swift (*Waterland* (1983)) reveal a reciprocal interest in the textuality, margins and footnotes of history and in self-reflexive fiction as critique and postmodern historicism.

## Postcolonialism/Postmodernism

The key themes of migrancy namely, heterogeneity, fragmented identity and hybridity that writers like Rushdie brought to the fore were equally important to literary postmodernism. As Rushdie observed, diasporic writers were in a sense postmodern *avant la lettre*: 'those of us who have been forced by cultural displacement to accept the provisional nature of all truths, all certainties, have perhaps had postmodernism forced upon us'. Rushdie locates this 'rootlessness' as emblematic of the late twentieth century, not just of individuals like himself: 'As I look around, I see many people linking two places in their minds. Neither is home, yet both become home'. However, it was Rushdie, alongside Timothy Mo (1950–) (*The Monkey King* (1978) and *Sour Sweet* (1982)), Kazuo Ishiguro (1954–) (*A Pale View of the Hills* 1982), Caryl Phillips and Hanif Kureishi who emerged in the 1980s and 1990s as the most compelling, important 'new' British novelists, internationalizing the British novel drawing in part on their respective non-metropolitan backgrounds. This is a trajectory reflected in the less-celebrated, accomplished novels by Sri Lankan writer Romesh Gunesekera and Sunetra Gupta among others.

In a parallel move, diasporic poets including David Dabydeen, Moniza Alvi, Denise Riley, Jackie Kay, Linton Kwesi Johnson, Fred D'Aguiar and Merle Collins invigorated British poetry, interrogating received notions of 'Britishness' and defiantly contest exclusionary attitudes, alongside their Scottish and Irish contemporaries Carol Ann Duffy, and older writers Seamus Heaney, Tom Paulin and Paul Muldoon, whose poems explore plural cultural identities outside the paradigm of migrancy.

Moniza Alvi's first collection of poems *The Country at My Shoulder* (Oxford University Press 1993) came to the fore as part of the influential New Generation promotion in 1994. Her poems in *The Country at My Shoulder* straddle the Pakistani and English landscapes of her childhood, while examining her own mixed-raced inheritance and broader issues of cultural hybridity. Her poems 'The Double City', 'The Asian Fashion Show' and 'Under the Brick' explore the duality of migrants' perspectives and the nature of diasporic lives in the city:

I live in one city,
but then it becomes another.
The point where they mesh –
I call it mine. 'A Double City' from *A Bowl of Warm Air*. (OUP 1996: p. 4)

Merle Collins' poem 'No Dialects Please' contests the exploitation of 'African Slaves Please!' and concomitant rejection 'No African Languages Please!' Her poem 'When Britain had its GREAT' (1992) underscores the building of Britain at the expense and suffering of the enslaved:

Some people yearn for simple things
Like
Putting the GREAT back into Britain
They cannot hear the strangled hunted voices
Of infant sisters
And brothers
Who died because enslaved mothers loved too much
To watch them grow to mate, unloved, unloving
To build GREAT Britain's greatness.

. . . And you
would you, then,
be part of the GREAT British nation, too,
when Britain regains its GREAT. (Collins 2000: pp. 206–7)

The afterlife of histories of slavery is similarly explored in Benjamin Zephaniah's poem 'A Modern Slave Song' (1992).

## Cultural Hybridity and Transnational, Globalized Fictions

The spate of literary texts and films that emerged from the early 1980s onwards (a crucial moment in defining a new identity politics in Britain) seemed to define contemporary British hybridized culture, stemming from a shared concern with reconfiguring dominant, exclusive monocultural constructions of Britain and Britishness. Rushdie's novel *The Satanic Verses* contests the amnesiac, exclusive constructions of British heritage and identity drawing attention to the marginalization of black contributions to history: 'See, here is Mary Seacole, who did as much in the Crimea as another magic-lamping lady, but, being dark, could scarce be seen for the flame of Florence's candle' (Rushdie 1988: p. 292).

Rather than simply signal the presence of minority 'ethnic' communities, or merely assert their right to equal citizenship, films *My Beautiful Laundrette*

(1985), *Sammy and Rosie Get Laid* (1988), *Handsworth Songs* (1986), and more recent novels, Bernadine Evaristo's *Lara* (1997) and Charlotte William's *Sugar and Slate* (2003) emphasize how these new elements are transforming what it means to be British. Meera Syal and Gurinder Chadha's screenplay *Bhaji on the Beach* (1993) explores the discoveries that Asian women from three different generations experience during a day trip, organized by the earnest feminist Simi of the Saheli Women's Centre, to the quintessentially English seaside town of Blackpool, which reminds one character of Bombay. Like so many of these texts, *Bhaji's* multigenerational focus at a thematic and structural level achieves a complex, shifting sense of the changing historical and cultural conditions of migrant experience, and of the different strands of histories and contemporary *globalized* consciousness that make up cultural identity in contemporary Britain. The texts are not only thematically but also formally hybrid: *Bhaji on the Beach* is influenced by the social-realist films of Ken Loach and Tony Richardson, and reminiscent of Bollywood movies.

The foregrounding of hybridity is tied up with the deconstruction of dominant configurations of the nation, and can be seen in terms of Stuart Hall, Homi K. Bhabha and Rushdie's theorizing of post-colonial migration to the metropolis as the subversion of the centre at its very heart both culturally and demographically. Rushdie observes:

> . . . hybridity, impurity, intermingling, the transformation that comes of new and unexpected combinations of human beings, cultures, ideas, politics, movies and songs. . . . Mélange . . . is *how newness enters the world.* It is the great possibility that mass migration gives to the world. (Rushdie 1991: p. 394)

For Saladin Chamcha one of the protagonists of *The Satanic Verses* the question of dealing with one's origins as a migrant involves an acceptance of hybridity and a rejection of models of assimilation.

Rushdie, who straddles contemporary British fiction and Indian writing in English, maps cultural hybridity in multicultural *and* postcolonial societies. However, the emphasis of many 'second generation' writers' work including, Joan Riley, Caryl Phillips, Mike Phillips, Merle Collins, Meera Syal, Diran Adebayo and Zadie Smith is predominantly on the contemporary results of immigration reconfiguring British culture and on mapping late twentieth century multi-cultural Britain. These writers' work embodies, complicates and resists Bhabha's and Rushdie's emphasis on the liberatory potential of cultural hybridity.

Kureishi avers that notions of Asian and British cannot be defined separately. Yet his protagonists experience both the potentials and the pitfalls of mixing and metissage. His novel *The Buddha of Suburbia* (1990) parodies the idea of homogenous, distinct racially defined communities, satirizing the assumptions made about mixed-race Karim, and the reductive attempts to categorize him according to ethnic boundaries. The novel turns on the ironies that arise from the gap between how Karim sees himself and how he is perceived.

If Rushdie's incendiary portrait of institutional racism and cultural condescension in Thatcher's Britain in *The Satanic Verses* (1989), simultaneously extols a hybridized post-colonial London, then hybridity and urban thematics are similarly interwoven in Hanif Kureishi's cartography of London in works such as *My Beautiful Laundrette* and *The Buddha of Suburbia* with its sustained exposure of London's underbelly, dereliction and violence, as well as its celebration of the capital's freedoms, potential for self-reinvention, energizing creativity and multi-cultural possibilities. These are tropes and themes revisited and reworked by younger writers Zadie Smith, Monica Ali and Gautam Malkani in their different versions of hybrid London in the twenty-first century. While some of these recent writers focus on Britain, their fictions also depict how constructions of identity and nation are refigured within a transnational context. Monica Ali's slice of London East End is counterpointed with Nazneen's sister Hasina's struggle to survive in Dhaka. Kiran Desai's Booker prize-winning novel *The Inheritance of Loss* (2006) with its myriad perspectives and split settings between Kalimpong, New York and imperial Britain enacts its interest in globalization and the integration of First and Third worlds. Roma Tearne's family saga *Bone China* (2008), tracing Sri Lanka's 25 year civil war, spans Britain and Sri Lanka while Kamila Shamsie's *Salt and Saffron* (2000) and *Kartography* (2002) examine Pakistani cultural identity in Karachi and London, and the tensions between those who stay and leave. The popularity and international visibility of these acclaimed prize-winning writers suggest how far expectations of what constitutes contemporary fiction have shifted.

As in James Joyce, G. V. Desani, Sam Selvon and Salman Rushdie before them, the co-existence of Standard English and non-standard varieties of spoken Englishes in Scottish writers James Kelman's *The Burn* (1991) and Irvine Welsh, Irish writer Roddy Doyle's *Paddy Clarke Ha Ha Ha* (1993) and Zadie Smith's *White Teeth* (2000), the Punjabi-inflected English of Daljit Nagra's recent collection of poems *Look We Have Coming to Dover* (2007) marks a 'postcolonial' syncretism and a linguistic politics that defies earlier demands that writing must be in 'unadulterated' Standard English. These younger writers have displaced and reformed Standard English in a regional 'postcolonial' mode. The articulation of national identity in the British novel can be read as part of the demand for a negotiation of British identity in the context of the process of devolution in 'Disunited Britain'.

## Writing After the Fatwa

For Rushdie *'The Satanic Verses* . . . rejoices in mongrelisation, and fears the absolutism of the Pure' (Rushdie 1991: p. 394). Yet his phrase the 'absolutism of the Pure' forges a link between his contestation of notions of purity (of origins) and his critique of the absolutism of religious faith. For Rushdie, if hybrid identities contest or destabilize claims to mono-cultural identities, this is a parallel process to undermining the monologism of faith central to certain versions of Islam that do not allow hybridity. The most vociferous protest to his novel *The Satanic Verses* – interpreted as blasphemy – was voiced by those British Muslims anxious to separate themselves from the intellectual hitherto constructed as their representative and marked the beginning of the Rushdie Affair.

The mass protests and public book-burnings by mostly non-readers in Bradford, Islamabad and India were partly inspired, and were in turn backed up by the ageing Ayatollah Khomeini's politically motivated, infamous *fatwa* which pronounced against Rushdie and all those involved with the publication of *The Satanic Verses* on 14 February 1989. The *fatwa* provoked a widespread discussion of issues of freedom and responsibility in writing, both in the West and among Muslim intellectuals. The British Muslim protests provoked debates on multiculturalism, definitions of Britishness and highlighted the gap between citizenship and integration. The post-*fatwa* homogenizing of Muslims equated Islam with intolerance and overlooked the differentiated nature of Muslim responses.

The liberal press and many writers, including those such as Farrukh Dhondy, Hanif Kureishi and Tariq Ali who interrogated and explored the *fatwa* and its impact in their own writing, backed Rushdie. In his novel *The Black Album* (1995) and screenplay *My Son the Fanatic* (1997) Kureishi examines the rise of radical Islam among young British Muslims (mostly men) who seek to reassert the religious traditions and prohibitions their quasi-liberal parents have abandoned. The furore shifted the literary and cultural landscape irreparably. One legacy of the Rushdie Affair is the recently passed law against incitement to religious hatred perceived by many writers as a curb on artistic expression. It also contributed to fashioning a political identity of 'British Muslim', distinct from 'British Asian' and the political signifier of 'Black' invoked in the 1970s and early 1980s.

## After 9/11 and 7/7: Writing in an Age of Anxiety

Concerns over the status and identity of Muslims in the west heightened during the Rushdie Affair, became even more so after the terrorist attacks in September 2001 and July 2005, and the global 'War on Terror' that inflame and conflate questions of Islam, immigration and security. In the context of the continued projection of a 'clash of civilizations' between a 'secular' west and 'Islamic fundamentalism' with conceptions of diasporic British Muslim identity polarized between non-believers and extremists and contained by a narrow discursive focus, literary texts have an important role to play in allowing for a more complex picture of the cultures of the Islamic diaspora in postcolonial Britain to emerge. Both Monica Ali's *Brick Lane* (2003) and Nadeem Aslam's *A Map for Lost Lovers* (2004) recreate self-enclosed, segregated, alienated British Muslims characters. Aslam's novel politicizes the condition of working-class British Muslims without directly invoking the political backdrop. Their sympathetic rich, textured portraits are particularly important in the context of Martin Amis and other writers' hysterical pronouncements on Islam and diasporic Muslims, as well as Rushdie's own shift towards reinscribing monolithic versions of Islam which serve to polarize the debate: 'When murder is ordered in the name of god you begin to think less well of the name of god' (Rushdie 2002: p. 235).

There has been a sudden governmental reverse-gear about multiculturalism, alongside some confusion about what multiculturalism might mean, looking at the confused accounts given in the media (including some of the self-satisfied contrasts with France), which often contradict the panic about 'British' bombers. If the goal of integration seemed problematic before 7/7, this is no longer the case. And it is integration, or rather its failure, that forms the subject of Gautam Malkani's debut novel *Londonstani* (2006). Two decades on from the white, masculinist backdrop of South London recreated in Hanif Kureishi's *My Beautiful Laundrette* (1986), *Londonstani* explores 'rudeboy' ethnic subculture in its tale of four swaggering teenagers in an established Asian community in Hounslow. The intervening decades have seen the reconfiguration of the race–relations landscape around issues of religion, and the reification of cultural 'difference': so the novel has different concerns of modern tribalism and inter-ethnic religious tensions. *Londonstani* exposes the way the idea entrenched in rudeboy culture – the equation of education with abandoning roots and selling out to white society (like the 'gorafied desis' who read the news on TV') – warps these young men's relationship with the world. Their failure to integrate (which is distinguished from assimilating into white Britain) but to engage with 'mainstream, multicultural society' disempowers them. As their former teacher tells them, trying to jolt the teenagers out of their apathy and disconnection with society 'you'll never change anything if you don't care. You'll get crappy jobs and end up working at the airport like everyone else' (Malkani 2006: p. 130).

Anti-Muslim prejudice is, of course, only one strand in the discourses of exclusion evident in the increasing demonization of the 'floods' of 'asylum seekers' and 'economic migrants' including white migrants since the 1990s.

Marina Lewycka's novel *Two Caravans* (2007), George Szirtes' poems and films such as Stephen Frears' *Dirty Pretty Things* contribute to and reshape our understanding of Britain as a multicultural nation in the twenty-first century, charting Britain's uneasy relationship with its existing and new migrant communities. Other writers such as Mohsin Hamid (*The Reluctant Funda-mentalist* (shortlisted for the Man Booker Prize in 2007) are feeling their way out of the 'postcolonial' and into the rather different dynamics of the 'War on Terror' and the second Intifada. In the context of ongoing fraught polemics over blasphemy, art and the sacred which traverse the debates on radicaliza-tion, the death of multiculturalism and anxieties about Muslims, the novel's fictionalized hero's monologue delineating his coming of age and political consciousness under the impact of 9/11 is one of a number of literary and non-literary auto-biographical, semi-biographical and fictionalized voices and narratives on the subject from diverse perspectives. The post-9/11 sens-ibility is still nascent, rather than fully developed and although race and its ramifications continue to be the central issue of our times, religious identity has come to the fore.

# 10 Mapping the Current Critical Landscape: Theory – The Final Frontier

*Sean Matthews*

---

**Chapter Overview**

---

The thesis of this paper is that there are limits, exceeding which in one direction literary criticism ceases to be literary, and exceeding which in another it ceases to be criticism.

T. S. Eliot, 'The Frontiers of Criticism' in *On Poetry and Poets* (London: Faber, 1957)

In his 1956 lecture, 'The Frontiers of Criticism', T. S. Eliot surveyed the critical and theoretical currents of the previous three decades and concluded that it had been 'a brilliant period' (Eliot 1956: p. 118). Although self-deprecating about his own contribution, he acknowledged that he had played a role in the radical changes which had taken place in the field – both in the modes and assumptions of literary criticism, and in its professional and institutional position. However, he argued that his own critical work, which he termed 'workshop criticism', was distinct from the main influences on contemporary thinking about literature because it had been directed towards clarifying and explaining his creative practice as a poet.

The primary determinants of the large changes in critical habits and priorities, he suggested, had been 'the [increasing] relevance of the social sciences to criticism, and [. . .] the teaching of literature (including contemporary literature) in the colleges and universities' (Eliot 1956: p. 114). About the latter development he was equivocal, noting simply that 'it means that the critic today may have a somewhat different contact with the world, and be writing for a somewhat different audience from that of his predecessors' (Eliot 1956: p. 105). It was the impact on literary study of the techniques and methodologies of social scientists which more particularly concerned him. He argued that, from the 1920s, an age of 'impressionistic' criticism had given way to a period in which critical modes had begun to focus more closely on the examination and interpretation of texts, on the explanation of their meanings and forms. He further identified two opposing currents in such work. The first, already in Eliot's day more commonly known as New Criticism, he called the 'lemon-squeezer school of criticism' (Eliot 1956: p. 113), because of its intense focus on the elucidation of the words on the page, to the exclusion of extraneous detail and concerns. The second he designated the 'criticism of explanation by origins' (Eliot 1956: p. 107), on account of its dependence on contextual (historical, biographical), or intertextual material to explicate the literary text.

Broad approval of the new professionalism and attention to detail which these emergent critical modes involved was tempered by anxiety that such work often left the impression that 'someone had taken a machine to pieces and left me with the task of reassembling the parts' (Eliot 1956: p. 114). Drawing distinctions between 'explanation' and 'understanding', between 'interpretation' and 'enjoyment', Eliot's essay posed as its central question whether 'there are limits, exceeding which in one direction literary criticism ceases to be literary, and exceeding which in another it ceases to be criticism' (Eliot 1956: p. 103).

This is not a question we often ask ourselves these days, at least in anything like this form, which may mean that Eliot was right and that we have ceased, for one reason or the other, to do 'literary criticism'. Of course such a sentence itself immediately begs the question as to who 'we' are, and I should make clear that I am a lecturer in a School of English Studies, and I am assuming that you, the reader, are either studying English at school, college or university, or working professionally in the field as a teacher, academic or journalist. These roles matter, and determine the mode and organization of my own writing, just as much as the context and purpose – or desired outcomes – of your reading. It is important to remember that I am not writing in a newspaper or magazine, or on my blog; I am presupposing, and the editors of this volume are anticipating, a shared level of professional and scholarly interest and knowledge, a level which is different from the level one might expect of a general readership in the print media, or on a television programme. That is the material and institutional context of my writing, and your reading, and it establishes conventions, expectations and limits, some of which I am transgressing, in fact, in drawing such overt attention to them.

## Literary Criticism

Eliot's essay, as we have already seen, pointed out that 'serious criticism' (Eliot: p. 105) would be more and more restricted to the institutional context, and his argument was in many ways directed towards people (that is to say, 'us'), who are more or less professionally concerned with literary criticism. However, few of my colleagues working within English Studies, or the students whom we teach, would readily define their work within the limits Eliot appears to suggest, circumscribed on the one side by 'literary' and on the other by 'criticism', and urged not to stray too far beyond these frontiers. We live in an interdisciplinary age, peculiarly suspicious of limits or restrictions to our freedom of academic research and reading modes, and, for that matter, of our speech generally. Nor, for his part, would Eliot recognize much of their (or our, or my) work as, in his terms, literary criticism, because so much of what happens in English is now almost indistinguishable from the (inter)disciplinary habits of other Humanities subjects (particularly History and Cultural Studies), and Social Sciences fields (above all Geography, given claims for the recent 'spatial turn' in criticism, and the impact of ecocriticism), but also because we no longer appear to have any explicit interest in questions of value, questions which were central to Eliot's understanding of literature.

The limits of Eliot's definition of 'literary' remain largely implicit in his essay, though his work as a whole defines and defends a literary tradition which we now recognize as centrally 'canonical', even if at the time some of his preferences appeared quirky and even controversial and have been subject to radical challenge in the intervening years. For the most part, today, canons are also out of fashion because they involve excluding or marginalizing some writing in favour of other writing. Since there are no absolute or scientific criteria for such exclusions, and previous exclusions seem not unrelated to white, imperial, heterosexual, upper-middle class prejudices generally (or at least have been primarily articulated by people with some or all of these attributes), it is, on the whole, thought best not to have them, and certainly much work that would not hitherto have been available or accessible has been included in the syllabus and brought to a wider readership as a result. One consequence, however, is that it is difficult, if not now impossible, for us to point confidently at something which anyone might agree *is* literature, except with the intention of exposing – as I just did – someone else's preconceptions about the matter for their (white, imperial, etc.) limitations, prejudices and assumptions (What, no *Harry Potter*? You don't include non-fiction? Unpublished drafts? Film adaptations?).

As for 'criticism', Eliot insisted on its conventional sense as involving distinctions of relative literary value, but while everyone nowadays, including us, would probably agree that literary journalism and literary prize juries, with their responsibilities to rank and place books, are self-evidently places where 'criticism' in this judgemental mode takes place, few would look to university lecturers in English for an indication of the 'best' books or the 'must reads', except when we write for newspapers and magazines, which is very different from our day job. The Mann Booker Prize and the Orange Prize, for example, occasionally have token academics on their juries, and a few university professors of English contribute regularly to the mass media, but these are the exception (creative writers have a special status, being honorary non-academics on account of their appointment being predicated on their position as writers, as I discuss below). In universities, any explicit commitment to evaluation, selection or judgement in terms of literary quality has long been off the syllabus, despite the fact that one might argue that syllabuses are inherently selective; it is simply that the criteria by which selection is made are no longer concerned with anything overtly resembling literary value.

The very name for the subject which currently predominates – English Studies, or English, which is gradually replacing English Literature – implies learning, reflection, observation and scholarship, rather than the assessment of relative importance. Many schools and departments around the country have variations of this title, but there are none that I can find which market themselves under the title 'Literary Criticism'. Are we unique in the academy in that we are unable even to agree on who we are? Historians do History, Geographers do Geography, Linguists do Languages, but those in English seem never to be quite sure of their identity, except that it might appear, as Eliot anticipated might happen, that we are no longer prepared confidently to state our commitment to literary criticism.

There is another perspective, however, from which Eliot seems to have accurately identified the tensions which still characterize our practice. What Eliot described as 'serious criticism' (Eliot: p. 105), which is what you and I are doing now, he believed would inevitably take place predominantly in universities and colleges. In one sense, that sounds like an elitist position, as if intelligent attention to literature cannot take place elsewhere, but that is to mistake Eliot's emphasis (even if he was a rather patrician figure): the point is that there is an unusual and dedicated concentration on such work in the academy. It remains the case that because, as Eliot commented, 'serious literary journalism is an inadequate, as well as precarious means of support for all but a very few' (Eliot: p. 105), when we talk of literary criticism and theory today we are concerned with a professional and academic practice. Popular literary journalism remains largely untouched by the controversies within our departmental walls, except where comically abstruse but always violently expressed donnish arguments might make for sensational copy, much as in the 'Structuralism controversy' or the 'Derrida affair' (which M. Derrida quite properly retorted was in fact actually another 'Cambridge affair'). One might go further, and argue that it is in universities and colleges that the *only* 'serious criticism' of the type Eliot envisages – a professional, theoretically informed reading – takes place. Even James Wood, who for many years was the only professional freelance literary journalist working independently of the academy (D. J. Taylor prefers to think of himself as a novelist first and critic after), has now taken a post, in addition to his contracts with the *London Review of Books, New Yorker* and *New Republic*, as Professor of the Practice of Literary Criticism, at Harvard University.

It is thus quite possible to argue that literary criticism has, in the years since 'The Frontiers of Criticism', developed in ways which relate readily to the pattern Eliot identified. Literary critics continue to press against, and beyond, the limits he sketched in both intellectual mode (borrowing ideas and methods from other disciplines, primarily but not exclusively those developed within the social sciences), and institutional situation (overwhelming professionalization and academicization of literary critical work). The impact of epistemological and methodological changes taking place elsewhere in the social sciences and humanities continues to be strong, evident not only in the emergence from within English of the independent disciplines of Cultural Studies, Communications Studies, and Film, TV and Media Studies, but also in a steady cross-fertilization among the faculties of methodologies and materials.

The flourishing of the general reading public, as a result of successive educational reforms in the latter part of the nineteenth century and the first half of the twentieth, has accompanied the prodigious expansion of further and higher education, with 'English' in its many forms and variants a robust disciplinary presence, one of the most popular subjects in schools and colleges. The most marked divergence from Eliot's account, in terms of his taxonomy of critical currents, has in fact been the growth of Creative Writing courses and the establishment of practitioner-critics (writers) at the heart of the academy, bringing 'workshop criticism' into still closer and more explicit relation to academic criticism and theory. This is a process already in train when he was writing, if one considers the influence of his own critical work, or that of such writers such as Henry James, Virginia Woolf, and E. M. Forster. The writer of a survey of the current state of literary criticism and theory cannot ignore the discourse of contemporary practitioners, nor are these 'creative writers' unaware of the plethora of competing theoretical modes within the literary critical field, although in many departments it remains the case that a mutual suspicion characterizes relations between the two groups.

Attention to the institutional or material history of the subject, as Eliot inferred, thus offers an important corrective to a 'pure' history of ideas or theory, which restricts itself solely to changing theoretical and method-ological practices. The tendencies which Eliot plotted, towards institutional-ization and towards theoretical rarefaction, have accelerated in the intervening decades. The gap between the academic critic or theorist and the ordinary reader, or even between what goes on in universities and what constitutes criticism in newspapers and magazines, is often a cause for complaint from those who find the difficulty of much contemporary theory, above all the obscurity of its terminology, elitist and obfuscatory. It is important to note that, within any single department of English, there will be those who undertake 'theoretically informed' criticism, and those who contribute 'pure' theory, but outside the academy such a distinction often seems hazy.

Such concerns were, of course, already evident in Eliot's reservations about 'lemon-squeezing' and 'explanation by origins', but with nothing like the intensity with which they are articulated these days. Beyond the confines of the seminar and class rooms, reading has never been so popular, if we are to believe library lending figures and book sales statistics; the readership for fiction and poetry appears to grow every year, and our appetite for reading groups and literary festivals seems insatiable. However, the dual impact of criticism and theory's academicization, and its thoroughgoing symbiosis with other academic disciplines, has led to much of the research in the field – Eliot's 'serious criticism' – being inaccessible, never mind comprehensible, to the Ordinary Reader (and even some students, though not to you, needless to say). It is therefore, with an irony Eliot would have enjoyed and doubtless intended, the practitioner-critics who now generally represent the public face of academic literary criticism. For the most part they use a familiar if informed idiom of discussion (rather than a technical or theoretically sophisticated language), write for the newspapers and magazines, appear on television and radio, and perform (if that is the right word) at literary festivals. It is only in these contexts and through these people that professional and academically informed criticism and theory still occasionally connects with the wider read-ing public. University students of English occupy a difficult in-between zone, neither Ordinary Readers nor paid-up academics, they often find the subject troubling in the way it unravels conventional expectations of what reading involves, and replaces it with something different, disturbed and not always altogether satisfactory.

## 'Theory'

Eliot did not use the word 'theory' in his essay, although the term was already becoming current (Austin Warren and Rene Wellek's *Theory of Literature* was published in 1949), but we recognize and categorize 'The Frontiers of Criticism' as theoretical writing, rather than literary criticism, just as his earlier, more famous essay, 'Tradition and the Individual Talent', has since been routinely anthologized in volumes of critical theory, and is a staple of Theory courses. 'The Frontiers of Criticism' takes as its subject the practices and priorities of criticism, rather than engaging directly in the reading or discussion of literary texts themselves. The essay locates the origins of many of our ways of thinking about literature and criticism in a tradition deriving from Coleridge, who 'established the relevance of philosophy, aesthetics and psychology' (Eliot: p. 104) to critical work and would, Eliot argued, 'were he alive now, take the same interest in the social sciences and in the study of language and semantics, that he took in the sciences available to him'. This sense of the 'scope and variety of the interests which Coleridge brought to bear on his discussion of poetry', of the diverse extra-literary pressures and determinants on our reading, is characteristic of theoretical thinking. Eliot plainly approved of these 'interests', and he advertised the fact that he is engaged in a similar mode of thinking. He isolated the variety of intellectual and material pressures on literary critical work but also, in his representation of them, articulated a challenge at a further, conceptual level. Although wary of the schematization of criticism as a result of pedagogic necessity or the influence of social science methodology, he was nonetheless contributing to the necessary meta-discourse of criticism, the discourse about criticism, which is Theory.

Specifically, reading his own essay closely, assessing its critical method, we see he built his argument through the examination of a sequence of oppositions: between impressionism and scholarship; between scholarship and criticism; between explanation and understanding; between text and context; between academic reading and amateur reading; and ultimately between institutional/material history and intellectual history. When he suggests that we stray in one direction out of the category of 'literary', and in another beyond the modes of 'criticism', he is doing so on the grounds of this series of binaries that are, on closer examination, more the abstracted limit points of a spectrum than points of absolute opposition. Moreover, in building the case this way he is demonstrating the necessity of theoretical discourse, even as, paradoxically, he is arguing if not against theory, then certainly for a less theoretical emphasis in literary criticism.

Describing 'The Frontiers of Criticism' in this way serves to make it more conformable to our expectations of literary theory, even if some of the terminology and phrasing seems rather old-fashioned – or pre-theoretical. It is, indeed, typical of a sub-genre of theory, to which the piece you are reading also belongs, concerned with the state of criticism and theory. This is a distinct genre of writing which reflects on the history, function and practice of criticism, and the theories which underlie them. Such writing has a long history, and conventionally contains the following elements: history or chronology; categorization or conceptualization; polemic; and, for want of a better word, confession (if you take the time to study this essay, you will also find that it contains all four of these elements). The historical or chronological narrative sets recent changes in the context of a longer, or revised, perspective of intellectual history (or, as Eliot called it, 'tradition'). Categorization or conceptualization presents a synoptic view offering schematization of the totality, the whole contemporary scene, ordinarily at a higher level of abstraction than the specific techniques under examination, and utilizing a set of explanatory terms and methods distinct from those under discussion. The polemical aspect typically offers an evaluation of the material, or aligns the author explicitly in relation to contrasting schools, currents of thought or parties. The confessional mode is generated by the more or less extreme self-consciousness about form and voice which is generally the burden of the writer of the piece, and this last element is perhaps the hallmark of the genre. It is impossible to survey the state of criticism and theory without becoming particularly alert to the determinants of one's own position. Such an exercise demands the heightened reflexivity, the intensified attention to one's assumptions, training and perspective, which epitomizes both theoretical and critical modes.

On the principle that such subjectivity is inherently tendentious or flawed, however, there have been many efforts to establish literary criticism and theory on an objective, scientific footing. Many such efforts, as Eliot indicated, have drawn their inspiration from social science methodology. Literary linguistics or stylistics (and the 'cognitive poetics' which derives from them), or narratology and semiotics, for example, have certainly developed quantitative and empirical methods to an impressive degree. In the earlier part of our period, as I discuss further, literary theories related to the science of historical materialism, the Marxist methodology which sought to offer a rational and totalizing account of the whole course of social and economic existence, also offered to present an objective account of the meanings of texts, albeit an account in which those texts played a secondary or subsidiary function to the political narrative.

Despite this work, it remains the case that for most readers the gap between 'explanation' and 'understanding' is still an important one, and the best of these practices leave us with choices to make in our relation to the text before us. At the most extreme point, there is a decision to be made even about what might constitute the object for criticism to criticize. As we remarked earlier, even the question 'What is a text?' is far from settled. We may no longer concern ourselves with Eliot's distinction between 'interpretation' and 'enjoyment' (the pleasures of the text being less and less of scholarly or academic concern), and his injunction that the good reader must rely upon 'sensibility, intelligence and capacity for wisdom' (Eliot: p. 117) seems rather quaint, but we are still faced with myriad choices and decisions every time we open a book. It is the nature and form of such decisions which are the matter of literary theory, but one might say that in one direction they cease to be theoretical, being subjective expressions of taste or preference, and in the other they have little to do with literature, being in essence predicated on extra-literary or non-literary principles, above all, in our time, politics or ethics.

Such decisions form the more or less explicit framework for literary criticism, and they provide the authors of surveys and position pieces such as this (or 'The Frontiers of Criticism'), with more than the usual graphophobia, since writing about the conflicting and contradictory principles which underlie our contemporary practices can come to resemble nothing more than sawing off the branch upon which one is perched. For this reason a characteristic of the genre is, as I have already suggested, a polemical relation to the subject: the very act of engaging in such a survey forces you to work out where you stand, to make a stand. For Eliot this involved, in his account of where the currents he had defined might lead, insisting upon the specificity of the practices of literary criticism, practices which might, as we have seen, cease to be literary or critical depending on which direction one strayed into. He felt his contemporaries were showing tendencies to move in both directions. It is striking that, in 'The Frontiers of Criticism', Eliot not only warns explicitly against such trends, but also reproduces the admonition at the level of the very form of his writing, keeping separate the two central categories which underpin his analysis in such a way as to enact the critical limit he is defining.

The conceptual and categorical distinction which structures 'The Frontiers of Criticism' is between: on the one hand, the variations in institutional or material context which determined changes in the practices of reading and criticism; on the other, the intellectual or epistemological shifts which were also driving those changes. That is to say, Eliot's lecture effectively dissociated the impact of material processes, the ways in which literary criticism changed as a result of its becoming an increasingly academic and institutional activity, from the intellectual or methodological influences, which arose from the interdisciplinary interactions of the social sciences, and creative writing, with the discipline of literary criticism. At some level, of course, there is certainly a relationship between these two elements. Work as an academic in a university is obviously different from work as a journalist in a newspaper, and the literary criticism produced in these contrasting environments is correspondingly distinct. The difference between the two literary critical practices is a function, result or effect of the different contexts, a relation which might be broken down into a combination of commercial, cultural, aesthetic, political, social, generic and intellectual factors. Yet Eliot refused to be drawn into speculating about, or exploring, such connections between material context and intellectual product, and this refusal is absolutely constitutive of the form and content of his lecture.

Having identified the two key determinants of change as the influence of social science methodologies and the increasing institutionalization of literary criticism, he says nothing about their interrelation, and his silence on the matter precisely reproduces the essential theme of his lecture. There is a danger, he argued, that the further we press to explain something (literary criticism; a poem), either in terms of its internal characteristics (form; style) or of its external determinants (context, be that biography or history), the more likely we are to lose touch with the thing itself (criticism; the poem; literature). Satisfied that he had identified the two primary determinants in his own time, Eliot did not examine them further, or even articulate a connection between them, because to do so, to his way of thinking, would be beyond the frontiers of literary criticism, would *not be* literary criticism. The single most significant change between his critical or theoretical moment and our own is thus embodied in the distance we have travelled from Eliot's position. In the intervening half century, the exploration of the complex connection or interrelation between the material and the intellectual elements of literature has become the predominant, almost one might argue the only, theoretical issue in literary criticism and theory.

To state that the dominant question for literary critics and theorists of our time has concerned the nature of the relations between material or historical and intellectual or aesthetic processes is not, however, to pretend that it is a new or original question. Speculation about 'where a poem comes from', or 'how a writer came up with that story', or 'what the relation might be between this fiction to that real event', is as old as the hills. What is new in our period is the way in which the terms through which such questions began to be formulated in the immediate post-war period have established a paradigm for the subsequent controversies around new historicism, structuralism, interdisciplinarity and many of the 'issue-led' forms of criticism (such as feminism; postcolonialism; ecocriticism) which now constitute English Studies. This paradigm, moreover, has also provided the horizon which has bounded most thinking about literary criticism for the last fifty years. For Eliot, as we have seen, the issue determined the deep structure and form of his argument, and he made clear that he thought attempting to elucidate the complex relations of determination between material and intellectual components in a literary work an illegitimate and ultimately self-defeating goal: 'If in literary criticism, we place all the emphasis upon *understanding*', he maintained, 'we are in danger of slipping from understanding to mere explanation. We are in danger even of pursuing criticism as if it were a science, which it never can be' (Eliot: p. 117). He accepted the inherent value of literary scholarship which makes use of the epistemological advances and insights of other disciplines, and as we have seen he saw his own work in a tradition stretching back to Coleridge which admitted the strong relevance of such extra-literary interests. Nonetheless, he stressed that such extra-literary work ultimately did not itself constitute literary criticism, and it ought not to determine the agenda for literary criticism, it was 'to be judged as a contribution to psychology, or sociology, or logic, or pedagogy, or some other pursuit – and it is to be judged by specialists, not by men of letters' (Eliot: p. 116).

We need, again, to be careful in our account of this position. He was not excluding historical scholarship (or philosophy, or politics, or sociology) from consideration in the processes of understanding a literary work, but warning of the potential for the literary work itself, and the qualities which distinguish it as a literary work (which are not self-evident, and may be properly part of the concern of literary critics), to become a secondary, or irrelevant, element in the act of reading if literary criticism itself became largely determined by non-literary objectives. For Eliot, as we have seen, the very question of the relations between the material and the intellectual determinants in the formation of a literary work led rapidly, if not immediately, beyond the frontiers of literary criticism.

## Culture Wars

It is symptomatic of the current paradigm of English Studies that it is a critical commonplace not simply to characterize Eliot's literary critical, theoretical and aesthetic positions, quite apart from his explicitly political remarks, as conservative and reactionary, but for that characterization, with more or less supporting detail, to seem a sufficient and final critical assessment. Indeed, since he famously described himself as 'classicist in literature, royalist in politics, and Anglo-catholic in religion' (Eliot 1928: p. 7), such a characterization is hardly an astonishing or even controversial insight, although the self-deprecating sentences which follow those lines are less frequently recalled: 'the first term is completely vague, and easily lends itself to clap-trap; [...] the second term is at present without definition, and easily lends itself to what is almost worse than clap-trap, I mean temperate conservatism; the third term does not rest with me to define'. There has been much debate about the extent of Eliot's sympathies with fascism, his anti-Semitism, and his mistreatment of his first wife, and the disapproval of our contemporary liberal consensus of such political views and personal conduct has become a legitimate, even necessary, aspect of our account of his literary achievement. We read, indeed, from the man to the writing and back, and find evidence in each which confirms, albeit with a rather obvious circularity, a largely negative political and personal judgement on both (unless we are ourselves classicist, Anglo-catholic and royalist). What is significant is the extent to which such assessments have come to constitute, to dominate, much of what passes for literary criticism today: if there *is* something evasive about Eliot's comments about the three categories above, is that because he is hiding something? As we saw earlier, few academic literary critics would now recognize an account of their own practice in the mode of criticism Eliot describes, or endorse his authoritarian establishment and policing of the 'frontiers' of literary criticism, and many have argued that his efforts to challenge or even refute the rise of historical and contextual approaches to literature were motivated by those same personal and political reflexes of elitism and conservatism (and the rest) which we condemn in his life. Eliot's literary critical position is thus inherently compromised politically, a judgement which somehow serves to disqualify it from consideration in any terms other than the elucidation of the patterns and forms of its complicity with his distasteful or unacceptable views.

Thus Eliot's attempt in 'The Frontiers of Criticism' to describe literary criticism, to offer a definition of it, which necessarily involves drawing distinctions between what it is, and what it is not, soon begins to appear from our modern perspective to have been motivated by a more dubious impulse. He is intent on binding the literary critic's thoughts and desires, on excluding or repressing the liberative and democratic potential of the discipline. In absolute contrast to Eliot's hesitancy, his defining metaphor in this essay of restraint and limit (the 'frontier'), the primary and largely uncontested ambition of our contemporary criticism, which has become the second nature of our research and teaching (as a thousand examination criteria, module specifications and subject benchmarks reveal, as Peter Barry (2007) has demonstrated), has been to refuse disciplinary or intellectual boundaries, to challenge the imposition of limits to knowledge, and – above all – to attempt to bring into focus the political and historical issues that were pre-empted by Eliot's foreclosing of the difficult questions involved in the interrelation of the material and aesthetic domains.

'The Frontiers of Criticism' was a lecture delivered at precisely the moment when the challenge to the dominant disciplinary formation in literary criticism with which Eliot was clearly associated was gaining force and momentum. This challenge, which came from critics who demanded more explicitly historical and political modes of literary criticism, a greater attention to the whole context of production (intellectual, social, economic, cultural) of a literary work, was grounded in the conviction that these aspects, which were crucial to a proper understanding not only of literature but also literature's cultural function, were elided or even repressed in conventional criticism, and that the purpose of such a repression was fundamentally political, in that it perpetuated an idea of English Literature, and by extension Englishness, which was limited and controlled by a small and unrepresentative elite, what

Raymond Williams – a key figure among these critics – was to call 'Eliot, Leavis and the whole of the cultural conservatism that had formed around them – the people who had pre-empted the culture and literature of this country' (Williams 1979: p. 112). Literary criticism, through its central position in the education system and in its influence on general habits of reading, contributed significantly to the formation of national and individual identity, but the discussion of its political functions was wholly occluded within the discipline itself. Again, such arguments had been around for many years, but had new vigour and relevance. During the 1920s and 1930s, Marxist criticism in Britain, with its central theory of base and superstructure, had struggled to develop a sophisticated or convincing account of the function of literature, not least because there seemed more important things to be doing, politically, than fussing about poems. Where Marxists did concern themselves with literature, it was therefore largely to reiterate a straightforward position: the economic base, as Marx had argued, which was embodied in the primary economic realities of the ownership of the means of production, determined the economic relations and consciousness of the people. Literature was but one element of the superstructural complex of ideology, false consciousness and illusion which was generated to mediate, maintain and vindicate those relations of production, the realities of power.

During the 1950s, however, the expansion of the education system encouraged the development and emergence of a new generation of working-class academics, many of whom sought to reconcile their socialist convictions, and solidarity with the working-class, with the disciplinary practices of their intellectual work. In History and English, above all, this involved radical challenges to the dominant modes of thinking of both the academic disciplines themselves, and the often undeveloped or formulaic Marxist thinking which had hitherto been the extent of socialist engagement with them.

In 1951, F. W. Bateson, a stalwart socialist and veteran of the political and the literary critical debates of the pre-war period, founded the academic literary critical journal *Essays in Criticism* with precisely such a goal in mind. He stated in his editorial manifesto, 'The Function of Criticism at the Present Time' (1953), that the journal's objective was to develop a new form of literary criticism, which would be distinguished by a commitment to a new 'discipline of historical context' (Bateson 1953: p. 14), and by the conviction that 'the skilled reader of literature will tend, by the nature of his skill, to understand and appreciate contemporary social processes better than his neighbours'. Bateson argued that the understanding of any text depended on the critic's ability to articulate and bring into play several levels of scholarship and contextual knowledge – verbal, literary, intellectual, social – which would enable, by a series of moves back and forth between text and context, the arrival at 'the correct meaning, the object as in itself it really is, since it is the product of progressive corrections at each stage of the contextual series' (p. 18). It was an ambitious programme, and at its foundation was the conviction that the New Criticism, which divorced texts from their historical contexts and read them 'as though the language in which they were written and on which their existence depends had no immediate connection with everyday human reality' (p. 25), was aberrant, indeed 'irresponsible' (the word is repeated several times).

The project of understanding literary work as an element of the culture and history, in contrast, was an inherently progressive and politically enabling process, it demonstrated *intellectual clarity, spiritual integrity, social conscience* (Bateson's emphasis) (p. 2). This model of critical practice and these claims for its value were forcefully rebutted by F. R. Leavis, in his own journal, *Scrutiny*. Leavis unpicked the way Bateson moved from 'the commonplace assumption that a poem is in some way related to the world in which it was written' to the 'assumption that the way to achieve a correct reading of a poem – of say, Marvell's or Pope's – is to put it back in its "total context" in that world' (Leavis 1953: p. 173). For Leavis, it was not only the case that the 'total "social context" that he [Bateson] postulates is an illusion', but also that the very ambition was flawed: '[T]o make literary criticism *dependent* on the extra-literary studies (or to aim at doing so, for it can't be done) in the way Mr. Bateson proposes is to stultify the former and deprive the latter of the special profit they might have for the literary student' (p. 174).

Although Leavis had the better of the exchange, it was clear that he was fighting a losing battle – *Scrutiny* ceased publication with the following number – against a widespread pressure to extend the range and focus of literary studies. By the end of the decade, the publication of two enormously popular and successful books by literary critics, Richard Hoggart's *The Uses of Literacy* (1957), and Raymond Williams's *Culture and Society* (1958), indicated that the rising generation was taking literary studies far beyond the frontiers proposed by Eliot or Leavis. This new work broke with the established forms of criticism in favour of an attention both to the historical context of literary forms (a context more broadly conceived than even Bateson suggested), and above all addressing the very interactions of the material and the intellectual which Eliot had deprecated, and the political implications of literature's function in contemporary culture.

The subsequent publication of Williams's *The Long Revolution*, in 1961, and the establishment of the Birmingham Centre for Contemporary Cultural Studies, in 1964, made clear that Eliot's borders had been utterly overrun. Williams tellingly defined his critical objective as 'the study of relationships between elements in a whole way of life' (Williams 1961: p. 46). This bold programme, needless to say, conceived the elucidation of the relations between material and intellectual elements as a central matter for study, and explicitly refused priority to any single element, least of all the literary text.

Williams and Hoggart were in the vanguard of this work, but the articulation of theoretical bases for understanding this set of relations became the preoccupation of a generation. Similar work was emerging from continental Europe, particularly from France, and the 1960s and 1970s were marked by a thrilling conviction that political change and such intellectual work were closely connected, indeed that the universities would be the forefront of social revolution. In particular, the work emerging from structuralist and Marxist traditions of thinking associated with critics such as Roland Barthes (whose work brought together insights from anthropology, narratology and philosophy to challenge our assumptions about authorship, textuality and reading), Michel Foucault (above all in his conceptualization of 'discourse' and related terms), and Louis Althusser (in his theoretization of structural causality, a revision and complication of the Marxist notion of determination), appeared to offer the means and methodology to structure and take forward the ambitious programme Williams and others had envisaged. During the 1970s, developments in psychoanalytic and linguistic theory, and especially in philosophy, extended further the range and ambition of these critical movements. Underpinning the whole process was, as Eliot had anticipated, an effective evacuation or denial of 'literature' (and with it, literary criticism), as an inherently conservative and ideologically obfuscatory category, in favour of analyses which explained elements of cultural activity in terms of their mutual and overdetermined interrelations: 'Broad non-literary notions such as "power", "culture", "gender", "politics", and "history" began to set the agenda (in the titles of books and conference) and, as the decade [the 1980s] progressed, the literary work itself seemed to become merely the written context of items of historical context narrowly conceived' (Barry 2007: p. 19).

The formal and intellectual challenge to the surveyor of the state of contemporary literary criticism and theory today is not just, therefore, that the course of the last half century involves a fissiparous narrative of such complexity that even T. S. Eliot would have struggled to make sense of it, but that this history now literally and theoretically *defies* narrative; the contemporary scene resists characterization. The dominant mode in research and teaching in the discipline appears to demand levels of competence and knowledge in a large range of humanity and social science fields, as well as a commitment to making the world a better place (a commitment which is, it is assumed, broadly left-liberal in form). Critics and theorists, just as much as novelists, have been questioning more than ever our conventional conceptions of cause, effect and influence, unpicking the familiar modes of recounting stories or events, challenging the foundations of any disciplinary identity for English, even attacking the bases of what we ordinarily call reading. It is commonplace to deny the coherence or existence of a stable object that criticism might criticize, or the stable subjectivity from which it might be criticized, and the deconstruction of a text (the demonstration that it does not, indeed can not, mean what it appears to say), is a necessary skill for undergraduates. The proliferation of challenging and esoteric theories, often in conflict with each other, are evidently the traces and products of profound ideological and philosophical divisions which have marked our era – Stanley Fish has argued persuasively that they are also the direct result of the professionalization of critical work which Eliot originally noted: 'The emergence of the *profession* of literary studies is thus a recent accomplishment of roughly the last 100 years, but the accomplishment has not been without its costs and the chief cost has been the increasing difficulty of connecting up specifically literary work with the larger arenas in which it was once able to intervene' (Fish 1995: p. 43).

Much critical work has, one should emphasize, been done that is powerful, liberatory, and original, but much more merely, unreflectively conforms to a historicizing and politicizing imperative. Plotting the course of the institutional history only further exposes the complexity of this intellectual history: even if we were able to sketch a chronology or map of when and where things happened, 'an explanation by origins', we would still be as far away as ever from, as Eliot inferred, any understanding of why they have occurred, or what the pattern means. This is not to fall into political quietism or to surrender to despair, but to acknowledge that it is very difficult to offer a summary of the nature or function of literary criticism. It will not have escaped your notice that in this assessment I have concentrated on critical debates which date from the 1950s, a period which is often regarded as a backwater, the time Before Theory, when literary critics were still mired in the humanist and idealist conventions which were compromised by, or complicit with, the ethos and values of the late-imperial world. It is for you to assess whether or not the questions which concerned Eliot, Leavis, Bateson and the rest are still important – my own position, or confession, should be apparent.

Eliot's use of the metaphor of the 'frontier' which bounds literary criticism is significant. Frontiers are territorial markers, which define the limits of our domain, beyond which we may find ourselves in hostile or unknown terrain, and they also indicate to outsiders that they are entering a distinct territory. Most of my colleagues in English Studies, I have suggested, would find such metaphors inherently repressive and conservative, only to be utilized in order to be dissolved, as in the context of a further metaphor of confederacy, of the happy united continent of interdisciplinarity, a land without border patrols or immigration controls – cultural geographers and spatial theorists would have interesting things to say about all these metaphors, I am sure. But there are signs that dissatisfaction with the dominant assumptions within English Studies is growing, and not merely in the bemusement expressed in student satisfaction surveys and in the derision to which we are often subjected in the media: even Edward Said, pre-eminent as a result of his foundational work in postcolonial studies, argued in his late work for a return to the humanistic bases of the subject (Said 2004).

To state such a thing is to invite charges of conservatism and wishful thinking at the same time, but the current reflex of political reading, which so often devolves into the self-righteous and rebarbative rhetoric of 'speaking of truth to Power', particularly in the default form which characterizes so many of our student essays, academic lectures and scholarly articles or monographs, effectively reduces texts to instances, to their representation of ideology, to the manner in which they construct identity, or to their relation (liberatory or complicit, sometimes both) to the prevailing organization of Power (which is always synonymous with repression). Our contemporary model of 'explanation by origins', with its appetite for context that grows by what it feeds on, with its ready assertion of intellectual, political and moral superiority to all that it engages, is – to repeat Eliot's terms – neither literary nor critical. It is – to echo Leavis – 'irresponsible' in the way it makes impossible demands of us as readers while at the same time so diminishing the singularity of that which is read, of our literature.

# Appendix: Teaching, Curriculum, and Learning

This Chapter is available online at
www.continuumbooks.com/resources/9780826495020

# Notes on Contributors

**Dr Claire Chambers** is Senior Lecturer in English Literature at Leeds Metropolitan University and soon to be course leader for the MA in Contemporary Literatures. She specializes in South Asian literature written in English and in literary representations of British Muslims. Claire is currently on research leave, supported by a HEFCE Promising Researcher Fellowship, and is completing a book entitled *British Muslim Fictions: Interviews with Contemporary Writers*. She has published widely in such journals as *Postcolonial Text, Journal of Commonwealth Literature* and *Journal of Postcolonial Writing*. She is also working on a monograph tracing the development of artistic depictions of Muslims in Britain, 1966–2009. She has been a subject editor for the 'Indian Subcontinent and Sri Lanka' section of *The Year's Work in English Studies* and a judge for the Muslim Writers Awards 2009, and is on the editorial board of *The Journal of Commonwealth Literature*.

**Dr Katharine Cockin** is Reader in English at the University of Hull where she is the convenor of the MA in Modern and Contemporary Literature. Her research interests range from the nineteenth century to the present day. She has published widely on women's writing, women's suffrage literature and theatre, editing two volumes of women's suffrage literature (Routledge 2007). Her articles include studies of Jackie Kay and contemporary fiction and she has edited two special issues of *Critical Survey* on contemporary fiction. She has published the biography of Edith Craig (Cassell 1998) and a monograph, *Women and Theatre in the Age of Suffrage* (Palgrave 2001). Her AHRC project, the Ellen Terry and Edith Craig Database is now online at http://www.ellenterryarchive.hull.ac.uk and she is currently editing *The Collected Letters of Ellen Terry* (Pickering and Chatto, 2010 onwards; 8 vols). She is a member of the editorial board of the *Journal of Gender Studies* and a member of the Arts and Humanities Research Council's Peer Review College.

**Dr Donna Cox** is Lecturer in English Literature at Grimsby Institute of Further and Higher Education where she is Programme Leader of the M.A. in Children's Literature. Her research interests are primarily in the area of critical theory and psychoanalytical approaches to textuality and culture with a particular interest in positions of rhetoric inhabited in relation to analysis. Published articles have ranged from readings of the early work of Freud, linguistic negotiation in rap and hip hop, and the role of phantasy in children's literature. She is currently completing a monograph on hysteria and critical analysis.

**Dr Katharine Cox** is Lecturer in Popular Culture and English at the University of Wales Institute Cardiff (UWIC). Her Ph.D. thesis examined the significance of the maze and labyrinth in contemporary fiction, connecting narrative complexity with early archaeological and literary examples. In September 2006 she organised and co-hosted the first conference dedicated to the work of Iain (M.) Banks, held at the University of Westminster, in conjunction with the UK Network for Modern Fiction Studies. Her teaching and research interests include children's literature, detective fiction, the interrelation of architecture and space in contemporary fiction, and contemporary writing especially the fictions of Jeanette Winterson and Iain Banks.

**Dr Julie Ellam** taught at undergraduate and masters level in English at the University of Hull for a number of years and is now employed as a freelance writer. She has had work published in various outlets including the *Times Literary Supplement*, Literature Online and the British Council Contemporary Writers' website at www.contemporarywriters.com. She has also written book-length study guides on *Birdsong* by Sebastian Faulks for Advanced York Notes (Longman 2009) and on *Atonement* by Ian McEwan (Continuum 2009). Her research interests are mainly concerned with modern and contemporary fiction. Her Ph.D. thesis, 'Representations of Love in Jeanette Winterson's Novels', is to be published (forthcoming, Rodopi).

**Dr Michael Greaney** is Senior Lecturer at the University of Lancaster. He has taught on The Theory and Practice of Criticism, From Decadence to Modernism, Contemporary Fiction and Critical Theory, and Contemporary British Fiction. His research interests lie in modern/contemporary fiction and theory. His first book, *Conrad, Language, and Narrative* (Cambridge University Press, 2002), received the Joseph Conrad Society of America's Adam Gillon Award for the most significant work in Conrad studies from 2001–4. *Contemporary Fiction and the Uses of Theory* (Palgrave, 2006) is a study of the reception and representation of theoretical ideas in literary fiction since the 1960s. His current research is on narratives of insomnia in contemporary fiction and film.

**Dr Sean Matthews** is Lecturer in Modern and Contemporary Literature, and Director of the D.H. Lawrence Research Centre. He has published widely on cultural theory and twentieth century literature, and has taught on these topics in Britain, Japan, the US, and, for the British Council, in Hungary, Romania, and Bulgaria. His *Raymond Williams* is forthcoming in the Routledge Critical Thinkers series (ed. Robert Eaglestone). His anthology of critical theory, *Theories: A Reader*, edited with Aura Sibisan of the University of Brasov, Romania, was published in 2003, and included his introductory essays and apparatus. He has recently directed events on contemporary studies for the British Council; the CCUE Annual Conference; ESSE; and the Learning and Teaching Support Network, LTSN. He is a contributor to www.contemporarywriters.com, and reviews for a number of newspapers and journals. He directed the 2007 D.H. Lawrence International Conference, 'Return to Eastwood', and co-curated the exhibition 'Lawrence Among the Women' at the Weston Gallery.

**Dr Jago Morrison** is Senior Lecturer in English at Brunel University, with expertise in post-war and contemporary fiction. His published books are all current references in the field. *Contemporary Fiction* (Routledge, 2003) is a study of fiction since 1975, discussing key period themes and offering fresh readings of nine influential writers. *Scandalous Fictions: The Twentieth Century Novel in the Public Sphere* (Palgrave, 2006) is a collection of essays co-edited with Susan Watkins, which re-assesses the twentieth century novel as a form shaped by its problematic, often scandalous relationship to the public sphere. *The Fiction of Chinua Achebe* (Palgrave, 2007) is a guide to the complex field of Achebe studies. Jago regularly works as a reviewer for major academic journals and publishers and is a member of the Arts and Humanities Research Council's Peer Review College.

**Jayne Murphy** is a doctoral student in the School of Arts at Brunel University. Her main research interests are contemporary women's fiction, historical fiction, gender and queer theory. Her first academic paper, on Sarah Waters' *The Nightwatch*, was presented at Leeds University in 2007.

**Dr Ruvani Ranasinha** is Senior Lecturer at King's College London, the author of *Hanif Kureishi: Writers and their Works Series* (Northcote House in association with The British Council, 2002) and *South Asian Writers in Twentieth-Century Britain: Culture in Translation* (Oxford University Press, 2007). Ruvani specialises in postcolonial literature and theory, especially relating to South Asia and the South Asian diaspora. Her research interests are in post-1945 and contemporary fiction and film, particularly as they relate to immigration, gender and/or book history. At present, she is working on an AHRC-funded project *Making Britain: South Asian Visions of Home and Abroad, 1870–1950* with Susheila Nasta, Open University and Elleke Boehmer, Oxford University, the British Library and the Courtauld Institute (2007–2010). She is also interested in the cultural representation of Muslim identity in the West. She is on the editorial board of *Interventions: International Journal of Postcolonial Studies*.

**Professor Patricia Waugh's** special interests are in twentieth-century literature, relations between modernism and postmodernism, women's writing and feminist theory, utopianism, literary criticism and theory, and literature, philosophy and science. She has published numerous articles and several books including: *Metafiction: The Theory and Practice of Self-Conscious Fiction* (Methuen, London and New York, 1984; 2nd edition,1988; 3rd edition, forthcoming Routledge; Japanese edition; Taiwanese edition, 1988); *Feminine Fictions: Revisiting the Postmodern* (Routledge, London and New York, 1989); *Practising Postmodernism and Reading Modernism* (Edward Arnold, London and New York, 1992); *The Harvest of the Sixties: English Literature and its Backgrounds 1960–90* (Oxford University Press, Oxford and New York, 1995); *Revolutions of the Word: Intellectual History and Twentieth Century Literature* (Arnold, 1997). Cultura, Scientza, Hpertext (ligouri,

Bologna) with D. Carpi, G. Hartmann and J. Hillis Miller. She is currently completing two books for publication in 2009–2010: *Beyond the Two Cultures: Literature, Science and the Good Society*; and *The Blackwell History of British Fiction 1945-present*.

**Dr Susan Watkins** is Reader in Twentieth Century Women's Fiction at Leeds Metropolitan University. She is the author of (2001) *Twentieth-Century Women Novelists: Feminist Theory into Practice* Basingstoke: Palgrave Macmillan, and co-edited with Jago Morrison (2006) *Scandalous Fictions: The Twentieth-Century Novel in the Public Sphere* Palgrave Macmillan. She has written widely on authors such as Doris Lessing, Margaret Atwood, Alison Lurie, Virginia Woolf, Radclyffe Hall and Charlotte Bronte. Susan's main research interests are in the field of twentieth-century women's fiction and feminist theory. She is currently working on a new monograph on Doris Lessing for Manchester University Press's Contemporary World Writers series, looking particularly at the treatment of race, nation, gender and genre in Lessing's writing. She is a founder member of the Contemporary Women's Writing Network (http://www.cwwn.org.uk/) and Associate Editor for the *Contemporary Women's Writing Journal*.

# Annotated Bibliography

Abrams, M. H. (1999), *A Glossary of Literary Terms*, Fort Worth: Harcourt Brace College. Abrams' glossary is a valuable reference tool to accompany any English Literature degree. The volume is regularly updated and clearly indicates topics, critical approaches, key words and literary theorists in an approachable manner. It should be used in conjunction with commentators on literary theory or with the theoretical material itself.

Appignanesi, Richard and Zarate, Oscar (1999), *Introducing Freud*, Cambridge: Icon. This graphic presentation of Freud's work is a highly accessible starting point for thinking about the far-reaching theories of psychoanalysis. It offers a humorous and enlivened presentation of the body of Freudian theory.

Barry, Peter (2000), *Contemporary British Poetry and the City*, Manchester: Manchester University Press. A lively, wide-ranging study, notable for its willingness to engage theoretically (via Bakhtin and others) with recent urban poetry.

Barthes, Roland 1973 (1974), *S/Z*, Richard Miller (trans.), Oxford: Blackwell.

—— 1968 (1977), 'The death of the author' in *Image Music Text*, Stephen Heath (trans.), London: Fontana. 'The Death of the Author' and 'From Work to Text' in this collection of cultural essays have had a massive impact on the field of literary criticism as these essays consolidate poststructuralist approaches to the author and his/her writing.

Belsey, C. and Moore, J. (1989), *The Feminist Reader: Essays in Gender and the Politics of Literary Criticism*, Basingstoke: Macmillan. A selection of essays covering the relationship between feminist politics and literature; interesting if comparing feminist perspectives to those of postfeminist critics.

Bowie, Malcolm (1991), *Lacan: Fontana Modern Masters*, London: Fontana. Bowie's overview offers an effective and sensible elucidation of the main areas of Lacanian theory. It explains the sometimes cryptic theories of Lacan clearly yet accurately without seeking to add to the already arcane reputation of Lacanian thought.

Brannigan, John (1998), *New Historicism and Cultural Materialism*, Basingstoke and London: Macmillan. This gives a thorough overview of the similarities and differences between the two theories and also applies them in relation to texts such as *Heart of Darkness* by Joseph Conrad and 'Easter 1916' by W. B. Yeats.

—— 2003, *Orwell to the Present: Literature in England, 1945–2000*, Basingstoke: Palgrave. Compact, accessible exploration of post-war literature from a variety of thematic perspectives, including time, memory, feminism and trauma. Includes a detailed chronology of the period that correlates major literary, cultural and political events.

—— (1996), *Postmodernist Culture: An Introduction to Theories of the Contemporary* (revised edition) [1989], Oxford: Basil Blackwell. Connor's work on postmodernism is very accessible and also recommended is his edited collection: *The Cambridge Companion to Postmodernism* (2004), particularly his introduction to the volume, while the breadth of the selected essays is particularly relevant to Cultural Studies students.

Butler, Judith (1999), *Gender Trouble: Feminism and the Subversion of Identity* (second edition), New York: Routledge. A fundamental text of queer theory that introduces the concept of performativity and its subversive potential.

—— (1993), *Bodies That Matter: On the Discursive Limits of 'Sex'*. New York: Routledge. Useful for discussion of the social processes by which the concept of the 'normal' sexed body is produced and accepted.

Cixous, H. (1980), 'The Laugh of the Medusa', in Elaine Marks and Isabelle de Courtivron (eds), *New French Feminisms*, Brighton: Harvester. A key text for those interested in French Feminism; this is a short piece which suggests the subversive potential for women of a new style of writing and itself provides a useful demonstration of this new expressive form.

Corcoran, Neil (1993), *English Poetry since 1940*, Harlow: Longman. An inclusive and incisive chronological study.

Culler, J. (2007), *On Deconstruction: Theory and Criticism after Structuralism* [1998], London: Routledge. This revised edition of Culler's important publication brings his original work up to date by assessing deconstruction's position alongside contemporary theoretical trends. The writing is insightful, straightforward and offers a bridge between Derrida's often complex intellectual narratives and the practice of his thinking.

Derrida, J. 1967 (1997), *Of Grammatology*, Gayatri Chakravorty Spivak (trans.), Baltimore: John Hopkins University Press. In this philosophical, literary and linguistic work Derrida presents his argument concerning language and thought, and in the process undermines traditional Western hierarchies that place writing above speech. This book outlines (as far as Derrida is prepared to go to explain his position) the practice of deconstruction around the blind spots of a text's construction. Derrida lays bare language as the artificial repository of 'truth' and exposes 'truth' itself as a sign, and in doing so fundamentally undermines the position and status of the author and reader. For a more accessible introduction to Derrida's writing see 'Structure, Sign and Play on the Discourse of the Human Sciences' in *Writing and Difference* first.

—— 1967 (1973), *Speech and Phenomena and Other Essays on Husserl's Theory of Signs*, Evanston, IL: Northwestern University Press. A difficult work that directly confronts the philosopher Husserl's premise that language is founded on logic; instead Derrida uses the opportunity to advance his thesis on a philosophy of language that is based on rhetoric.

—— 1967 (2001), *Writing and Difference*, Alan Bass (trans.), London: Routledge Classics. Perhaps the most accessible of Derrida's writing on deconstruction, this is Derrida at his playful best; the collection of essays allows the reader to dip in and out of his critical thinking and as a result is not burdensome.

Dollimore, Jonathan, and Sinfield, Alan (eds) (1985), *Political Shakespeare: New Essays in Cultural Materialism*. Manchester: Manchester University Press. This is one of the earliest collected works of cultural materialist and new historicist critics.

Eagleton, Terry 1985 (1996), *Literary Theory: An Introduction*, Oxford: Blackwell. Eagleton's introduction to literary theory has been a mainstay on the majority of English Literature degrees since its publication. The second edition covers the basics of literary theory in an accessible but fulsome manner. The chapter on psychoanalysis is particularly effective in its explanation of the connections between psychoanalysis and poststructuralist thinking.

Foucault, Michel (1972), *The Archaeology of Knowledge*, London: Tavistock/ Routledge. In this work, Foucault defines his approach to historicism and this has helped to shape new historicist thinking.

Gamble, S. (2001), *The Routledge Companion to Feminism and Postfeminism*, London: Routledge. Contains essays on a variety of feminist and postfeminist concerns. Also offers a concise but thorough glossary of terms, concepts and names likely to be encountered.

Greenblatt, Stephen (1980), *Renaissance Self-Fashioning: From More to Shakespeare*, Chicago and London: University of Chicago Press. This is regarded as a defining work of new historicist criticism.

Haffenden, John (1985), *Novelists in Interview*, London: Methuen. Illustrious interviewees in this collection include Angela Carter, William Golding, Ian McEwan, Iris Murdoch and Salman Rushdie.

Hawthorn, Jeremy (1996), *Cunning Passages: New Historicism, Cultural Materialism and Marxism* in the *Contemporary Literary Debate*, London: Arnold. *Cunning Passages* is influenced by Marxist theory and engages with complex definitions of history and ideology and has an accessible explanation of Foucault's influence on new historicism.

Head, Dominic (2002), *The Cambridge Introduction to Modern British Fiction, 1950–2000*, Cambridge University Press. A lucid and exceptionally wide-ranging study that is notable for its emphasis on the ongoing significance of socially engaged realism in contemporary British fiction.

Irigaray, L. (1985), *Speculum of the Other Woman*, G. Gill (trans.), New York: Cornell University Press. Useful for those interested in French Feminism, *écriture feminine*, and associated essentialist concepts.

—— (1985), *This Sex Which Is Not One*, Catherine Porter (trans.), New York: Cornell University Press. Short essay which calls on women to celebrate the plurality of female sexuality and withdraw from a masculine and male-dominated economy; interesting for its association of femininity and feminine qualities with the female body.

King, Bruce (2004), *The Internationalization of English Literature*, The Oxford English Literature History, Vol. 13: 1948–2000, Oxford: Oxford University Press. Complementing Randall Stevenson's book in the same series, this study provides a chronological overview of the work of colonial, postcolonial and immigrant writers who have figured in the British literary scene. Dozens of poets, novelists and dramatists are covered, included such major figures as V. S. Naipaul, Salman Rushide and Zadie Smith.

Kristeva, Julia (1982), *Desire in Language: A Semiotic Approach to Literature and Art* [1969], Columbia: Columbia University Press. This edition contains essays from her earlier work in semiotics (1969 and 1977) and so acts as a useful overview of her theoretical approach to text which she views as a conflicted and contested product. Her concept of intertextuality is outlined here as a means of seeing the text in a network or dialogue with other texts and references.

—— (1984), *Revolution in Poetic Language* [1974], Columbia: Columbia University Press. Drawing on Lacanian approaches to self, *Revolution in Poetic Language* advocates a new way of writing and analysing to deal with the notion of a subject which is unstable or in process.

Lechte, J. (1990), *Julia Kristeva*, London: Routledge. A clear and very helpful exposition of Kristeva's early work, including the concept of the *semiotic*.

Lyotard, J. F. 1979 (1984), *The Postmodern Condition: A Report on Knowledge*, G. Bennington and B. Massumi (trans.), Manchester: Manchester University Press. In this publication, Lyotard views the changing approaches to the power and status associated with knowledge in societies entering the postmodern age. In the post-industrial society, knowledge has become a commodity and its very existence constructed and mediated by language games.

Minsky, Rosalind (ed.) (1996), *Psychoanalysis and Gender*, London: Routledge. This anthology places a collection of key texts on gender by Freud, Klein, Winnicot, Lacan, Kristeva and Irigaray alongside commentaries and discussions of the selected texts. It is accessible and extremely useful for the undergraduate student of literature or gender. Minsky's introduction on psychoanalysis and the unconscious is also effective in interconnecting psychoanalytical theories while carefully addressing the subject in a balanced overview of different perspectives.

Moi, Toril (ed.) (1986), *The Kristeva Reader*, London: Routledge. This is a useful compendium of some of the main areas of Kristevan theory. The general introduction is clear and concise and each excerpt is prefaced by a clear introduction which contextualises the work from which it is taken.

—— (2002), *Sexual/Textual Politics* (second edition), London: Routledge. A clear but detailed discussion of the differences between early Anglo and French forms of feminism and their implications for literary criticism.

Morrison, Blake (1980), *English Poetry and Fiction of the 1950s: The Movement*, London: Methuen. Still the standard introductory work on the literature of this period.

Morrsion, Jago and Watkins, Susan (2006), *Scandalous Fictions: The Twentieth-Century Novel in the Public Sphere*. Basingstoke: Palgrave Macmillan. Innovative collection of essays exploring the nature of fiction as a public form in the twentieth century. Includes discussion of such issues as the re- and mis-appropriation of texts by their readerships, the nature and limits of authorial control, censorship and literary scandal.

Munt, S. (1992), *New Lesbian Criticism: Literary and Cultural Readings*, Hemel Hempstead: Harvester Wheatsheaf. Contains a selection of cultural readings

from lesbian perspectives; not all readings refer to literary works, but the introduction provides useful insights on the relationship between literature and
lesbianism.

Rabey, David Ian (2003), *English Drama since 1940*, Harlow: Longman. A spirited
and thoroughgoing survey of six decades of English drama that convincingly
deals with issues of language, stagecraft and historical context. Includes a
chapter on Irish drama.

Ryan, Kiernan (1996), *New Historicism and Cultural Materialism: A Reader*, London
and New York: Arnold. The introduction to these essays is useful for the
background it gives to the two theories and is also welcome for its critical
questioning of how its theorists have moved perhaps too far from close reading
the literary text.

Showalter, E. (1978), *A Literature of Their Own: British Women Novelists from Bronte
to Lessing*, London: Virago. A key text of early feminist criticism which looks
at a selection of women writers now considered canonical and suggests a new
aesthetics to be applied to women's writing.

—— (1986), *The New Feminist Criticism: Essays on Women, Literature, and Theory*,
London: Virago. A similar work to the above which provides a further
exposition of Showalter's position.

Sinfield, Alan (1989), *Literature, Politcs and Culture in Postwar Britain*, Oxford:
Blackwell. A pungently written piece of cultural history from an avowedly
dissident perspective, in which British literature since World War II is located
in multiple contexts, from the Welfare State and the Cold War to the emergence
of new homosexual subcultures and the rise of pop music.

—— (1992), *Faultlines: Cultural Materialism and the Politics of Dissident Reading*,
Oxford: Oxford University Press. This is a significant example of cultural
materialism in practice.

Stevenson, Randall (2004), *The Last of England?* The Oxford English Literary
History, Vol. 12: 1960–2000, Oxford: Oxford University Press. Scholarly, wide-
ranging survey of post-war literature, with an introductory section on social,
intellectual and cultural contexts, and major sections on poetry, drama and
prose narrative. Includes a set of informative biographical notes on several
dozen major authors.

Veeser, H. Aram (ed.) (1994), *The New Historicism Reader*, London: Routledge. This
is a recommended collection of new historicist essays.

Waugh, Patricia (1995), *Harvest of the Sixties: English Literature and its Background 1960
to 1990*, Oxford: Oxford University Press. A measured overview of both cultural
history and the history of ideas from the *Chatterley* trial to the Rushdie affair.

Whelehan, I. (2005), *The Feminist Bestseller: From Sex and the Single Girl to Sex and
the City*, Basingstoke: Palgrave MacMillan. Provides an interesting discussion
of various female authored texts commonly considered popular rather than of
literary merit. Whelehan suggests that such works may be read as developments of the early feminist consciousness-raising novels and as such reflect
changes in the women's movement and the onset of postfeminism.

Williams, Raymond (1977), *Marxism and Literature*, Oxford: Oxford University
Press. Williams' work in the uses of Marxism in the criticism of literature has
helped to define the course of cultural materialism.

Williams, Raymond (1980), *Problems in Materialism and Culture: Selected Essays*. London: Verso. Williams' definition of cultural materialism appears here.

Wright, Elizabeth (1998), *Psychoanalytic Criticism: A Reappraisal* (second edition), Cambridge: Polity. The second edition of this book provides a carefully updated and useful critical overview of the field of psychoanalytical theory. It is useful in explaining how aspects of psychoanalysis might be employed critically in producing literary readings.

Zeifman, Hersch and Zimmerman, Cynthia (2003), *Contemporary British Drama 1970–1990*, Basingstoke: Palgrave. A collection of some twenty articles from *Modern Drama*. Playwrights covered include Pinter, Shaffer, Ayckbourn, Stoppard and Churchill.

# References

**Primary Texts**

Achebe, Chinua (1958), *Things Fall Apart*, Oxford: Heinemann.
Aldiss, Brian (1973), *Frankenstein Unbound*, New York: Random House.
Ali, Monica (2003), *Brick Lane*, New York: Scribner.
Allnutt, Gillian, D'Aguiar, Fred, Edwards, Ken and Mottram, Eric (eds) (1988), *The New British Poetry*, London: Paladin.
Alvarez, A. (ed.) (1962), *The New Poetry*, Harmondsworth: Penguin.
—— (1974), *The Savage God*, Harmondsworth: Penguin.
Alvi, Moniza (1993), *The Country at My Shoulder*, Oxford: Oxford University Press.
—— (1996), *A Bowl of Warm Air*, Oxford: Oxford University Press.
Amis, Kingsley (1961), *Lucky Jim*, Harmondsworth: Penguin.
Amis, Martin (1975), *Dead Babies*, London: Cape.
—— (1981), *Other People*, New York: Viking.
—— (1984), *Money: A Suicide Note*, Harmondsworth: Penguin.
—— (1989), *London's Fields*, New York: Harmony.
—— (1991), *Time's Arrow*, London: Vintage.
—— (2002), 'The Adventures of Augie March', in *The War Against Cliché: Essays and Reviews 1971–2000*, London: Vintage.
—— (2006), 'The Last Days of Mohammed Atta', www.martinamisweb.com/documents/lastdays_one.pdf and www.martinamisweb.com/documents/lastdays_two.pdf.
—— (2008), *The Second Plane*, London: Jonathan Cape.
Armitage, Simon 2006 (2008), *Out of the Blue*, London: Enitharmon.
Aslam, Nadeem (2004), *A Map for Lost Lovers*, London: Faber & Faber.
Atwood, Margaret 1985 (2004), *The Handmaid's Tale*, Philadelphia: Chelsea House.
—— (2003), *Oryx and Crake*, London: Bloomsbury.
Auden, W. H. (1962), *The Dyer's Hand*, New York: Random House.
Austen, Jane 1814 (2006), *Mansfield Park*, London: Penguin.
Banks, Lynne Reid (1960), *The L-Shaped Room*, London: Chatto and Windus.
Barker, Pat (1986), *The Century's Daughter*, London: Virago.
—— (1991), *Regeneration*, London: Viking.
Barnes, Julian (1998), *England, England*, London: Jonathan Cape.
—— (1984), *Flaubert's Parrot*, London: Jonathan Cape.
—— (1989), *A History of the World in 10½ Chapters*, London: Jonathan Cape.

Bradbury, Malcolm (2000), *To the Hermitage*, London: Picador.
Brontë, Charlotte 1847 (2007), *Jane Eyre*, London: Penguin.
Brontë, Emily 1847 (2004), *Wuthering Heights*, London: Penguin.
Brooke-Rose, Christine (1966), *Such*, London: Michael Joseph.
—— (1986), *Xorandor*, Manchester: Carcanet.
—— (1990), *Verbivore*, Manchester: Carcanet.
—— (1991), *Textermination*, Manchester: Carcanet.
Bryson, Bill (1995), *Notes From a Small Island*, New York: Doubleday.
Burford, Barbara *et al.* (1984), *A Dangerous Knowing: Four Black Women Poets*, London: Sheba Feminist.
Burgess, Antony (1962), *A Clockwork Orange*, London: Heinemann.
Bushnell, Candace (1996), *Sex and the City*, New York: Atlantic Monthly.
Carroll, Lewis 1865 (2007), *Alice's Adventures in Wonderland*, London: Penguin.
Carter, Angela 1967 (1981), *The Magic Toyshop*, London: Virago.
—— 1977 (1982), *The Passion of New Eve*, London: Virago.
—— (1979a), *The Bloody Chamber and Other Stories*, Harmondsworth: Penguin.
—— (1984), *Nights at the Circus*, London: Picador.
—— (1991), *Wise Children*, London: Chatto and Windus.
Chatwin, Bruce (1977), *In Patagonia*, New York: Summit.
Churchill, Caryl (2002), *A Number*, London: Methuen.
Cobham, Rhonda and Collins, Merle (eds) (1987), *Watchers and Seekers: Creative Writing by Black Women in Britain*, London: The Women's Press.
Conquest, Robert (1963), *New lines 11*, London: Michael Joseph.
Conrad, Joseph 1899 (2007), *Heart of Darkness*, London: Penguin.
Crace, John (2004), *Arcadia*, London: Jonathan Cape.
Dabydeen, David (1991), *The Intended*, London: Secker & Warburg.
—— (1993), *Disappearance*, London: Secker & Warburg.
D'Aguiar, Fred (1994), *The Longest Memory*, London: Vintage.
Delaney, Sheila 1959 (1962), *A Taste of Honey*, London: Methuen.
Desai, Kiran (2006), *The Inheritance of Loss*, London: Hamish Hamilton.
Dhingra, Leena 1986 (1988), *Amritvela*, Toronto: Women's Press.
Dick, Philip K. 1968 (1996), *Do Androids Dream of Electric Sheep?* New York: Ballantine.
Doyle, Paddy (1993), *Paddy Clarke Ha Ha Ha*, London: Secker & Warburg.
Eliot, T. S. 1936–42 (2004), *The Four Quartets*, London: Faber.
Emecheta, Buchi (1972), *In the Ditch*, London: Heinemann.
—— 1974 (1994), *Second Class Citizen*, London: Heinemann.
Enright, D. J. (ed) (1955), *Poets of 1950s*, Tokyo: Kenkyusha.
Evaristo, Bernardo 1997 (2009), *Lara*, Highgreen: Bloodaxe.
Farrell, J. G. (1973), *The Siege of Krishnapur*, London: Weidenfeld & Nicolson.
Fielding, Helen (1996), *Bridget Jones's Diary*, London: Picador.
Forster, E. M. 1924 (2005), *A Passage to India*, London: Penguin.
French, Marilyn (1977), *The Women's Room*, New York: Summit Books.
Froer, Safran (2005), *Extremely Loud and Incredibly Close*, New York: Houghton Mifflin.
Fowles, John (1969), *The French Lieutenant's Woman*, London: Jonathan Cape.
Gibbon, Lewis Grassic 1934 (2008), *A Scots Quair*, Edinburgh: Canongate.

Gibson, William (1984), *Neuromancer*, New York: Ace Books.

Gilroy, Beryl 1976 (1994), *Black Teacher*, London: Bogle-L'Ouverture.

Golding, William (1954), *Lord of the Flies*, London: Faber & Faber.

Gorman, Dave (2004), *Googlewhack Adventure*, New York: Overlook.

Gourevitch, Philip (1998), *We Wish to Inform You That Tomorrow We Will Be Killed With Our Families*, New York: Farrar, Straus & Giroux.

Gray, Alasdair 1981 (2007), *Lanark*, Edinburgh: Canongate.

Greene, Graham (1951), *The End of the Affair*, London: Heinemann.

Griffiths, Niall 2000 (2001), *Grits*, London: Vintage.

Hall, Radclyffe 1928 (1982), *The Well of Loneliness*, Alison Hennegan (ed.), London: Virago.

Hamid, Mohsin 2007 (2008), *The Reluctant Fundamentalist*, London: Penguin.

Harris, Wilson (1960), *Palace of the Peacock*, London: Faber.

—— (1996), *Jonestown*, London: Faber.

Heppenstall, Rayner (1962), *The Connecting Door*, London: Barrie & Rockliffe.

Hornby, Nick 1992 (2005), *Fever Pitch*, London: Penguin.

Huxley, Aldous 1932 (2004), *Brave New World*, London: Vintage.

—— (1954), *The Doors of Perception*, London: Chatto & Windus.

Isherwood, Christopher (1964), *A Single Man*, London: Methuen.

Ishiguro, Kazuo (1982), *A Pale View of the Hills*, London: Faber.

—— (1989), *The Remains of the Day*, London: Faber.

—— (1995), *The Unconsoled*, London: Faber.

—— (2005), *Never Let Me Go*. London: Faber.

Jhabvala, Ruth Prawer (1975), *Heat and Dust*, London: John Murray.

Johnson, B. S. (1969), *The Unfortunates*, London: Secker & Warburg.

Johnson, Linton Kwesi (1975) *Dread, Beat an' blood*, London: Bogle-L'Ouverture.

—— (1980), London: Race Today.

—— 2002 (2006), *Mi Revalueshanary Fren*, Kene, NY: Ausable.

Joyce, James 1922 (2000), *Ulysses*, London: Penguin.

Kay, Jackie (1991), *The Adoption Papers*, London: Bloodaxe.

Kelman, James (1989), *A Disaffection*, London: Secker & Warburg.

—— (1991), *The Burn*, London: Secker & Warburg.

—— (1994). *How Late It Was, How Late*, London: Vintage.

Kerouac, Jack (1957), *On the Road*, New York: Viking.

Kunzru, Hari (2002), *The Impressionist*, London: Hamish Hamilton.

Kureishi, Hanif (1985). 'Dirty Washing', *Time Out* 795 (14–20 November), 25–26.

—— (1990), *The Buddha of Suburbia*, London: Faber.

—— (1995), *The Black Album*, London: Faber.

—— (1996), *My Beautiful Laundrette and Other Writings*, London: Faber.

Larkin, Philip (1954), *The Whitsun Weddings*, London: Faber.

—— (1988), *Collected Poems*, London: Faber.

Lawrence, D. H. (1960), *Lady Chatterley's Lover*, Harmondsworth: Penguin.

LeGuin, Ursula K. 1969 (1992), *The Left Hand of Darkness*, London: Macdonald & Co.

Lessing, Doris (1952–1969), 'Children of Violence', 5 Vols: *Martha Quest*, London: Michael Joseph, 1952; *A Proper Marriage*. London: Michael Joseph, 1954; *A Ripple from the Storm*. London: Michael Joseph, 1958; *Landlocked*. London: MacGibbon and Kee, 1965; *The Four-Gated City*. London: MacGibbon and Kee, 1969.

—— 1960 (1993), *In Pursuit of the English*, London: Flamingo.

—— 1962 (1993), *The Golden Notebook*, London: Flamingo.

—— (1973), *The Summer Before the Dark*, London: Jonathan Cape.

Levin, Ira 1976 (1998), *The Boys From Brazil*, London: Bloomsbury.

Levy, Andrea (2004), *Small Island*, London: Headline.

Lewis, Norman (1951), *A Dragon Apparent*, London: Eland.

Lewycka, Marina (2007), *Two Caravans*, London: Penguin.

Lodge, David (1975), *Changing Places*, London: Secker & Warburg.

Lucie-Smith, Edward (ed.) (1970), *British Poetry Since 1945*, Harmondsworth: Penguin.

MacInnes, Colin 1957 (1958), *City of Spades*, New York: Macmillan.

—— (1959), *Absolute Beginners*, London: Macgobbon & Kee.

Malkani, Gautam (2006), *Londonstani*, London: Fourth Estate.

Manzurul, Syed (1997), *The Mapmakers of Spitalfields*, Leeds: Peepal.

Márquez, Gabriel García 1967 (1970), *One Hundred Years of Solitude*, London: Jonathan Cape.

Marriott, Edward (2000), *Wild Shore: Life and Death with Nicaragua's Last Shark Hunters*, London: Picador.

McEwan, Ian (2005), *Saturday*, London: Jonathan Cape.

Mehmood, Tariq (1983), *Hand on the Sun*, New York: Penguin.

Michael, Livi (1992), *Under a Thin Moon*, London: Secker & Warburg.

Mo, Timothy (1978), *The Monkey King*, New York: Morrow.

—— 1982 (1985), *Sour Sweet*, New York: Vintage.

Mohin, Lilian (ed.) (1979), *One Foot on the Mountain: An Anthology of British Feminist Poetry, 1969–79*. London: Onlywomen.

Morrison, Blake and Motion, Andrew (eds) (1982), *The Penguin Book of Contemporary British Poetry*, Harmondsworth: Penguin.

Murphy, Dervla 1965 (1986), *Full-Tilt: Ireland to India with a Bicycle*, Woodstock, NY: Overlook.

Nagra, Daljit (2007), *Look We Have Coming to Dover*, London: Faber.

Naipaul, V. S. 1961 (1969), *A House for Mr Biswas*, Harmondsworth: Penguin.

—— (1967), *The Mimic Men*, Harmondsworth: Penguin.

—— 1979 (1988), *A Bend in the River*, Harmondsworth: Penguin.

—— (1980), *A Congo Diary*, Los Angeles: Sylvester and Orphanos.

Namjoshi, Suniti (1988), *The Blue Donkey Fables*, London: Women's Press.

Newby, Eric 1958 (2008), *A Short Walk in the Hindu Kush*, London: Picador.

Nichols, Grace (1984), *The Fat Black Woman's Poems*, London: Virago.

Orwell, George (1949), *1984*, London: Secker & Warburg.

—— (1968), *The Collected Essays, Journalism and Letters*, Vol. 2, Sonia Orwell and Ian Angus (eds), London: Secker & Warburg.

—— (1949), *Nineteen Eighty-four*, Harmondsworth: Penguin.

Osborne, John (1956), *Look Back in Anger*, London: Methuen.

Parsons, Tony (1999), *Man and Boy*, London: Harper Collins.

Paskin, Sylvia, Ramsay, Jay and Silver, Jeremy (eds) (1986), *Angels of Fire: An Anthology of Radical Poetry*, London: Chatto and Windus.

Pax, Salam (2003), *The Baghdad Blog*, London: Atlantic.

Pearson, Allison (2003), *I Don't Know How She Does It*, New York: Random House.

Philips, Caryl (1986), *A State of Independence*, London: Faber.

—— (1992), *Cambridge*, New York: Knopf.

Piercy, Marge 1976 (1987), *Woman on the Edge of Time*, London: Women's Press.

—— (1991), *He, She and It*, New York: Knopf.

Plath, Sylvia (1963), *The Bell Jar*, London: Faber.

Quin, Ann 1964 (2001), *Berg*, Chicago: Dalkey Archive Press.

Raban, Jonathan (1979), *Arabia: Through the Looking Glass*, London: Collins.

Randhawa, Ravinder (1987), *A Wicked Old Woman*, London: Women's Press.

Roberts, Michele (1993), *Daughters of the House*, London: Virago.

Rhys, Jean (1966), *Wide Sargasso Sea*, Harmondsworth: Penguin.

Rumens, Carol (ed.) (1985), *Making for the Open: The Chatto Book of Post-Feminist Poetry 1964–1984*, London: Chatto.

Rushdie, Salman 1981 (1995), *Midnight's Children*, London: Vintage.

—— (1983), *Shame*, London: Vintage.

—— (1988), *The Satanic Verses*, London: Viking.

Salinger, J. D. (1951), *The Catcher in the Rye*, Boston: Little Brown.

Scott, Paul 1977 (1984), *Staying On*, London: Heinemann.

Selvon, Sam 1956 (1987), *The Lonely Londoners*, London: Longman.

Seth, Vikram (1993), *A Suitable Boy*, London: Phoenix House.

Sexton, Ann (1981), *The Collected Poems*, Boston: Houghton Mifflin.

Shakespeare, William 1611 (2007), *The Tempest*, London: Penguin.

Shamsie, Kamila (2000), *Salt and Saffron*, London: Bloomsbury.

—— (2002), *Kartography*, London: Bloomsbury.

Shelley, Mary 1832 (1969), *Frankenstein*, Oxford: Oxford University Press.

Sillitoe, Alan (1958), *Saturday Night and Sunday Morning*, London: W. H. Allen.

Smith, Ali (2005), *The Accidental*, London: Hamish Hamilton.

Smith, Zadie (2000), *White Teeth*, London: Hamish Hamilton.

Spark, Muriel 1959 (1961), *Memento Mori*, Harmondsworth: Penguin.

—— 1961 (1999), *The Prime of Miss Jean Brodie*, Harmondsworth: Penguin.

—— 1966 (1975), *The Girls of Slender Means*, Harmondsworth: Penguin.

—— 1970 (1974), *The Driver's Seat*, London: Macmillan.

Sterne, Lawrence 1767 (2003), *The Life and Opinions of Tristram Shandy*, Harmondsworth: Penguin.

Stoppard, Tom (1967), *Rosencrantz and Guildenstern are Dead*, London: Faber.

Swift, Graham (1983), *Waterland*, London: Picador.

Syal, Meera (1996), *Anita and Me*, New York: New Press.

—— (1999), *Life Isn't All Ha Ha Hee Hee*, New York: Doubleday.

Tearne, Roma (2008), *Bone China*, London: Harper Press.

Thesiger, Wilfred (1959), *Arabian Sands*, New York: Dutton.

Thiong'o, Ngugi Wa (1964), *Weep Not, Child*, London: Heinemann.

—— (1967), *A Grain of Wheat*, London: Heinemann.

Thomas, D. M. (1981), *The White Hotel*, New York: Viking Press.

Thomas, Dylan (1936), 'The Hand that Signed the Paper', in *Twenty Five Poems*, London: Dent.

Thwaite, Anthony (1992), *Selected Letters of Philip Larkin, 1940–1985*, London: Faber.

Wain, John (1953), *Hurry on Down*, London: Secker & Warburg.

Warner, Marina (1992), *Indigo: Or, Mapping the Waters*, London: Chatto.

Waters, Sarah (1999), *Tipping the Velvet*, London: Virago.
—— (2006), *The Night Watch*, London: Virago.
Waugh, Evelyn (1948), *The Loved One*, Boston: Little Brown.
—— (1962), *Brideshead Revisited*, Harmondsworth: Penguin.
Weldon, Fay (1989), *The Cloning of Joanna May*, London: Fontana/Collins.
Wells, H. G. 1898 (1986), *The War of the Worlds*, Harmondsworth: Penguin.
Welsh, Irvine (1993), *Trainspotting*, London: Minerva.
Wheeler, Sarah (1996), *Terra Incognita: Travels in Antarctica*, New York: Random House.
William, Charlotte (2002), *Sugar and Slate*, Aberystwyth: Planet.
Williams, Raymond 1960 (1964), *Border Country*, London: Chatto and Windus.
Wilson, Angus (1956), *Anglo-Saxon Attitudes*, London: Secker & Warburg.
Wilson, A. N. (2005), *A Jealous Ghost*, London: Hutchinson.
Winterson, Jeannette 1987 (2001), *The Passion*, London: Vintage.
—— (1991), *Oranges Are Not the Only Fruit*, London: Vintage.
—— (2000), *The Power.Book*, London: Jonathan Cape.
Woolf, Virginia 1929 (1945), *A Room of One's Own*, Harmondsworth: Penguin.
—— (1941), *Between the Acts*, London: Hogarth Press.

## Secondary Sources

Abrams, M. H. (1999), *A Glossary of Literary Terms*, Fort Worth: Harcourt Brace College.
Allen, Sheila (1994), 'Race, Ethnicity and Nationality: Some Questions of Identity', in Haleh Afshar and Mary Maynard (eds), *The Dynamics of 'Race' and Gender: Some Feminist Interventions*, London: Taylor & Francis, pp. 85–105.
Alvarez, A. (2005), 'The myth of the artist' in Corinne Saunders and Jane Macnaughton (eds), *Madness and Creativity in Literature and Culture*, Basingstoke: Macmillan, pp. 194–201.
Anderson, Perry (1964), 'Origins of the Present Crisis', *New Left Review* 1 (23): 26–54.
Annesley, James (2006), *Fictions of Globalization*, London: Continuum.
Appignanesi, Richard and Zarate, Oscar (1999), *Introducing Freud*, Cambridge: Icon.
Arendt, Hannah (1951), *The Origins of Totalitarianism*, New York: Harcourt Brace.
—— 1963 (1964), *Eichmann in Jerusalem*, London: Viking.
Ashcroft, Bill, Griffiths, Gareth and Tiffin, Helen (1989), *The Empire Writes Back: Theory and Practice in Post-colonial Literatures*, London: Routledge.
Attridge, Derek (2004), *The Singularity of Literature*, London: Routledge.
Barry, Peter (2000), *Contemporary British Poetry and the City*, Manchester University Press.
—— (2007), *Literature in Contexts*, Manchester: Manchester University Press.
Barthes, Roland 1973 (1974), *S/Z*, Richard Miller (trans.). Oxford: Blackwell.
—— 1968 (1977), 'The Death of the Author', in Stephen Heath (trans.), *Image Music Text*, London: Fontana.
Bateson, F. W. (1953), 'The Function of Criticism at the Present Time', *Essays in Criticism* 3 (1): 1–26.

Baudrillard, Jean 1983 (1994), *Simulations*, Paul Foss, Paul Patton and Philip Beitchman (trans.), New York: Semiotext(e).

—— (2002), *The Spirit of Terrorism*, London: Verso.

—— (2005), 'The Matrix revisited' in Sylvère Lotringer (ed.), *The Conspiracy of Art*, Ames Hodges (trans.), New York: Semiotext(e).

Benjamin, Walter 1936 (2002), 'The Storyteller: Reflections on the Works of Nikolai Leskov', in *Selected Writings, Vol. 3, 1935–1938*, Cambridge, MA: Harvard University Press.

Bentley, Nick (2008), *Contemporary British Fiction*, Edinburgh: Edinburgh University Press.

Bergonzi, Bernard (1970), *The Situation of the Novel*, London: Macmillan.

Berlin, Isaiah (1958), *Two Concepts of Liberty*, Oxford: Clarendon Press.

Bernstein, Stephen (2005), 'Never Let Me Go', *Review of Contemporary Fiction* 25 (1): 139.

Bhabha, Homi K. (1990), *Nation and Narration*, London: Routledge.

—— (1994), *The Location of Culture*, London: Routledge.

—— (1996), 'Of Mimicry and Man: The Ambivalence of Colonial Discourse', in Philip Rice and Patricia Waugh (eds), *Modern Literary Theory: A Reader*, London: Arnold.

Blackman, Stuart (2006), 'Human 2.0', *Focus* 169 (October): 35–51.

Bloom, Harold (1994), *The Western Canon: The Books and Schools of All the Ages*, New York: Harcourt Brace.

Boehmer, Elleke (1995), *Colonial and Postcolonial Literature: Migrant Metaphors*, Oxford: Oxford University Press.

Bowie, Malcolm (1991), *Lacan: Fontana Modern Masters*, London: Fontana.

Bradbury, Malcolm (1987), *No, Not Bloomsbury*, London: Deutsch.

—— (1993), *The Modern British Novel*, London: Secker & Warburg.

Brannigan, John (1998), *New Historicism and Cultural Materialism*, Basingstoke and London: Macmillan.

—— (2003), *Orwell to the Present: Literature in England, 1945–2000*, Basingstoke: Palgrave.

Bristow, Joseph and Broughton, Trev (1997), *The Infernal Desires of Angela Carter: Fiction: Femininity, Feminism*, Harlow: Longman.

Burke, Seán (1998), *The Death and Return of the Author: Criticism and Subjectivity in Plato, Foucault and Derrida*, Edinburgh: Edinburgh University Press.

Butler, Judith (1977), *The Psychic Life of Power: Theories in Subjection*, Stanford: Stanford University Press.

—— (1990), *Gender Trouble: Feminism and the Subversion of Identity*, London: Routledge.

Caputi, Jane (2006), 'Responses to 9/11', *Journal of American Culture* 28 (1): 1–127.

Carter, Angela (1979b), *The Sadeian Woman*, London: Virago.

Castle, Terry (1993), *The Apparitional Lesbian: Female Homosexuality and Modern Culture*, New York: Columbia University Press.

Childs, Peter (2005), *Contemporary Novelists: British Fiction Since 1970*, Basingstoke: Palgrave.

Childs, Peter and Williams, R. J. Patrick (1997), *An Introduction to Post-colonial Theory*, London: Prentice Hall/Harvester Wheatsheaf.

Cochrane, James (ed.) (1977), *Kipling: Poems*, Harmondsworth: Penguin.

Cockin, Katharine (2003), 'Rethinking Transracial Adoption: Reading Jackie Kay's *The Adoption Papers*', *a/b: Auto/Biography Studies* 18 (2): 276–91.

—— (2007), 'Chicks and Lads in Contemporary Fiction', in *Teaching Contemporary British Fiction* (eds) Steven Barfield, Anja Muller-Wood, Philip Tew and Leigh Wilson, anglistik & englischunterricht 69, Heidelberg: Universitätsverlag Winter, pp. 107–24.

Collins, Merle 1992 (2000), 'When Britain had its great', in James Proctor (ed.), *Writing Black Britain*, Manchester: Manchester University Press, pp. 206–7.

Connor, Steven (1996), *The English Novel in History, 1950–1995*, London: Routledge.

—— 1989 (1996), *Postmodernist Culture: An Introduction to Theories of the Contemporary* (revised edition) [1989] Oxford: Blackwell.

—— (2000), *Dumbstruck: A Cultural History of Ventriloquism*, Oxford: Oxford University Press.

—— (2004), *The Book of Skin*, London: Reaktion.

Corcoran, Neil (1993), *English Poetry since 1940*, Harlow: Longman.

Culler, J. (2007), *On Deconstruction: Theory and Criticism after Structuralism* [1998], London: Routledge.

De Beauvoir, Simone 1949 (1977), *The Second Sex*, Harmondsworth: Penguin.

Deleuze, Gilles 1963 (2002), *Nietzsche and Philosophy*, London: Continuum.

Derrida, J., 1967 (1997), *Of Grammatology*, Gayatri Chakravorty Spivak (trans.), Baltimore: Johns Hopkins University Press.

—— 1967 (1973), *Speech and Phenomena and Other Essays on Husserl's Theory of Signs*, Evanston, IL: Northwestern University Press.

—— 1967 (2001), *Writing and Difference*, Alan Bass (trans.), London: Routledge Classics.

Dirlik, Arif (1994), 'The Postcolonial Aura: third world criticism in the age of global capitalism', *Critical Inquiry* 20 (winter): 328–56.

Doan, Laura L. (2000), ' "Sexy greedy is the late eighties": Power systems in Amis's *Money* and Churchill's *Serious Money*' (1990), in Nicolas Tredell (ed.), *The Fiction of Martin Amis: A Reader's Guide to Essential Criticism*, London: Palgrave.

Doan, Laura and Waters, Sarah (2000), 'Making up lost time: contemporary lesbian writing and the invention of history', in David Alderson and Linda Anderson (eds), *Territories of Desire in Queer Culture: Refiguring Contemporary Boundaries*, Manchester: Manchester University Press.

Dollimore, Jonathan (1983), 'The Challenge of Sexuality', in Alan Sinfield (ed.), *Society and Literature 1945–1970*, London: Methuen, pp. 51–85.

Dollimore, Jonathan, and Sinfield, Alan (eds) (1985), *Political Shakespeare: New Essays in Cultural Materialism*, Manchester: Manchester University Press.

Dowson, Jane and Entwhistle, Alice (2005), *A History of Twentieth-Century British Women's Poetry*, Cambridge: Cambridge University Press.

Douglas, Mary 1966 (2005), *Purity and Danger: An Analsyis of the Concepts of Pollution and Taboo*, London: Routledge.

Eagleton, Mary (1986), *Feminist Literary Theory: A Reader*, Oxford: Blackwell.

—— (1991), *Feminist Literary Criticism*, London: Longman.

—— (2005), *Figuring the Woman Author in Contemporary Fiction*, Basingstoke: Palgrave Macmillan.

Eagleton, Terry 1985 (1996), *Literary Theory: An Introduction*, Oxford: Blackwell.

—— (1986), *Against the Grain: Essays 1975–85*, London: Verso.

—— 2005, *Holy Terror*, Oxford: Oxford University Press.

Eliot, T. S. 1920 (1997), 'Hamlet and His Problems', in *The Sacred Wood: Essays on Poetry and Criticism*, London: Faber.

—— (1928), *For Lancelot Andrewes*, London: Faber & Gwyer.

—— (1939), *The Idea of a Christian Society*, London: Faber.

—— (1949), *Notes Towards the Definition of Culture*, London: Faber.

—— 1956 (1957), 'The Frontiers of Criticism', *On Poetry and Poets*, London: Faber, pp. 103–118.

—— (1957), *On Poetry and Poets*, London: Faber.

Faludi, Susan (1991), *Backlash: The Undeclared War Against American Women*, London: Chatto and Windus.

Fanon, Frantz 1952 (1986), *Black Skin, White Masks*, Charles Lam Markmann (trans.), London: Pluto.

—— , 1961 (1965), *The Wretched of the Earth*, Constance Farrington (trans.), London: MacGibbon and Kee.

Fetterley, Judith (1978), *The Resisting Reader: A Feminist Approach to American Fiction*, Bloomington: Indiana University Press.

Firestone, Shulamith (1971), *The Dialectic of Sex: The Case for Feminist Revolution*, London: Paladin.

Fish, Stanley (1995), *Professional Correctness: Literary Studies and Political Change*, Oxford: Clarendon Press.

Foucault, Michel 1965 (2006), *Madness and Civilization: A History of Insanity in the Age of Reason*, London: Taylor & Francis.

—— (1972), *The Archaeology of Knowledge*, London: Tavistock/Routledge.

—— (1977), *Discipline and Punish: The Birth of the Prison*, Harmondsworth: Penguin.

—— 1979 (1998), *The History of Sexuality, Vol. 1: The Will to Knowledge*, Robert Hurley (trans.), Harmondsworth: Penguin.

—— 1988 (1995), 'Technologies of the self', in Luther H. Martin, Huck Gutman and Andrej Gasiorek (eds), *Post-War British Fiction: Realism and After*, London: Edward Arnold.

Freidan, Betty 1963 (1965), *The Feminine Mystique*, Harmondsworth: Penguin.

Freud, Sigmund 1908 (1983), 'Creative Writers and Day-dreaming', in Kurzweil, Edith, and William Phillips (eds), *Literature and Psychoanalysis*, New York: Columbia University Press, pp. 19–23.

Fryer, Peter (1984), *Staying Power*, London: Pluto Press.

Fukuyama, Francis 1989 (1992), *The End of History and the Last Man*, London: Free Press.

—— 2002 (2003), *Our Posthuman Future: Consequences of the Biotechnology Revolution*, London: Profile Books.

Gasiorek, Andrzej (1995), *Post-War British Fiction: Realism and After*, London: Arnold.

Gikandi, Simon (1992), *Writing in Limbo: Modernism and Caribbean Literature*, Ithaca, NY: Cornell University Press.

Gillis, Stacey, Howie, Gillian and Munford, Rebecca (2004), *Third Wave Feminism: A Critical Exploration* (second edition), Basingstoke: Palgrave Macmillan.

Greenblatt, Stephen (1980), *Renaissance Self-Fashioning: From More to Shakespeare*, Chicago and London: University of Chicago Press.

Greer, Germaine 1970 (1971), *The Female Eunuch*, London: Paladin.

—— (1999), *The Whole Woman*, London: Doubleday.

Gregson, Ian (1996), *Contemporary Poetry and Postmodernism: Dialogue and Estrangement*, Basingstoke: Macmillan.

Gutman, Huck and Hutton, Patrick H. (eds) (1988), *Technologies of the Self: A Seminar with Michel Foucault*, London: Tavistock Publications.

Haffenden, John (1985), *Novelists in Interview*, London: Methuen.

Haraway, Donna (1985), 'Manifesto for Cyborgs: Science, Technology, and Socialist Feminism in the 1980s', *Socialist Review* 80: 65–108.

Hawthorn, Jeremy (1996), *Cunning Passages: New Historicism, Cultural Materialism and Marxism in the Contemporary Literary Debate*, London: Arnold.

—— (2000), *A Glossary of Contemporary Literary Theory*, London: Arnold.

Hayles, N. Katherine (1999), *How We Became Posthuman: Virtual Bodies in Cybernetics, Literature and Informatics*, Chicago: University of Chicago Press.

Head, Dominic (2002), *The Cambridge Introduction to Modern British Fiction, 1950–2000*, Cambridge: Cambridge University Press.

—— (2007), *Ian McEwan*, Manchester: Manchester University Press.

—— (2008), *The State of the Novel: Britain and Beyond*, Chichester: Wiley Blackwell.

Henderson, Mae Gwendolyn (1993), 'Speaking in Tongues: Dialogics, Dialectics and the Black Woman Writer's Literary Tradition', in Patrick Williams and Laura Chrisman (eds), *Colonial Discourse and Post-colonial Theory: A Reader*, Hemel Hempstead: Harvester Wheatsheaf, pp. 257–68.

Hennessey, Peter (2006), *Never Again: Britain 1945–51*, Harmondsworth: Penguin.

—— (2007), *Having It So Good: Britain in the Fifties*, Harmondsworth: Penguin.

Hite, Shere (1977), *The Hite Report: A Nationwide Survey of Sexuality*, London: Summit Books.

Hobsbaum, Philip (1996), *Metre, Rhythm and Verse Form*, London: Routledge.

Hoggart, Richard (1957), *The Uses of Literacy: Aspects of Working Class Life with Special Reference to Publications and Entertainments*, London: Chatto and Windus.

Holderness, Graham (1992), *Shakespeare Recycled: The Making of Historical Drama*, Hemel Hempstead: Harvester Wheatsheaf.

hooks, bell (1982), *Ain't I A Woman: Black Women and Feminism*, London: Pluto Press.

Howe, Stephen (2002), *Empire: A Very Short Introduction*, Oxford: Oxford University Press.

Huggan, Graham (2001), *The Post-Colonial Exotic: Marketing the Margins*, London: Routledge.

Hutcheon, Linda (1988), *A Poetics of Postmodernism: History, Theory, Fiction*, London: Routledge.

Irigaray, Luce 1985 (1991), 'The Power of Discourse and the Subordination of the Feminine', in Margaret Whitford (ed.), *The Irigaray Reader*. Oxford: Blackwell.

Israel, Nico (2006), 'Tropicalizing London: British Fiction and the Discipline of Postcolonialism', in James F. English (ed.), *A Concise Companion to Contemporary British Fiction*, Oxford: Blackwell, pp. 83–99.

Jameson, Fredric (1991), *Postmodernism or the Cultural Logic of Late Capitalism*, London: Verso.

Joannou, Maroula (2000), *Contemporary Women's Writing: From the Golden Notebook to the Color Purple*, Manchester: Manchester University Press.

Jordan, Michael (2005), 'The Hum Inside the Skull, Revisited', *New York Times* 16 Jan (Section 7): 8.

Karl, Frederic (1963), *A Reader's Guide to the Contemporary English Novel*, London: Thames & Hudson.

King, Bruce (2004), *The Internationalization of English Literature*, The Oxford English Literature History, Vol. 13: 1948–2000, Oxford: Oxford University Press.

King, Jeannette (1989), *Doris Lessing*, London: Edward Arnold.

—— (2005), *The Victorian Woman Question in Contemporary Feminist Fiction*, Basingstoke: Palgrave Macmillan.

Klein, Melanie 1928 (1948), 'Early Stages of the Oedipus Conflict and of Super-ego Formation', in *Contributions to Psycho-Analysis, 1921–45*, London: Hogarth Press.

—— (1957), *Envy and Gratitude: A Study of Unconscious Sources*, New York: Basic Books.

Klotzko, Arlene Judith (2005), *A Clone Of Your Own? The Science and Ethics of Cloning*, Oxford: Oxford University Press.

Koedt, Anna (1968), 'The Myth of the Vaginal Orgasm', in Anne Koedt, Ellen Levine and Anita Rapone (eds), *Radical Feminism*, New York: Quadrangle, pp. 198–207.

Kristeva, Julia (1982), *Powers of Horror: An Essay on Abjection*, New York: Columbia University Press.

—— (1982), *Desire in Language: A Semiotic Approach to Literature and Art* [1969], Columbia: Columbia University Press.

—— (1984), *Revolution in Poetic Language* [1974], Columbia: Columbia University Press.

Laing, R. D. (1971), *The Divided Self*, Harmondsworth: Penguin.

Lawton, Graham (2006), 'The Incredibles', *New Scientist* 13 May: 32–8.

Leavis, F. R. (1948), *The Great Tradition: George Eliot, James and Conrad*, Harmondsworth: Penguin.

—— (1953), 'The Responsible Critic: Or the Function of Criticism at Any Time', *Scrutiny* 19 (3): 162–83.

—— 1952 (1962), *The Common Pursuit*, Harmondsworth: Penguin.

Lejeune, Philippe (1991), 'The Autobiographical Contract', in Tzvetan Todorov (ed.), *French Literary Theory Today*, Cambridge: Cambridge University Press.

Lessing, Doris 1963 (1994), 'To room nineteen', in *To Room Nineteen: Collected Stories*, Vol. 1, London: Flamingo.

Lodge, David (1977), *The Modes of Modern Writing: Metaphor, Metonymy and the Typology of Modern Literature*, New York: Cornell University Press.

—— (ed.) (1988), *Modern Criticism and Theory: A Reader*, London: Longman.

—— (1992), *The Art of Fiction*, London: Secker & Warburg.

Low, Gail and Wynne-Davies, Marion (eds) (2006), *A Black British Canon?* Basingstoke: Palgrave.

Lyotard, J. F. 1979 (1984), *The Postmodern Condition: A Report on Knowledge*,

G. Bennington and B. Massumi (trans.), Manchester: Manchester University Press.

Macaulay, Thomas B. 1835 (1995), 'Minute on Indian Education', in B. Ashcroft, G. Griffiths and H. Tiffin (eds), *The Post-Colonial Studies Reader*, London: Routledge, pp. 428–30.

Marcuse, Herbert 1965 (1968), *Repressive Tolerance*, Berkeley: Berkeley Commune.

—— (1969), 'Repressive Tolerance', in Robert Paul Wolff, Barrington Moore, Jr and Herbert Marcuse (eds), *A Critique of Pure Tolerance*, Boston: Beacon Press, pp. 95–137.

McClintock, Anne (1995), *Imperial Leather: Race, Gender, and Sexuality in the Colonial Contest*, New York: Routledge.

McLeod, John (2000), *Beginning Postcolonialism*, Manchester: Manchester University Press.

Millett, Kate 1970 (1977), *Sexual Politics*, London: Virago.

Minsky, Rosalind (ed.) (1996), *Psychoanalysis and Gender*, London: Routledge.

Mitchell, Juliet (1984), *Women: The Longest Revolution*, London: Virago.

Moi, Toril (ed.) (1986), *The Kristeva Reader*, London: Routledge.

Montgomery, Martin (2005), 'The Discourse of War after 9/11', *Language and Literature: Journal of the Poetics and Linguistics Association* 14 (2): 149–80.

Morrison, Blake (1980), *English Poetry and Fiction of the 1950s: The Movement*, London: Methuen.

Morrison, Jago (2003), *Contemporary Fiction*, London: Routledge.

Morrison, Jago and Watkins, Susan (2006), *Scandalous Fictions: The Twentieth-Century Novel in the Public Sphere*, Basingstoke: Palgrave Macmillan.

Motion, Andrew (1993), *Philip Larkin: A Writer's Life*, London: Faber.

Mullan, John (2006), 'Never Let Me Go', *Guardian*, 18 March.

Nicholson, N. (ed.) (1970), *Harold Nicholson: Diaries and letters 1939–45*, London: Fontana.

Norris, Christopher (1992), *Uncritical Theory: Postmodernism, Intellectuals, and the Gulf War*, London: Lawrence & Wishart.

Palmer, Paulina (1989), *Contemporary Women's Fiction: Narrative Practice and Feminist Theory*, Hemel Hempstead: Harvester Wheatsheaf.

—— (1993), *Contemporary Lesbian Writing: Dreams, Desire, Difference*, Buckingham: Open University Press.

—— (1999), *Lesbian Gothic: Transgressive Fictions*, London: Cassell.

Petersen, Kirsten Holst and Rutherford, Anna (eds) (1986), *A Double Colonization: Colonial and Post-colonial Women's Writing*. Mundelstrup: Dangaroo Press.

Phelan, Peggy (1993), *Unmarked: The Politics of Performance*, London: Routledge.

Phillips, Deborah (2006), *Women's Fiction 1945–2005: Writing Romance*, London: Continuum.

Phillips, Mike and Phillips, Trevor (1988), *Windrush: The Irresistible Rise of Multi-Racial Britain*, London: HarperCollins.

Prakash, Gyan (1992), 'Postcolonial Criticism and Indian historiography', *Social Text* 31/32: 8–19.

Procter, James (2003), *Dwelling Places: Post-war Black British Writing*, Manchester: Manchester University Press.

Rabey, David Ian (2003), *English Drama Since 1940*, Harlow: Longman.

Reading, Peter (1984), *C*, London: Secker & Warburg.

Rich, Adrienne (1980), 'Compulsory Heterosexuality and Lesbian Existence', *Signs* 5: 631–60.

Riviere, Joan S. 1929 (1966), 'Womanliness as Masquerade', in Hendrik M. Ruitenbeek (ed.), *Psychoanalysis and Female Sexuality*. New Haven: College and University Press, pp. 209–220.

Rolph, C. H. (ed.) (1961), *The Trial of Lady Chatterley: Regina v. Penguin Books Ltd.*, Harmondsworth: Penguin.

Rushdie, Salman (1991), *Imaginary Homelands*, London: Granta.

—— 1993 (2002), 'The Last Hostage', *Step Across This Line*, New York: Random House.

Ryan, Kiernan (1996), *New Historicism and Cultural Materialism: A Reader*, London and New York: Arnold.

Sage, Lorna (1992), *Women in the House of Fiction: Post War Women Novelists*, London: Routledge.

—— (ed.) (1994), *Essays on the Art of Angela Carter: Flesh and the Mirror*, London: Virago.

—— (ed.) (1999), *The Cambridge Guide to Women's Writing in English*, Cambridge: Cambridge University Press.

—— (2001), *Moments of Truth: Twelve Twentieth Century Women Writers*, London: Fourth Estate.

Said, Edward W. 1978 (1995), *Orientalism: Western Conceptions of the Orient*, Harmondsworth: Penguin.

—— (2004), *Humanism and Democratic Criticism*, New York: Columbia University Press.

—— (2005), *Power, Politics and Culture: Interviews with Edward W. Said*, London: Bloomsbury.

Sandhu, Sukhdev (2003), *London Calling: How Black and Asian Writers Imagined a City*, London: HarperCollins.

Saunders, Corinne J. and Mcnaughton, Jane (ed.) (2005), *Madness and Creativity in Literature and Culture*, Basingstoke and New York: Palgrave.

Saussure, Ferdinand de 1916 (2005), *General Course in Linguistics*, New York: McGraw Hill.

Sayers, Valerie (2005), 'Spare Parts', *Commonweal* 132 (13): 27–8.

Sedgwick, Eve Kosofsky (1990), *Epistemology of the Closet*, Berkeley, CA: University of California Press.

Sinfield, Alan (1989), *Literature, Politics and Culture in Postwar Britain*, Oxford: Blackwell.

—— (1992), *Faultlines: Cultural Materialism and the Politics of Dissident Reading*, Oxford: Oxford University Press.

—— (1994), *Cultural Politics: Queer Reading*, London: Routledge.

—— (2004), *Literature and Culture in Post-War Britain*, London: Continuum.

Singer, Elyse (1991), 'Hanif Kureishi: A Londoner, But Not a Brit', in Melissa Biggs (ed.), *In the Vernacular: Interviews at Yale with the Sculptors of Culture*, Jefferson: McFarland and Co.

Smith, Patricia Juliana (1997), *Lesbian Panic: Homoeroticism in Modern British Women's Fiction*, New York: Columbia University Press.

Spivak, Gayatri Chakrabarty (1988), 'Can the subaltern speak?', in C. Nelson and L. Grossberg (eds), *Marxism and the Interpretation of Culture*, Basingstoke: Macmillan Education, pp. 271–313.

—— (1992), 'Asked to talk about myself . . .', *Third Text: Third World Perspectives on Contemporary Art & Culture* 19 (Summer): 9–18.

—— (1993), *Outside in the Teaching Machine*, New York: Routledge.

Squires, Claire (2007), *Marketing Literature: The Making of Contemporary Writing*, Basingstoke: Palgrave.

Stanley, Liz (1992), *The Auto/biographical I*, Manchester: Manchester University Press.

Sterling, Bruce 1986 (1994), *Mirrorshades: The Cyberpunk Anthology*, New York: Arbor House.

Stevenson, Randall and Cairns Craig (2001), *Twentieth-century Scottish Drama: An Anthology*, Edinburgh: Canongate.

Stevenson, Randall (2004), *The Oxford English Literary History vol. 12, 1960–2000: The Last of England?*, Oxford: Oxford University Press.

Stevenson, Randall and McHale, Brian (eds) (2006), *The Edinburgh Companion to Twentieth-century Literatures in English*, Edinburgh: Edinburgh University Press.

Stoler, Ann (1995), *Race and the Education of Desire: Foucault's 'History of Sexuality' and the Colonial Order of Things*, Durham: Duke University Press.

Sutherland, John (1982), *Offensive Literature: Decensorship in Britain 1960–1982*, London: Junction Books.

Tew, Philip, Mengham, Rod and Lane, Richard (2003), *Contemporary British Fiction*, Cambridge: Polity.

Tew, Philip and Mengham, Rod (2006), *British Fiction Today*, London: Continuum.

Tew, Philip 2004 (2007), *The Contemporary British Novel*, London: Continuum (revised second edition).

Thurley, Geofrey (1974), *The Ironic Harvest: English Poetry in the Twentieth Century*, London: Edward Arnold.

Thwaite, Anthony (1957), *Essays on Contemporary English Poetry: Hopkins to the Present Day*, Tokyo: Kenkyusha.

Thwaites, Tony (2000), 'Miracles: Hot Air and Histories of the Improbable', in Niall Lucy (ed.), *Postmodern Literary Theory: An Anthology*, Oxford: Blackwell.

Tillyard, E. M. W. (1944), *Shakespeare's History Plays*, New York: Macmillan.

Toffoletti, Kim (2007), *Cyborgs and Barbie Dolls: Feminism, Popular Culture and the Posthuman Body*, London: I. B. Tauris.

Tredell, Nicholas (ed.) (2000), *The Fiction of Martin Amis: A Reader's Guide to Essential Criticism*, London: Palgrave.

Trevenna, Joanne (2002), 'Gender as Performance: Questioning the "Butlerification" of Angela Carter's Fiction', *Journal of Gender Studies* 11 (3): 267–76.

Veeser, H. Aram (ed.) (1994), *The New Historicism Reader*, London: Routledge.

Visram, Rozina (1986), *Ayahs, Lascars and Princes*, London: Pluto.

—— (2002), *Asians in Britain: Four Hundred Years of History*, London: Pluto.

Walter, Natasha (1998), *The New Feminism*, London: Little Brown and Company.

Warren, Austin and Wellek, Rene (1949), *Theory of Literature*, New York: Harcourt, Brace.

Watkins, Susan (2001), *Twentieth-Century Women Novelists: Feminist Theory into Practice*, Basingstoke: Palgrave Macmillan.

Waugh, Patricia and Rice, Philip (eds) (1989), *Modern Literary Theory: A Reader*, London: Edward Arnold.

Waugh, Patricia (1984), *Metafiction: The Theory and Practice of Self-Conscious Fiction*, London: Methuen.

—— (1989), *Feminine Fictions: Revisiting the Postmodern*, London: Routledge.

—— (1992), *Practising Postmodernism: Reading Modernism*, London: Edward Arnold.

—— (1995), *Harvest of the Sixties: English Literature and its Background 1960 to 1990*, Oxford: Oxford University Press.

Whelehan, Imelda (2000), *Overloaded: Poplar Culture and the Future of Feminism*, London: Women's Press.

Williams, Raymond (1958), *Culture and Society, 1780–1950*, London: Chatto and Windus.

—— (1961), *The Long Revolution*, London: Chatto and Windus.

—— (1973), *The Country and the City*, London: Chatto and Windus.

—— (1976), *Keywords*, London: Fontana.

—— (1977), *Marxism and Literature*. Oxford: Oxford University Press.

—— (1979), *Politics and Letters: Interviews with the New Left Review*, London: New Left Books.

—— (1980), *Problems in Materialism and Culture: Selected Essays*, London: Verso.

Wilson, Edmund 1941 (1965), *The Wound and the Bow: Seven Studies in Literature*, New York: Oxford University Press.

Wolf, Naomi (1990), *The Beauty Myth: How Images of Beauty are Used Against Women*, London: Chatto and Windus.

Woolf, Virginia (1942), *The Death of the Moth and Other Essays*, London: Hogarth Press.

Wright, Elizabeth (1998), *Psychoanalytic Criticism: A Reappraisal* (second edition), Cambridge: Polity.

Young, Robert (1995), *Colonial Desire: Hybridity in Theory, Culture, and Race*, London: Routledge.

—— (2001), *Postcolonialism: An Historical Introduction*, Oxford: Blackwell.

Zeifman, Hersch and Zimmerman, Cynthia (2003), *Contemporary British Drama 1970–1990*, Basingstoke: Palgrave.

Zeleza, Paul Tiyambe (1997), 'Fictions of the postcolonial', *Toronto Review of Contemporary Writing Abroad* 15.2 (Winter): 19–29.

Zizek, Slavoj (2002), *Welcome to the Desert of the Real! Five Essays on 11 September and Related Dates*, London: Verso.

# Index

Please note that titles of publications beginning with 'A' or 'The' will be sorted under the first significant word